Please renew or return items by the date
shown on your receipt
www.hertsdirect.org/libraries
Renewals and enquiries: 0300 123 4049
Textphone for hearing or 0300 123 4041
speech impaired users:

ROGER MOORE: A BIOGRAPHY

Also by Roy Moseley

MY STARS AND OTHER FRIENDS
MERLE: A biography of Merle Oberon
(with Charles Higham)*

* New English Library

ROGER MOORE:

A BIOGRAPHY

Roy Moseley

with
Philip and Martin Masheter

NEW ENGLISH LIBRARY

Copyright © 1985 by Roy Moseley with
Philip and Martin Masheter

First published in Great Britain in 1985 by
New English Library, Mill Road, Dunton Green, Sevenoaks, Kent.
Editorial office: 47 Bedford Square, London WC1B 3DP.

Typeset by Rowland Phototypesetting Ltd,
Bury St Edmunds, Suffolk

Printed in Great Britain by
St Edmundsbury Press, Bury St Edmunds, Suffolk

British Library C.I.P.
Moseley, Roy
    Roger Moore: a biography.
    1. Moore, Roger, *1927–*   2. Moving-picture
    actors and actresses—Great Britain—Biography
    I. Title   II. Masheter, P.   III. Masheter, M
    791.43′028′0924   PN2598.M62

ISBN 0-450-06114-0

To my Mother and Father, with love
Roy Moseley

and to Heather and Harry, with love
Philip and Martin Masheter

Acknowledgements

Janet de Cordova, Harold Schwab, Tony Curtis, Ross Hunter, David Hedison, Noele Gordon, H.S.H. Prince Rainier of Monaco, Robert Brown, Peter Moore, Fred de Cordova, Jack Davies, Barbara Broccoli, Peter Hunt, David Wardlow, Alan Harris-Quelch, Dave Medrano of the Luxury Line of Beverly Hills, Jerry Pam, Shirley James, Sir John Mills, John Marven, Robert Baker, Leslie Charteris, Euan Lloyd, John Howard Davies, Brian Desmond Hurst, Terence Young, Eleanor Summerfield, Daniel Massey, Bob Simmons, Sylvia Syms, Albert R. Broccoli, Leslie Bricusse, Ian Bevan, Glenn Ford, Sheila Rawstorne, Elspeth March, Joe Baker, Jane Seymour, Charles Juroe, Hazel Court, Lindsay Hatchett, Jack Kelly, David Stoner, Bryan Forbes, Fred Newby, Anthony Perkins, William Tyler, Jean Kent, Yusef Hurst, Dinah Sheridan, Christian Roberts, Charles Isaacs, Dennis Van Thal, Dennis Selinger, Irma Logan, Sally Bullock, Keith McConnell, Harry Masheter, Lewis Gilbert, Leslie Martinson, Doorn Van Steyn, Lea Brodie, Ray Danton, Patricia Bickford, Brian Durban, Bruce Cohn Curtis, Virginia McKenna and Bill Williamson.

All the above mentioned were most generous with their time and help. The authors would like to pay special tribute to Roberta Rubenstein for her marvellous contribution to this book; to Milton Goldman, the King of his profession; to our esteemed representative Mitchell Douglas and editor Colin Honnor; to Rian O'Connell for his happy and timely arrival; to Heather Masheter and Dorothy Colgate who tirelessly and perfectly typed the manuscript and, last but by no means least, to Roger Moore who, with his usual generosity and good humour, allowed this book an easy progress.

Prologue

On June 12th, 1944, six days after D-Day and amid fearful attacks by the dreaded V-1 bombers, filming began at Denham, the heart of the British film industry since Alexander Korda opened the studios there in 1936, on the most expensive and elaborate British film ever made up till that time. This was *Caesar and Cleopatra*, Gabriel Pascal's third screen dramatisation of a George Bernard Shaw play and a film on which such great hopes rested and where all eyes in the British film industry were focused.

Gabriel Pascal always enlisted the aid of a partner to co-direct these ventures – Leslie Howard was responsible for *Pygmalion* in 1938, David Lean made his directional debut with *Major Barbara* in 1941, and the famed Brian Desmond Hurst was at the helm of this most ambitious of the three.

The British film industry seemed set to reach a new peak with this venture, with a cast that included the beautiful and legendary Vivien Leigh, and Claude Rains and Flora Robson both recently returned from Hollywood, as well as the young Stewart Granger, then Britain's most popular romantic hero.

On one bright summer's day, amidst hundreds of bustling extras, Mr Hurst was rehearsing a scene with Vivien Leigh and Claude Rains on the spectacular set for the port of Alexandria on the back-lot of Denham, nestling in the beautiful Buckinghamshire countryside just nineteen miles from the centre of London. The director glanced about him and noticed a tall figure standing on the edge of an enormous set.

Soon a break was called, and Mr Hurst saw two men approaching him. The older of the two was the man Hurst had already become aware of and it was he who addressed the director:

'Do you mind if I speak to you, sir? I am Detective Sergeant Moore.'

Recognising him immediately, Hurst replied, 'Not at all.'

And then, drawing round the young man who stood partially hidden behind him, the detective sergeant introduced the youth to the eminent Mr Hurst:

'This is my son Roger. He wants to be an actor.'

One

IN THE London of 1940 barrage balloons stood out on the skyline, suspended above streets where houses had been reduced to rubble. Shops would open despite having their windows smashed or doors broken. All around were the signs of a country at war: the propaganda and the public information posters on the walls, notices pointing out air raid shelters and the strain on the faces of the people queuing for food after another sleepless night as the bombs rained down on London.

Every evening, as shops and offices closed, Londoners would silently make their way home and report to their posts for the long night ahead. Fire watchers, ambulance men and air raid wardens would all then wait for the German bombers. When darkness fell and sirens howled, the distant drone of the engines would be heard approaching the capital. Searchlights shot out of the darkness sweeping across the sky, trying to locate the German planes whilst the anti-aircraft guns outside London and in the city itself would boom out, lighting up the sky for a few brief seconds as if it were daytime. The guns pounded continuously in an attempt to cripple the enemy planes before their bomb load was dropped. But many planes broke through the fierce barrage, and houses which had looked solid before nightfall were by the next morning nothing but a pile of bricks, broken glass and timber. Bodies would be dragged out of the broken houses, bloodied and contorted in their death agonies. The sight of death and maiming became commonplace – as much a part of everyday life as seeing the postman on his daily round. Each morning was greeted by more rubble to clear away, and with each morning was the thought that the night to come could be your last.

At night it was usual to see the sky lit up with an orange glow from the fires raging all over the city, whilst in the background could be heard the frantic ringing of fire engine bells. At 2 a.m. on one such night during the late summer of 1940, policeman Fred Newby stood, as usual, on his doorstep in Albert Square, South London, reading his newspaper by the light of the city which was burning for miles around him. The solid Victorian terraced buildings which formed the square had not escaped damage. The

9

block opposite Mr Newby had been completely destroyed, while to his left half of one terrace had been ripped through, disfiguring the solid wall of the square which had once been a quiet enclave out of sight of the busy Clapham Road.

In the garden flat in the same terrace a mother and her young son were huddled in their claustrophobic shelter, waiting for the whine of the 'All Clear' sign when they could emerge into the night air, hot with the heat from the fires around them, to check that their house was still standing, and that friends they had seen only hours before were still alive. She would be hoping her husband was safe amid the raging inferno as he carried on with his duties as a Bow Street policeman. This is what life was like for Mr and Mrs George Moore and their thirteen-year-old son Roger – and for thousands of other families living in London during the Blitz.

Thirteen years earlier, on October 17th, 1927 the residents of 4, Aldebert Terrace had shared the joy of Mr and Mrs Moore over the birth of their son, Roger George Moore. The baby was delivered half a mile away at the Annie McCall Maternity Hospital in Jeffreys Road, an imposing Victorian construction with a heavy iron gate marking the entrance.

As Police Constable George Moore walked out of the hospital into the warm sunshine, where the pavement was drying out after an overnight rain shower, he could never have imagined that the chubby-faced young baby who had been looking up at him only minutes before would grow to be one of the most recognisable faces in the world.

South London had already produced a number of highly successful entertainers, who despite the 'sarf' London intonations with which they were surrounded in their childhood, all grew up to speak with clipped and pronounced English accents. They included Charlie Chaplin, who was born and raised in poverty just around the corner in Kennington, Noel Coward, who lived a couple of miles away down the river, Gertrude Lawrence, who lived in Clapham, and Gladys Cooper, who was born in Lewisham. Another outstanding figure in the theatrical world was still living in Stockwell: Lilian Baylis, the Manager of the Old Vic and Sadlers Wells Theatres, who lived at 27, Stockwell Park Road until her death in 1937. She was the great lady who had been responsible for the careers of so many of the greatest actors and actresses of the twentieth century, including Olivier, Gielgud and Richardson.

The year in which Roger was born was an exciting one. Only four months prior to his birth Charles Lindbergh had successfully made the first solo aeroplane crossing of the Atlantic, on May 20th–21st, in 'The Spirit of St Louis'. The flight had stimulated a great deal of public interest, and the enthusiasm for attaining new flight records was at its height when Roger Moore was born, with pilots of all nationalities attempting to emulate the achievement of Colonel Lindbergh. Early on the morning of October 14th two Frenchmen, Captain Costes and Lieutenant LeBrix, had begun their attempt to cross the South Atlantic, and in England that afternoon Mrs Keith Miller and Captain W. N. Lancaster left Croydon aerodrome to fly the 13,000 miles to Australia.

Other diversions from the harsh realities of life were the opening of the motor show at Olympia and a very good season for the West-End theatre. At His Majesty's Theatre Gertrude Lawrence was appearing in *Oh Kay*, which had been a hit on Broadway, written especially for her by George and Ira Gershwin; Tallulah Bankhead was in *The Garden of Eden* at the Lyric Theatre; Sybil Thorndike could be seen in *The Taming of the Shrew* at the Old Vic; and Gladys Cooper and Nigel Bruce were co-starring in *The Letter* at the Playhouse. This was Miss Cooper's first attempt at solo management after having been offered the play by W. Somerset Maugham himself. For cinemagoers the two main attractions were *Ben Hur* with Ramon Novarro at the Tivoli and *Seventh Heaven* with Charles Farrell and Janet Gaynor at the New Gallery. Both were silent films, but their days were numbered as only a week before, on October 7th, *The Jazz Singer* starring Al Jolson had opened at the Warner Theatre in New York, ushering in the new age of the 'talkies'.

In 1927 the world was getting smaller all the time. Apart from the numerous flights to points throughout the globe, communications were advancing rapidly, most notably with the introduction of contact by radio telephone across the Atlantic. This new era of better communications made it only too clear that the world into which Roger Moore had been born was not a happy one, toppling as it was on the brink of the Great Depression. On May 13th the German economic system had finally broken down on what was to become known as 'Black Friday'. It would be only a matter of six years before the Nazis had whipped up mass hysteria among the German people and taken over the country. It was a time of uncertainty and unrest throughout the world. Only a year before Britain had been brought to a standstill by the General

Strike of May 3rd–12th. The working classes were unhappy with their lot, although the situation would become worse as unemployment spiralled. In Russia less than ten years earlier the workers had revolted against and overthrown a corrupt autocracy in the hope of creating a better world, and in 1927 the Comintern was still striving towards International Socialism. All around the globe the old way of life was disappearing and new alternatives were being offered. Communists, Socialists, Fascists, Anarchists – all were trying to change what had gone before. This then was the background to the world in which Roger Moore would grow up.

George and Lily Moore had been man and wife for ten months when their son was born. They were married in a civil ceremony on December 11th, 1926 at the Register Office of St Giles in West Central London, near to where Lily had been living in Drury Lane. George was twenty-two at the time and his bride a year younger. Lily had been working as a cashier, and George was a Police Constable. George was a tall, slim man, just over 6ft, broad with an athletic build, who wore glasses and had a receding hairline. Lily was a handsome woman of medium height with a full figure. Her features were rounded and pleasant, with a lovely complexion and a good head of hair which her son would inherit – as well as the same broad friendly smile.

Both came from solid lower middle class backgrounds, and their ancestry on both sides was pure London. George's father, George Percy Moore, was a mechanical engineer, and Lily's father, William George Pope, was, at the time of his daughter's marriage, a Military Barrack Superintendent, although during World War I he had been a Senior Regimental Sergeant Major in the British Army. Prior to that he had served with the 4th Regiment, stationed in Calcutta – the hub of the British Army in India – where Lily was born in 1905.

Before his marriage George had been living in Judd Street in St Pancras, but now with a young wife to support he decided to move to larger quarters south of the Thames. The area he chose was the modest one of Stockwell, surrounded by Brixton, Clapham, Lambeth and Dulwich. Not a particularly fashionable place to live in then, it is considerably less so today. They rented a three-room flat on the first floor at 4, Aldebert Terrace, just off the busy South Lambeth Road. The terraces were three-storey Victorian buildings. The Moores had their own bath but shared a toilet with the tenants above. Not long after the birth of their son they moved into nearby 5, Albert Square, where they had a small back garden which ran next to a timber yard with a sawmill. And again just after Roger had started his schooling the family moved across the square to number 16 – again on the first floor, although the rooms were slightly larger. The flat at 16, Albert Square was only about seventy-five yards around the corner from the house to which Roger had been brought as a newborn baby. The flats on the square were considerably more desirable because of the secluded nature of living within the square itself, out of sight of the South Lambeth Road with its constant stream of heavy traffic in and out of the West End. The view was far more pleasant as it looked out on to a fairly large rectangle of grassland, dotted with a few trees and surrounded by ornate railings, which broke up the monotonous outlook of endless Victorian terraces that had been their lot in Aldebert Terrace.

The community in which the Moores lived was a good mixture of English and Italians – mostly professional men and their families – which included wood-workers, waiters, marble workers, mosaic workers, bus conductors, engineers, greengrocers, and policemen like George Moore and Fred Newby.

In this colourful setting Roger Moore was to grow up a happy, contented child, not spoilt but certainly doted on by both parents. Because of the nature of his father's work he was fortunate in being able to spend a great deal of time with both his parents during the day. George Moore was a plan-drawer at Bow Street police station. As Roger explains it:

When there'd been an accident or a murder, plans had to be drawn up of the crime. So he'd go out, do the measurements and then draw the plans. He worked at home mostly. In fact, I never thought he worked at all. Once a month, he'd have to go to court to swear his plans were accurate and that is the only time he'd put on his uniform.

To give himself time to spend with his growing son during the day, George would do most of his work in the evenings when Roger had gone to bed. So Roger was able to have an unusually close relationship with both his father and his mother. George also used the time during the day to practise his furniture-making skills, and many of the rooms in the flats they lived in were filled with furniture he had made.

Although an only child, Roger was certainly not lonely. He had a seemingly endless number of relatives and numerous friends of his own age among the families who lived in the square, among whom was his best friend, Reg, who lived in Aldebert Terrace, opposite to where the Moores lived for a short time. Neighbour Fred Newby remembers Roger and Reg as two very presentable young lads, always friendly and polite: 'It was a pleasure to see them pass by,' he recalls. Both were active and athletic, and would run around Albert Square together, doing all the things that healthy young boys do. As soon as they were able, both Roger and Reg joined the Cubs. One adventure that they had which Roger recalls is when they went camping on Wimbledon Common. They walked to the common from Stockwell, loaded up with their tent and some sandwiches. As soon as they arrived they pitched tent; having done this, they were just about to relax when a man poked his head inside and, looking at the fresh faced young boys, said, 'You've got nice knees.' Roger sensed that the man was a little strange and so made a bolt for it, leaving Reg to whatever fate awaited him. Later on, when he thought it was safe, Roger crept back to the tent. Reg met him there with a pained expression on his face – he had got away, but the man had eaten all their sandwiches.

The Moores are remembered as a very friendly but close-knit family, who generally kept themselves to themselves. Among their closest friends in the neighbourhood were Mr and Mrs Lanza, who lived next door to them at 17, Albert Square. Mr Lanza was a chef at one of the big hotels in the West End. Lily was extremely friendly with Mrs Lanza and continued to visit her long after she and George moved out of Stockwell.

With so many uncles, aunts and cousins there was a constant stream of visitors. Roger's favourite was his Uncle Jack, a regular soldier who travelled all over the world. Whenever he was in London he never failed to call in on George and Lily, and he would always have a present for the little boy; Roger would await his visits eagerly. Another uncle had a farm in Devon, and in the summer Roger used to go and stay with him and help him out; among other things he became experienced at milking a cow. Some relatives stayed with the Moores for a while too. For a short time his cousin Doreen, who was a couple of years older than Roger, stayed with them, and also an Aunt Nelly, who lived with them until she got married.

As an only child, Roger did not want for anything. Young son Roger, unlike his tall, lean father, was inclined to be overweight – a pampered child whose diet included generous portions of the inevitable fish and chips covered with plenty of tomato sauce. His love of sweets extended from bullseyes to the bars of chocolate which he had a weakness for munching. A particular favourite with him and his friends was baked potatoes. The boys became friendly with a nightwatchman where the road was being mended, and Roger and his friends would each grab a large potato from home and take them to be cooked over the nightwatchman's hot brazier. Roger's memories of his childhood seem to be deeply influenced by his insatiable appetite for all kinds of food. Another fond memory is seeing through the darkness at Christmas when his parents were ramming his stocking full of peanuts, tangerines and toffees. He would devour as much food as he could, even to the point of eating the bread that his mother had thrown out for the birds, having become addicted to the taste the bread had after having been dried by the sun. As a family they tended to enjoy the simple pleasures of eating, and Roger remembers that his father used regularly to tuck into a bar of Cadbury's Brazil Nut Chocolate every Sunday.

Roger's eating habits, however, caused him to be a rather fat little boy, and his father used to get furious with him and would pull the belt of his blue schoolboy's raincoat so tight that he would look like a sack of potatoes 'tied up ugly in the middle'.

His son's weight problem was of great concern to the fitness-conscious George Moore. Before joining the Police Force, he had been a physical training instructor with the YMCA, and although as a policeman he never actually walked the beat, he felt it his duty to keep himself in top physical condition and used to work out at the bar bells, horizontal bars and rings. He was also a strong swimmer and diver, a talent which he ensured he passed on to his son. He took him swimming frequently, and the boy became a good sprint swimmer in school championships and Police Federation boys' matches, rarely being beaten. His father also took him to the local park to play football and cricket, thus giving him a taste for the outdoor life. Lily, a keen roller skater in her youth, used to take Roger skating at the rink in nearby Tulse Hill, and often they would roller-skate all the way to Battersea and back.

They were a normal, everyday family. George Moore liked nothing better to relax him than to roll a cigarette with a light ale beside him for a drink. In common with other boys of his age, Roger had the prize possession of a Meccano set and a train set. He was also allowed to have a pet. When he was eight years old he was bought a wire-haired terrier called Pip, but tragically the dog was later run over by a taxi, to Roger's great distress. Pip's replacement was a dog called Ruff, predominantly an Irish Wolf-hound; this dog grew up with Roger, and they were devoted to one another.

As a family they enjoyed the cinema and used to go regularly. Lily's particular favourite film star was Richard Dix, while George was more attracted to Jean Harlow. In common with all boys of his age, Roger liked the adventure films made by Errol Flynn, as well as gangster films starring Humphrey Bogart and James Cagney. Another special favourite whom he admired and aspired to emulate was Gary Cooper, and later on, in the early 1940s, when Stewart Granger started making romantic British films, he too became another of Roger's idols. There were no family ties with the theatre except for an Aunt Fanny who sang opera; the only possible influence on Roger to follow an acting career, apart from his adulation of Gary Cooper and Stewart Granger, was the enthusiasm of his father for amateur dramatics. George Moore threw himself wholeheartedly into the organisation of the dramatic society for E Division and used to produce, direct, do the make-up, play the leads and build the scenery. Roger would always be in the audience watching.

Roger's formal education began at the Hackford Road Elementary School, about a quarter of a mile away from Albert Square across the Clapham Road. It was a typical Victorian school, built in 1886, with separate entrances for boys and girls. Roger was admitted on September 2nd, 1932 but unfortunately he went down with double pneumonia soon afterwards. The illness kept him away from school for so long that it was decided that, as he would have so much work to catch up on, it would be more sensible to wait and to be readmitted the following year. As a result, he again entered Hackford Road School on September 4th, 1933. Roger's illness was a trying time for both parents; in order to pay the medical bills, George was forced to sell the motor-cycle that he used to travel to and from Bow Street. When the doctor first saw the young boy he told the parents to prepare themselves for the worst, and fully expected to be signing the boy's death certificate the next day. But Roger rallied and was able to pull himself out of the critical period; his own memories of the illness are not clear, although he does have faint recollections: 'I remember the poultices being put on my chest and back, and the burning of them.' It was a long illness, during which Roger was confined to bed for a considerable time. Bad luck followed soon after his

16

recovery when he fell through the rusty roof of the coalshed in the backyard, cutting his legs severely; he still carries the scars to this day. Apart from this unfortunate time during his early life, Roger was to be free from any major illness, suffering only from common diseases such as measles which swept through the school periodically.

On April 17th, 1935 he was one of twenty-nine boys and twenty-eight girls who were promoted from the primary school to the senior school. At school, although he was good at most subjects, being a bright young boy, and was rarely out of the top three places in class, his favourite subjects were art and drawing, and it was generally accepted that he would make a career for himself in that field. Roger was also an avid reader – some of his particular favourites being the 'Saint' books written by Leslie Charteris. He was extremely happy at school and was fortunate that his time there coincided with a number of national events. All the pupils were given the day off for the glamorous wedding of Prince George, Duke of Kent, the younger son of George V, to Princess Marina of Greece in November 1934. In Roger's early schooldays he also celebrated the Silver Jubilee of King George V in 1935, and the following year the school was shut in mourning for the King's funeral. In 1937 he experienced the excitement of the coronation of George VI and Queen Elizabeth in May, for which they were given a three-day holiday. Along with the other children at the school he received a Coronation cup and saucer presented to him by the Mayor of Lambeth on behalf of the Borough Council.

From 1938 the talk of war was becoming more common. There was a special closure of the school because of the 'crisis excitement', and meetings were held with teachers concerning air raid precautions and evacuation procedures from the city of London. When Roger returned to school after the Easter break, the first duty on the timetable was an evacuation rehearsal. Soon after, on the evening of September 27th, gas masks were delivered to the school, to be distributed the following day. When Roger arrived at school the next morning, all the children were lined up and given a gas mask each. The masks must have looked strange to them, with their long noses with a grill on the end and the thin strip of cellophane which allowed the only view of the outside world. Trying the mask on, under directions, Roger would have placed it over his head, making sure that it was air-tight. The rubbery smell from the masks made the children feel as if they were suffocating, but they were told that if they did not put them on they would burn their throats when the Germans started dropping something called mustard gas. The holes at the end of the nose would prevent the gas from penetrating and allow them to breathe safely – if uncomfortably. Even in that late summer of 1938 it seemed that evacuation was imminent at any time and Roger, along with his classmates, was told one day to bring his belongings to school with him the next morning in readiness for evacuation, if necessary. By late afternoon, however, a message was received calling it off.

Amid all the excitement of the talk of war, life went on as usual. By 1939 Roger had earned himself a place at Battersea Grammar School, having succeeded in passing the entrance examination. However, he was not able to take advantage of the opportunity because on September 1st, two days before war broke out, evacuation finally became a reality.

Roger, a label tied to his collar with his name and destination, clutching his gas mask in its neat little case along with a meagre brown paper parcel of belongings, was taken to Victoria Station. That morning as all the children had assembled at the school, which for them was the evacuation point, they knew only that they were being sent away for their own good, before Hitler started dropping bombs over the area where they had grown up. Like many other parents, Lily was sobbing as she bid farewell to her son, amid the noise and bustle of hundreds of other London children being sent out of the capital to safety, while George had to bite his lip to stop himself from crying. None of the parents being parted from their children that day knew what was going to happen. As George and Lily watched the train start its journey to the south coast, seeing the waving hand of their son getting smaller as the train gathered speed, they must have wondered if they would live to see him again. Roger was too young to appreciate what was happening and did not know of the danger that his parents might be in by staying in the capital. He must have been carried along by the excitement of a new adventure which had more of the air of a school outing, with all of his friends in the same situation. The only doubt that might have crossed his mind was the talk of getting 'new parents' who would look after him until the war was over.

When the train arrived at the coastal town of Worthing, twelve miles west of Brighton, Roger was told that it was time for him to get off. The children who disembarked at Worthing were taken to a local school, and from there they were billeted with a family. By now the looks on the children's faces had become sad and dismal as the reality of the evacuation hit them. Roger heard his name called, and before he knew what was happening a woman from the Women's Voluntary Service, dressed in her distinctive green uniform, was leading him out to be introduced to his new family. Arriving at a house, she knocked on the door and when it opened nudged Roger forward while she handed a piece of paper to the lady inside, as a form of receipt for the boy. The new evacuee was now officially under the care of a total stranger. For taking him in the family received seven shillings and sixpence a week (37½ pence) from the government.

Away from his parents and friends, Roger felt terribly lonely and unhappy. Being put into the care of a family completely unknown to him was a traumatic experience which he shared with thousands of other London children who had been sent away from the city. He was alone for the first time in his life, since being an only child he did not have the luxury of a brother or sister with him to give him moral support. When he awoke next morning in an unfamiliar bed to the smell of breakfast cooking in the kitchen, he had only himself to confide in as he cautiously crept downstairs.

Roger was in Worthing on September 3rd when he heard Neville Chamberlain announce the outbreak of war between Britain and Germany. The night before the south coast of England had been hit by a violent thunderstorm, and with no mother or father to whom he could run for comfort he must have felt that his whole world was crumbling around him.

The family he stayed with were kind people who did their best to look after the young boy. But it was an uphill task when, like most other evacuees in Worthing, he only wanted to see his real parents again. And matters of etiquette, such as their disapproval of his habit of dipping his toast into his boiled egg at breakfast, must have become enlarged out of all proportion in his mind, making him feel that he was being persecuted unfairly for things which drew no comment at home. Roger's troubles were also compounded by the presence in the family of two sons, both of whom were older than Roger. They were at an age when a boy of Roger's age being around the house was a nuisance to them, upsetting their normal routine. As such they did little to make the young boy feel at home.

Roger had been in Worthing for only a few weeks when he

went down with impetigo, a nervous disease of the skin, and was immediately admitted to hospital. He had good reason to feel sorry for himself – alone, unhappy, and sick in hospital. He wrote a letter home, and George came down to visit his son. When his father arrived Roger looked so pathetic that George took pity on him and arranged to take him back home to London.

Back in Stockwell, Roger was confronted by the sight of barrage balloons hovering in the sky over the city. In the square there were no other children around, since they were scattered all over the country as evacuees. But Roger had little time to reflect on the changes he saw as George wasted no time in sending his son up to Chester to join his mother, whom he had sent there previously for her own safety.

Roger was much happier, and from then on he was not to be parted from his mother throughout the duration of the war. While he was spending his time contentedly in Chester, the news from London, which had experienced no bombing, made people think that it was a 'phoney war'. The initial apprehension of staying in the capital disappeared, and many families began to drift back to their homes. Among them were Lily and her son, Roger, who in the spring of 1940 returned to their flat in Albert Square.

No sooner were they back than the war began in earnest. The Nazis raced through France and before anyone knew what had happened Paris had fallen into their hands. They continued their push towards the coast, forcing the British troops to evacuate Dunkirk. Roger remembers seeing the trains going by Clapham North Station packed with tired and wounded soldiers. In the summer of 1940 the Battle of Britain was being fought in the skies above London. Roger was a witness to the first dog-fight over the capital. He recalls:

The planes came over and we saw them twisting and weaving in the sky as the Luftwaffe and the RAF fought it out. Once we had to fling ourselves into some bushes as we were strafed on the ground. God, the whine of those bullets as my father hunched himself over me in some kind of protection.

Roger also vividly remembers hearing the first bomb drop at the Elephant and Castle, a nearby district. In the back garden they had an Anderson air raid shelter in which they would all squeeze when the siren warned of the approaching German planes. 'In the following weeks things started to hot up. Houses in and around our square were bombed. And I can remember watching the first big blitz fire in the East End from the roof of our flats.'

George began to worry for the safety of his family, with the continual bombing raids over London, and it was decided that Lily should take Roger to live in Amersham, in the Buckinghamshire countryside about 25 miles from London. At night they could see the glow of London burning in the distance, knowing that somewhere in the middle of it was George carrying on with his duties. In Amersham Roger attended Dr Challoner's School, but he only stayed there for two unhappy terms because his mother fell out with the people with whom they were lodging. By this time the danger in London seemed less after the Battle of Britain had been won, and so Lily decided to return once again to her home in Stockwell.

Despite the end of the worst bombing in London, it still seemed to Roger that they spent every night in their shelter, where he recalls they fried sausages over an electric fire for dinner. 'I remember running around the garden a few times chasing after incendiary bombs with a bucket of water. Some mornings – too many mornings – we would wake up to find houses had disappeared. And the people with them.' The war would also rob Roger of his beloved Uncle Jack, who was killed during the Italian campaign, at Monte Cassino in 1944.

During his adolescence Roger had a few girl friends, but he admits that he was not particularly successful with the girls. He was ridiculed because of his minor weight problem, and with their gift for exaggeration Roger says, 'People used to call me too tall, fat and ugly.' However, he was on the brink of blossoming into an incredibly handsome young man.

Back in London, his education continued; he became a school prefect and passed the Royal Society of Arts examinations. Roger's natural intelligence carried him through school with comparative ease, as he admits: 'Whether it's a disadvantage or not to one's character development I always found that I never had to push myself a great deal, at school or later.'

His childhood had been an unusually contented and happy time for Roger; it had given him a very stable outlook on life, enabling him to look to the future with confidence. He was secure in the love his parents had for him and he for them. Unlike so many others who went on to become celebrated film stars, his early life was not marked by struggle or poverty; his was a very ordinary upbringing. Inevitably this has left its mark on the character of the man who is widely acknowledged to be very easy-going and tolerant, avoiding unpleasantness if he can, preferring a friendly and relaxed environment in both his work and his private life. It would also give Roger an inherent idleness, as Terence Young, the director who knew him from the middle of the 1940s, says: 'I've always thought that practically Roger's only defect as a human being is that he is basically idle – not lazy. He allows things to happen but always makes the major decisions in his life, and it's a very good way of going through life.' When Roger left school he had no particular ambition, but was content to drift into whatever presented itself.

Two

In 1943, at the age of fifteen, Roger decided to leave Vauxhall Central School which he had been attending since 1941, and to start to earn his living. The early dislocation of the war, being moved all over the country, and the air raids when living in London, had not created an atmosphere conducive to serious study, and his formal education suffered as a result. The only academic qualification that Roger Moore possessed was his certificate from the Royal Society of Arts examination he had taken. Having inherited a talent for drawing from his father, it was natural that his sights were set on a career as an artist. Through one of his father's colleagues, who had seen and liked Roger's Walt Disney-style drawings, the young man was given an introduction to Publicity Picture Productions in D'Arblay Street, Soho, situated between Oxford Circus and Piccadilly, and was subsequently offered employment.

Working in D'Arblay Street meant travelling into the West End of London every day by bus. On his way to work he would see the statue of Eros in Piccadilly Circus boarded up, the shops with their sparse window displays and the walls dirty and pock-marked after four years of war.

Roger's position at Publicity Picture Productions was that of junior trainee and general office boy. He was there to get an impression of what the business of making animated cartoons entailed, part of his duties being to help out on the more mundane tasks of producing the films, and he would often be called to trace and colour outlines drawn by the experienced artists. Otherwise his work was that of a general nature undertaken by a junior office boy and included running errands, carrying film stock, and making tea for the staff. Because of the attacks of the V-1 bombers over London at this time he was obliged to go fire spotting once a week, when he would stay up all night to deal with any fire that might break out in the building.

Working in D'Arblay Street was a good start for a young man just out of school with an interest in cultivating his potential as an artist. Since he was involved, in part, in the creative work of producing the animated films, he became a member of the studio workers' union, ACTT – the Association of Cinematograph and Allied Technicians, his membership of which he keeps up to this day. In later years it would prove a useful asset to be a member of the union, as it enabled him to direct episodes of *The Saint* and *The Persuaders* television series.

Roger was pleased, as any young boy is, to have money in his pocket which he had earned himself. Early on he saved enough to buy himself his first suit and also started smoking cigarettes. In his spare time he would go to the cinema and frequently spent evenings at the Locarno Ballroom in Streatham. Despite his newly-acquired affluence, his wage of £3.10s a week was not sufficient for him to forget such practical tips as meeting a girl on a date inside rather than outside the ballroom, so that she would have to pay her own admission. When he was working in Soho Roger would keep himself in trim by swimming a great deal, often getting up at six o'clock in the morning to swim at the local pool before going to work. At lunchtime, and occasionally after he had finished work, he would go to the Marshall Street Baths, close to the office in D'Arblay Street.

The highlight of the young man's stay with Publicity Picture Productions was a visit from Lieutenant-Colonel David Niven, who had been granted leave from his regiment to make possibly his finest film, *The Way Ahead*. The War Office had given the company a contract to make animated instructional films for the armed services, and Niven was working briefly with it in his capacity as technical adviser. For Roger it was a real thrill to see the famous actor, and he could hardly have realised that their meeting was his first personal contact with a man who would become, in later years, one of his closest friends. Niven, on his part, always maintained that he never recalled the teenage Roger Moore.

Although Roger enjoyed his time at D'Arblay Street, he was not destined to pursue a career in animation for long. One luckless day everything went wrong: he forgot to carry out one of the errands he was sent out for, the tea he made was cold, and he finally sealed his fate when he made a mistake on some celluloid.

Out of work, the early summer of 1944 was one of idleness for Roger, who spent most days at the local swimming pool in Brockwell Park. One day at the pool he was talking to a friend, Harry Caulfield, who told him about the opportunities available to work as 'extras' in crowd scenes on the mammoth production of *Caesar and Cleopatra*, being filmed at Denham. Roger was intrigued by the idea and took himself up to Wardour Street, feeling he would be a great asset to Central Casting, who were sorely in need of tall, handsome young men to work as extras, with so many abroad on active service. So, at the age of sixteen, Roger was now legitimately able to work in film studios as an actor, as well as a technician. He also knew that his father might be able to help him in some way.

George Moore's work in the Police Force had become busier than ever and was more varied as the war progressed. Amidst the generally shocking role that the London policeman had to play in the bomb-torn capital, there were the lighter reliefs of the police-man's ordinary tasks to perform. Robberies, both large and small, had to be dealt with by Detective Sergeant Moore in his capacity as a plan drawer. In 1944 George Moore was brought in on the case of a robbery suffered by the famous film director, Brian Desmond Hurst, not the first time the talented Irishman had been the victim of such a crime, as 'a man like myself is subject to this kind of nuisance'. Detective Sergeant Moore, tall, handsome and with the dignity and air of a man of military background, made a marked impression on Mr Hurst because of his control of the situation, as well as his sympathy and understanding.

Ulster-born Brian Desmond Hurst had, by the time war broke out, become one of the British film industry's most important directors. Terence Young, who was later to direct three of the early James Bond films, and was also a protégé of the active Mr Hurst, has a high regard for his talent: 'Brian Hurst in 1939 was the best director in England by a mile, streets ahead of Carol Reed, Michael Powell and Anthony Asquith.' Hurst's major contributions to the British cinema at this stage in his career had been *On the Night of the Fire,* starring Ralph Richardson and Diana Wynyard, made in 1940 and *Dangerous Moonlight* with Anton Walbrook and Sally Gray, the script for which had been written by Terence Young during seven days' leave from the services. The film became celebrated for its introduction of the 'Warsaw Concerto', which Hurst had commissioned British com-poser Richard Addinsell to write. This composition was in its own way to become as popular a piece of music as 'Lili Marlene' during World War II. In 1942 Hurst teamed Margaret Lockwood and James Mason for the first time in his fine murder mystery, *Alibi.* But his greatest contribution to the cinema is undoubtedly *Theirs is the Glory*, the ultimate British war documentary and a stirring tribute to the men who fought at Arnhem.

And so it happened that while Hurst was directing Vivien Leigh and Claude Rains in a scene for *Caesar and Cleopatra*, on a hot summer's day in 1944, George introduced his son to the victim of the robberies he had attended, saying, 'This is my son, Roger. He wants to be an actor.'

Brian Desmond Hurst recalls: 'I remember meeting Roger very well on the set of *Caesar and Cleopatra*. I took a look at him and said, "Have you any acting experience?" "No sir, I haven't," he said.'

Hurst liked the young man immediately and thought him exactly right for a part that was, in reality, little more than a spear carrier in the film. Hurst says: 'He was tall and slim, and over six foot and I wanted a tall handsome young man.'

And so Roger became a professional actor in the celebrated *Caesar and Cleopatra*. He later recalled his feelings at the time of this fateful meeting with Brian Hurst: 'It didn't occur to me *not* to be interested in being an actor. It was like walking in the dark towards an object you know to be there, and when you switch on a torch and see it suddenly in the beam it comes as no surprise to you.' Roger, in interviews, has been customarily modest about his being spotted by Brian Desmond Hurst and, giving his own explanation of how he came to the director's attention, has said: 'There was Stewart Granger running around in a red toga. And all of us extras had red togas and were carrying spears – my spear was longer, that's all there was to it!'

Hurst's interest in Roger was as a patron, most unusual for that between director and extra, and with the help of the older man Roger obtained work as an extra in two other films during the summer of 1944. He worked on *Gaiety George* which starred Richard Greene and Ann Todd, as a member of a theatre audience, and also appeared in *Perfect Strangers* (US title: *Vacation from Marriage*) with Robert Donat and Deborah Kerr. Roger was to recount later that he had to sit across from Miss Kerr for a scene in a railway carriage, playing a sailor for two days. Roger harboured a secret crush for the actress, little knowing that for the past two years, since playing opposite the celebrated Mr Donat at the Cambridge Theatre in Shaw's *Heartbreak House*, Miss Kerr and Mr Donat had been heavily drawn to one another. Roger was certainly one of the shipwrecked sailors in the lifeboat which was manned by Robert Donat and was placed directly beside Donat for this very important scene. To share screen time with an actor of Robert Donat's supreme status was not only a great experience for the young man, but he also had the distinction of being directed by Sir Alexander Korda – no mean feat for a seventeen-year-old beginner.

By this time Roger had become very friendly with Brian Desmond Hurst, who said,

'I am going to send you to the Royal Academy of Dramatic Art for one year.' I asked his father if he could support him at college whilst I paid the fees and his father said, 'Yes.'

Roger recalled going home and rushing up to his mother, barely able to control his excitement, shouting, 'I'm going to be Stewart Granger!'

Hurst says: 'I pulled strings for him when necessary to get him into the Academy and just telephoned and told them he was coming.'

This was quite a feat, particularly as the Principal of RADA at this time was the austere Sir Kenneth Barnes, brother of the famous Vanbrugh sisters, Dame Irene and Violet. RADA had been founded by Sir Kenneth in 1906, and he remained Principal until the early 1950s. He wanted his students to be ladies and gentlemen, and the atmosphere at the Academy was very much like a finishing school for gentlefolk. It was at RADA that any traces of a south London accent would be removed, as Roger had to learn 'standard' or 'received' English. RADA produced something called the RADA voice, which implied a mannered artificiality of tone. Although Barnes was secretly nicknamed 'Granny' by the students, he was most certainly a matriarchal 'Granny'.

Hurst continues:

I told him what to expect when he went to RADA and I coached him for his exams at my home at 26, Grosvenor Crescent Mews in Belgravia. He was very excited but quite calm and I said, 'All you have to do is work hard.' I changed everything: his speech – he didn't have a particularly heavy accent although he did talk a bit cockney but RADA cured all that; his clothes – I bought him clothing and saw that he changed from being the son of a police sergeant to a young gentleman. He was a very apt pupil.

Roger was in the fortunate position of knowing in July that he would be attending RADA in October.

His audition was on September 26th, 1944. He remembers, 'For my RADA audition I fell back on my schoolboy recital of *The Revenge*, and a piece from *The Silver Box* by Galsworthy. When I started RADA had been bombed out of its main theatre and was using a tiny place in Gower Street.' It is the hardest thing that an actor will ever do in his life when he goes to an audition for a drama school because he goes in completely cold, not knowing what anyone wants or expects of him. He is a total newcomer to a profession he knows absolutely nothing about.

During his time at RADA Roger lived with his family in Stockwell, but visited Hurst regularly. Hurst remembers him as a family boy who was very fond of his mother and father. Once Roger had decided on an acting career he was very diligent in his studies. Hurst says, 'He was willing to experiment in any direction. He would do almost anything to get on.' He was a very hard worker at RADA and was very much loved and respected for it, as well as for the mischievous side of his character which endeared him to many. Roger was keen to mix with people of culture and distinction, and Brian Hurst made sure that he was able to meet many influential and important people in the business. Hurst recalls:

He fitted in very well with my friends because he was so handsome, charming and always had lovely manners. He was wanted by everybody but he was very choosy. He wasn't a nun and he wasn't a play-about either. He took care of himself and was very highly respected by all of us because he did his work beautifully. His austerity was not oppressive.

Hurst introduced him to the celebrated critic, James Agate, and the ballet critic, Richard Buckle, and he often dined with them.

Roger and Desmond Hurst would often dine at the Caprice and a restaurant near Leicester Square, where Agate and Buckle also used to take him. James Agate told Roger at this time, 'You'll be successful – but you'll never be an actor. You'll be popular with the gallery and you'll never learn.' Hurst says of the circle in which he mixed:

I don't know whether he was intimate with any of them or not. I didn't ask him any questions, but I didn't want him to go along

the wrong path. In our business a handsome, tall young man is
the butt of many people's desires and I kept him clear of that.
They were all after him, but the one person he was close to was
me. Nobody got near him.

Despite the influential circle in which Roger moved, it was
Hurst who was the major influence on his early life. The director
relates: 'Sometimes I coached him privately in acting. He would
come to me with work that was proposed to him and I would
advise him, telling him what to do and how to handle the situation.'
George Moore also used to visit Hurst at his house to discuss the
progress of his son and to express his gratitude for what Hurst
was doing to help. When Hurst met George Moore he was at
pains to inform him of the uncertain profession that his son was
entering, and that after training it would not necessarily follow
that work would be at hand. He told George that Roger would
have to expect many periods when he would be totally without
work. But as Hurst says: 'He was not worried about his son. He
knew what lay ahead of him. He wasn't a police sergeant for
nothing. He was broad-minded and very dignified always.'

In the mid 1940s the West End stage was crammed as never
before with the greats of the British theatre: Olivier, Richardson,
Gielgud, Dame Sybil Thorndike and Noel Coward, as well as the
wonderful Cicely Courtneidge, Tommy Trinder, Vivien Leigh,
Flora Robson, Donald Wolfit and even the Lunts, who were in
and out of the West End frequently. Through Brian Desmond
Hurst Roger was, at the age of only seventeen, to meet almost all
of them.

Hurst sent Roger to the theatre regularly, paying for his tickets
out of his own pocket: 'I got him in the stalls, up close in the sixth
row back on the aisle, from where he could go for a pee if he
wanted to without any trouble. I took him into their dressing
rooms after. He met them all.' When introduced to such great
actors as Olivier and Richardson, Hurst remembers him as being
'a bit in awe of them but . . . cool about it. He examined them
and took what he wanted from them.'

Going to RADA each day during the bombing, Roger would
make his way across the river from Stockwell to Gower Street in
Bloomsbury. The continuous air raids did not deter him or his
fellow students. Amongst them were Lois Maxwell under her real
name of Lois Hooker, with whom he would be reunited some
thirty years later in a way he could not have envisaged. She

29

remembers that 'Every girl in the class was besotted with him. He was quite beautiful.' She said, 'We were both in the same class, and because I was taller than most other girls, I often had to play men's parts. I played Roger's uncle in *Henry V* and was almost always his fencing partner.'

At the end of his first term Roger had to perform four extracts from Shakespeare plays, to enable the Academy to give an assessment of his work. He was acknowledged to be physically good, but his acting was reported as being rather self-conscious, with room for a great deal of improvement. However, he did manage to get the part of a French policeman, and actually had to sing a couple of songs, in *The Italian Straw Hat* at the Arts Theatre during the Christmas break. His second try at the West End stage was in a small part in *Circle of Chalk*.

The time that Roger spent at RADA was one of the happiest periods of his life. He enjoyed the close *camaraderie* with the other students, all of them trying to make their money last by sharing meals, and supplementing what little they did have by getting jobs as waiters or washing-up in restaurants. Roger says: 'There were sixteen girls and four boys. I learnt a great deal about sex, but not much about acting.' Actress Fabia Drake, who was one of his tutors at RADA, directed him as the King and Bardolph in a production of *Henry V* in his last term, upon which the tutor commented: 'He speaks and moves badly. Still terribly self-conscious.' Years later she said of him: 'He was an extraordinarily good-looking boy with a strongly-developed sense of humour even then. It's this light-hearted manner that causes a lot of people to underrate him as an actor. I found that, under it all, he was a serious artist. His flippant manner simply disguises this seriousness.'

At the start of his second term at the Academy Roger made a point of studying the new intake of girls and was immediately struck by one in particular. 'A swift assessment of the incoming class sent me homing in on a very pretty girl with long blonde hair and a baby face. Her name was Doorn Van Steyn. She was five years older than me but she looked as young as the rest of us. She was quite a stunningly beautiful girl, and very soon we were dating heavily.'

Doorn would later admit that she was not a bit interested in 'younger men' like him and said of Roger, 'He was like a great sloppy puppy.' But despite this initial impression she soon fell under the spell of his youthful charm.

Doorn Van Steyn had been born in Streatham and christened Lucy Woodward. She was one of three sisters and one brother born to a Mr and Mrs William Woodward. Her father, apart from other work, took a keen interest in his role as an active trade union official in the Labour Party. By the time she met Roger she was calling herself Doorn Van Steyn, having changed her name by deed poll, and through her ice-skating skills had already appeared in a small part in the film, *The Wicked Lady*.

Of his courtship Roger says: 'Doorn was working, sometimes in stage shows, sometimes in ice shows. I had to learn to ice-skate to be near her during our courting days at RADA. I don't remember proposing. It just happened as a natural progression.'

At the end of his third term Roger was approaching his eighteenth birthday and knew that he would be called for National Service. With this in mind he saw little point in staying on and decided to get some practical experience. He secured an offer to do a season of George Bernard Shaw plays, including *Androcles and the Lion*, in repertory at Cambridge. Roger left for Cambridge pledging his undying love for Doorn. During this first season in repertory the director, who found Roger's ability to be as unimpressive as his tutors at the Academy had reported, gave him some practical advice, telling him: 'You're not very good are you? So smile when you come on.'

Some thirty years later Roger would say that he thought it much more useful to join a repertory company to learn the acting trade by experience, rather than academic training. But he said: 'I enjoyed the time spent there but they convinced me I didn't have any talent, and took away my self-confidence. I used to sidle into interviews and say I'd been to RADA, but it didn't mean anything so I stopped saying it.'

Completing his season of Shaw at Cambridge in the autumn of 1945, Roger, now eighteen, was called up to do National Service. His reluctance to enlist was looked on as rather a disgrace since he came from a family with strong military tradition. Before entering the army he was called for his medical, which coincided with an attack of yellow jaundice. Consequently he arrived for the medical with yellow eyes and jaundiced skin. He was asked to give a urine sample and remembers: 'It was a very strange sort of colour but they still passed me A1.' The war had caused a tremendous loss of manpower, and with numerous soldiers waiting for their demob papers the army could not afford to be too choosy. So Roger was passed as fit and was sent to Bury St Edmunds for six weeks' basic training. He was determined not to like army life.

At Bury St Edmunds Roger and other new recruits were lined up, still dressed in their civilian clothes, while the company commander looked them over. Roger was confronted by the Regimental Sergeant Major, who saw by his papers that he had been an artist. Appropriately, the first job he was given was to paint a wooden hut. They were all issued with their uniforms and in compliance with army regulations were obliged to have their hair cut very short. This particularly bothered Roger:

'I was only eighteen and with my small face and no nose and hardly any head to speak of I looked like a little pinhead sticking out of an enormous uniform.'

His six weeks at Bury St Edmunds are not remembered with any particular fondness by Roger, who had a gruelling time there in the bitter winter cold learning to march in step, how to use a rifle and being pushed through rigorous assault courses.

The Sergeant watched the progress of Private Moore and was sufficiently impressed to consider recommending him for the Intelligence Corps; he used to let him know of his intentions, as Roger recalls: 'The Sergeant would always say to me, "I. Corps for you, lad!" and I thought he meant I was going in the Opticians Branch of the Medical Corps.' When the Sergeant discovered what Roger's idea of the I. Corps was the matter was quickly dropped and not mentioned again. The task was then to find something for which Private Moore was suited, and he was put to work drawing Army Personnel posters.

Despite his initial blunder over the Intelligence Corps, by the end of his basic training Roger was requested to report to WOSBY – the War Office Selection Board, to ascertain whether he was suitable officer material. At WOSBY he spent three days going through various tests, each designed to bring out his qualities of leadership and intelligence, and was closely spied upon to evaluate his potential. He then returned to his unit to await the results.

A week later he was informed that he had been selected to be sent to OCTU to start his officer training. In the course of his training he was sent all over the country, including a period at Dartford to become familiar with Motor Transport, where, he claims, he lost control of a motorcycle and, unable to stop, went careering through a Woolworth's store. Christmas was spent at a desolate camp in North Wales set on a peninsula with the icy sea on three sides.

On his first leave from the army while at Officers' Training

School Roger was fortunate enough to secure a bit part in Herbert Wilcox's *Piccadilly Incident*, the first film to team Anna Neagle with Michael Wilding, who were to become one of the most popular romantic screen couples ever in British films. Roger's part in the film entailed sitting at a table with Michael Wilding, and earned him five shillings a day, which was a useful addition to his army pay. More important was that the great British film-maker, Herbert Wilcox, impressed by the young soldier, told Roger to look him up when he came out of the army. Roger says: 'Anna Neagle had seen me and I looked up and saw her talking to her husband, Herbert Wilcox. He came over to me and said they had been discussing me. He asked if I was an actor or a real soldier earning a few bob on the side. I said I was both and he told me to come and see him when I eventually was demobbed.'

At the age of nineteen Roger was commissioned a second lieutenant in the Royal Army Service Corps, although he modestly says, 'The only reason they commissioned me was I looked good in uniform and they felt they had to make me an officer. I looked like a hero.' As a second lieutenant his first posting was to Schleswig-Holstein in West Germany, where he was to command a small supply depot. This was Roger's first trip abroad to a country severely ravaged by war and on the verge of starvation, where for a time cigarettes were used as currency and girls, desperate for food, would sell themselves for a bar of chocolate. For those young men doing their National Service at this time it was a period of boredom and depression.

Second Lieutenant Roger Moore was, however, luckier than most in being put in command of a small depot. He was in charge of forty men and a troop of Polish soldiers.

Being in sole command, Roger was able to run the camp in his own way. Never liking what seemed to him excessive discipline and regard for red tape in the army, his post was run along much more informal lines, as he always preferred to work in a friendly, casual atmosphere. His example in leadership meant that the men under his charge were constantly being reported for having their buttons undone on their tunics or for not wearing their full kit. When charge sheets were brought to him Roger would just throw them in the waste paper basket and give those concerned a mild rebuke, telling them not to do it again. Second Lieutenant Moore was not interested in all the paper work which was inevitably involved if disciplinary action were to be taken. Apart from having no one senior to him in rank at the depot to tell him what to do,

Roger had another reason to be grateful: 'After years of sparse wartime rations, I found myself in possession of vast quantities of Libby's tinned fruit and evaporated milk, eggs and bacon.' Under such pleasant conditions he saw no reason to upset the men under his authority by going overboard on discipline. As commander of the supply depot it was his responsibility to make sure that the Officers' Messes in his territory were all kept well stocked with necessary foodstuffs, and he often travelled up to Copenhagen in Denmark in order to buy eggs, bacon and other supplies. Through being able to travel around he saw at first hand a country he had known only as an enemy; seeing people who had caused him to be sent away from home when he was evacuated, who had wreaked havoc and destruction among the streets he had grown up in and who had taken the life of his favourite relative, Uncle Jack. He must have viewed going over to Germany with some trepidation, but at the same time he must have felt considerable interest.

His days at Schleswig-Holstein were to come to an end when after six months he was transferred to the Main Supply Depot at Neumunster, sixty miles away, as Chief Stores Officer. This being a main depot, Roger was again under the command of higher ranking officers and was no longer able to run the depot in his own way. He was back in the army life of rules and regulations. Here his former casualness about discipline was not looked upon favourably, and he was frequently reprimanded for his indifferent attitude over whether or not he was saluted as an officer should be.

Life under the army discipline he so hated became miserable for him, and it was at this time that he began his numerous attempts to get a transfer to the CSEU – the Combined Services Entertainments Unit – but without success. The CSEU was, and still is, an off-shoot of the British Army which provided light entertainment for servicemen stationed at distant outposts, not to be confused with ENSA – the Entertainments National Service Association, which was formed by Basil Dean in 1939 as a purely civilian enterprise to despatch star entertainers to as many theatres of war as possible during wartime.

Unable to gain entry into the CSEU, Roger began producing his own welfare shows and quiz programmes in the evenings for the nearby camps. On one such evening, on his way back from one of his shows, he was involved in a severe jeep accident. Roger remembers nothing at all of what had happened, but was told that the wheel had come off the steering column and the jeep had

34

smashed, out of control, into a tree. Roger woke up a week later in hospital in Schleswig-Holstein to discover the awful truth: 'My head and jaw were split open. I was concussed and my sight badly affected by congealed blood around the eyeballs. My face was in a ghastly mess.'

Fortunately for Roger, the accident left him with no scars; it could have meant the end of his acting career, since he was counting on his handsome features to take him along the road to success. Despite having avoided permanent damage to his face, it was a long time before he was completely recovered from the accident. He had to spend seven weeks on his back in the hospital, and it was three months before he was well again, during which time he was transferred to a large military hospital in Hamburg.

On his first leave from Germany Roger married Doorn. The ceremony took place at Wandsworth Register Office on December 9th, 1946. It was a quiet occasion, with only close members of each family huddled in the office out of the bitter winter cold. George Moore was a witness, as was Doorn's sister, Fleur: Roger was just nineteen years old. Doorn says of their marriage: 'We were perfectly suited, physically and sexually.' However Roger was far too young to tackle the responsibilities and commitment that marriage entailed. Embarking on so insecure a career as that of an actor was no basis for a strong financial future. But at the time of their marriage towards the end of 1946 Roger was still in the army. The real strain would come when he came out of the services and resumed his attempts to get on in the acting world.

Never having had a proper honeymoon, Doorn came over to Hamburg as soon as he was released from hospital. Roger had been given three weeks' sick leave, and they intended to spend it in a servicemen's hotel in the city. However, this brief respite was not to last as almost immediately Roger was struck down with severe stomach pains and rushed to hospital again, to have his appendix out, leaving him with a six-inch scar. Roger spent his time in the hospital annoying the other patients, by riding around in his wheelchair playing 'In The Mood' on an old gramophone, and trying to avoid the attentions of members of the nursing staff in the hospital.

Discharged from hospital once again, he was informed that his next posting was as a welfare officer to No. 4 Training Brigade in Lippstadt. Having been through so much physical discomfort in the past few months, Roger was, for once, in a fighting mood and made it clear to the commanding officer that he wanted a transfer from the Royal Army Service Corps to the Combined Services Entertainments Unit. Knowing of the rough time that the young lieutenant had been through recently, the CO must have looked on Roger with compassion, as he allowed him to telephone the officer in command of CSEU.

The man Roger spoke to on the telephone was Colonel Sanders Warren, who was with the Unit's headquarters in Hamburg. Colonel Warren's theatrical career had reached its peak in the pre-war years when he played Red Shadow in a touring version of *The Desert Song*, of which he was very proud. The result of Roger's conversation with the Colonel was that he was transferred within twenty-four hours to the most outrageous unit in the whole of Europe.

The CSEU was much more to Roger's liking with its friendly, jokey atmosphere. It also had the advantage of putting him back into the world of the theatre. The army fought a losing battle trying to keep them all in line and discipline was notoriously lax. Most of the personnel in the unit had been in show business of one sort or another before being called up for their National Service. The most notable exception was the Adjutant, who was regular army and had been posted to the unit in an attempt to make sure that regulations were complied with and that all members behaved in a way appropriate to their position in His Majesty's Forces. Unfortunately, he had an impossible task.

The men in the unit, as well as disregarding regulations governing behaviour, took a similar attitude towards dress regulations. Many of them wore specially-tailored uniforms which enabled them to wear a collar and tie; they also wore their hair much longer than the army regulations allowed and favoured suede shoes rather than the army footwear with which they were supplied. Colonel Warren, known to the men affectionately as 'Bunny', would occasionally call a parade to remind them about discipline – but this was only a formality. He would get them all on the parade ground and lecture them: 'The place is like Fred Karno's army. You're all a shambles and from now on you'll respect officers and salute them. You are still in the army and they have got a commission!'

The Adjutant might smile to himself when the Colonel ticked the men off, but 'Bunny' Warren did little to encourage discipline. The Adjutant would put the men on charges and march them in front of the Colonel only to have him cry out, 'But you can't put this man on a charge. He's got dress rehearsal tomorrow!'

36

Bryan Forbes, who was to become one of the British cinema's most important screen writer/directors, was a Sergeant-Major in the Intelligence Corps and was transferred to CSEU. He recalls going to the Hotel zum Kron Prinzen in the Hauptbahnhof Platz in Hamburg, a bombed-out hotel which had been taken over by the unit. The hotel was used by all the officers and NCOs, the officers on the third floor and the NCOs on the second floor. Forbes was confronted by an incredibly dashing Second Lieutenant: Roger Moore. He says, 'We were so pleased to see each other that I flung my arms around him and we went into a tight embrace, whereupon the Adjutant put me under arrest for kissing an officer in a theatre of war. Fortunately the Colonel let me off the charge.'

Another Sergeant there was Joe Cunningham, who worked under the stage-name of Joe Baker and was to become a top comic in British music halls and subsequently moved to California. Like Forbes, he had known Roger vaguely in London before they were called up and was to fall victim to the pranks that Roger and the other officers would get up to: 'They used to come into my room at two o'clock in the morning and throw a bucket of water over me. Roger came in one night with a fire extinguisher and just put it all over me. We had to be careful what we did back to the officers in case the Adjutant found out.'

Joe Baker remembers one occasion when he got his revenge. Roger was showing a young officer, fresh out of training school, around the hotel and pointing out the various departments used for music, scenery and such. Then Roger led the young man out of the hotel, where Sergeant Baker happened to be walking down the road towards them with a kit big over his shoulder full of laundry. Baker recalls:

All of a sudden he saw me and, as always, the look on his face was one of slight fear of what I was going to do. As I got to him I saluted correctly, giving him a real regimental salute, and he looked very relieved. Then I just dropped the kit bag, flung my arms around him and said, 'Roger darling, I love you; kiss me!' and ran away. The young officer said, 'Put him on a charge!' but Roger said, 'It's alright – I'll speak to him later.' And, of course, he came into my room and gave me the biggest rollicking of my life. Then later that evening we had a drink together.

It was decided early on during his time with CSEU that Roger should be promoted to acting Captain, to give him more seniority among the ranks. As an officer Roger's duties were different to those of the NCOs like Bryan Forbes and Joe Baker. Army regulations forbade the participation of officers in an acting capacity in any of the productions which CSEU mounted, so Captain Moore had to be satisfied with working on the production side. Bryan Forbes says: 'I was the humble non-commissioned officer and the humble actor, while Roger was the exalted officer in production.' One of Captain Moore's presentations was *The Shop on Sly Corner*, which was a current West End hit.

As a senior officer Roger was also put in charge of much of the administrative work which needed to be carried out at the camp. This included the control of supplies, the taking of pay parade and the clearing and planning of travel arrangements for members of the unit when they went on their tours around West Germany, Austria and Italy. This was no easy task since groups could be on the road for as long as three months. Bryan Forbes had a lot of experience of these kinds of road shows: 'Once you were out on the road you were isolated. You didn't come back for two or three months, and in that time we would perform plays in twenty or thirty different places.' They would perform such plays as *Charley's Aunt* and *The Hasty Heart*, often on one-night stands from the back of a Bedford truck. Occasionally Roger himself would accompany groups on the train to Italy and Austria, but most of his time was spent in Hamburg, carrying out his duties there. Away from headquarters, or out of sight of other officers, Captain Moore would quickly relax into first name terms with the men. They, in turn, would call him 'Rodge' out of earshot of any regular army personnel, and would also drop the formality of saluting him.

The unit was full of young men who would later become celebrated entertainers in civilian life, including Sergeant Harry Secombe, who was making a name for himself with his popular shaving act, and also Spike Milligan and Terry Thomas.

Roger was fortunate that his superior rank meant that he would generally take charge of looking after visiting celebrities. One such star was Danny Kaye, who made a brief visit when he came over on a USO tour to entertain GIs in the American sector. He performed one night for the British troops at the Theatre Royal in Hamburg. On February 2nd, 1948 Danny Kaye had been a virtually unknown American entertainer chosen to headline the variety bill at the London Palladium, the foremost variety house in the world. Kaye's success there has never been emulated, before or since. He literally took London by storm and the critics' reaction to his ninety-minute stint was ecstatic. His two-week engagement turned into four weeks and then into six. For the first time a King and Queen of England sat in the stalls of a theatre for a performance, after the then Princess Elizabeth, having already seen his act, insisted that her parents sit in the front row. Danny Kaye became a show business legend overnight. Roger felt totally overwhelmed and honoured that he would be in charge of his visit to Hamburg.

Another celebrity, popular with the soldiers, who came out to play the same theatre, was Hollywood film star Yvonne de Carlo. Kay Kendall, who like Roger had been an extra in *Caesar and Cleopatra*, also came out to Hamburg, and sang and danced to entertain the troops. On first seeing Roger dressed immaculately in his Captain's uniform, she had shouted out, 'Look at the bloody Duchess!' The nickname stuck and was to be a constant source of ribbing, even after Roger had left the services.

The time that Roger spent with CSEU in Hamburg was a happy one for the aspiring young actor, pleased to be given the opportunity to mix with other hopefuls in the theatrical profession while doing his National Service. He was even fortunate in the last few months before his demob, at the end of 1948, when it was decided to relax the rules concerning what was considered appropriate for an officer, and he was permitted to do a little acting to keep his hand in for when he left the army. On leave again in England, five months before his demob, he heard of the much-publicised search for the male lead in the planned film version of *The Blue Lagoon*, about a young boy and girl shipwrecked on a desert island. Roger went to Pinewood Studios and was tested for the part of the young man, but his lack of experience let him down and the part, co-starring with a young Jean Simmons, went to Donald Houston, who was deemed to be more experienced for the role. Another young actor who tested for the role and lost was Larry Skikne, who soon after would change his name to Laurence Harvey. Like Roger, his career did not take off until he became involved with a woman much older than himself, in his case the brilliant, witty and outrageous West End star Hermione Baddeley, whom he would meet at about the same time Roger met Dorothy Squires.

Roger returned to Hamburg to complete his National Service,

and finally in the winter of 1948 he came back to England to live with the wife he had married two years before.

Looking back on his National Service, Roger would say, 'I was lucky, I managed to avoid fighting but I think the experience is very beneficial. It cuts the umbilical cord, if it hasn't already been cut. It is discipline and good for you, and you learn to stand on your own feet. It also gives you a common enemy – the Sergeant and the CO. I think it did me a world of good.'

It was not easy for Roger to come out of the relatively secure life of the army, where he had enjoyed privileges in accordance with his officer status, and be just one of the thousands of people in London looking for employment during the lean years after the war. In fact, Roger remembers one Christmas during this time, back in civilian life, when money was so short he was forced to hawk novelties in London's famous Oxford Street, having to keep one eye open for the police.

Being married to Doorn meant that he was unable to continue his companionship with the director Brian Desmond Hurst that he had enjoyed before he went into the army. Doorn could be of little influence in helping his career, struggling herself to get on. Only when Roger met Dorothy Squires would he find someone who was prepared to fulfil the role of Hurst, Agate, Buckle and their circle. In the interim period Roger would know what it was like to have to scrape together enough money to live. Although he and Brian kept in touch, the situation had changed too radically for him to be of more than passing help to the young actor, and Roger was often forced to turn to his parents for financial aid.

The marriage to Doorn, as well as being a surprise to Hurst, must have come as an equal jolt to his parents. They had looked after him throughout his life and had unhesitatingly entered into their private partnership with Brian Desmond Hurst in order to send Roger to RADA, which was a great drain on their resources. At the age of nineteen Roger had suddenly informed them, after a couple of extremely poorly paid jobs before joining the army, that he was going to marry a woman older than himself.

Roger's financial situation was negative. His parents lost him to the army, and he was not to return home again. Instead he returned to the squalor of his situation in Streatham, which must have been a dreadful disappointment to them. Like many newly-married couples in the immediate post-war years, Roger and Doorn were forced to lodge with relatives, as the large-scale destruction of housing in London during the war had caused a shortage of living space. The strain imposed on marriages by having to live in this way was a common cause of divorce among young couples. The lack of privacy and the inability to discuss problems openly, without having a family audience, inevitably meant that anger would be bottled up until they were alone and could talk privately. A situation where they were living on top of one another was no recipe for a successful marriage. Whether or not Roger loved Doorn is immaterial to the fact that he placed a heavy burden on himself – a burden with which he was certainly not in a position to deal. Roger was now plunging into what was to be the lowest point in his life.

The lack of work around at this time put an almost impossible strain on both Roger and Doorn, and the marriage soon ran into trouble. As Doorn recalled years later, 'We were broke. We had to live in a bed-sit at my parents' house.' Doorn also recalled with great bitterness that she used to take on any job that would bring in some cash while Roger stubbornly insisted on staying at home, waiting by the telephone for a call from his agent, Gordon Harbord. His answer to her fury was: 'You married me as an actor and I will never be anything else.' Angrily she would reply: 'You'll *never* be an actor. Your face is too weak, your jaw's too big and your mouth's too small.'

Roger remembers his first marriage differently. 'We were living in one room in Streatham. Yet we never bothered too much about being broke. We struggled along together and I always had the feeling that success wasn't very far away. There was a little electric grill in the corner of our room, which I surrounded with her mother's paintings to stop the fat spraying on to the wallpaper.'

They would eventually leave their little bed-sit and move into a £3-a-week council flat in Streatham. They were often so hard up that Roger would have to ask his mother to pay their milk bill, which she willingly did. Doorn has said that in the post-war years her career was progressing quite well and this caused trouble between them. She became a Rank starlet, did some modelling and continued to work in ice-skating spectaculars, which increasingly entailed long separations as Doorn had engagements to fulfil on the Continent. She also got a small part in the Anna Neagle/ Michael Wilding film, *Maytime in Mayfair*. When Roger heard this, he remembered Herbert Wilcox's remark about looking him up when he came out of the army, and asked Doorn to get him into the studio. Roger had met with little success in persuading the casting director on the film that Mr Wilcox had asked him to come and see him, and so as a last resort he turned to Doorn for help.

At the studio, Roger lunched with Doorn and then went off to stalk his quarry. When he spotted Herbert Wilcox he steeled himself to approach the great man, but just as he was walking up to him the object of Roger's attention turned away and disappeared into the toilet. Undaunted by this setback, Roger strode after him. He walked towards Mr Wilcox, stood beside him, then turned to him and said, 'Hello, Mr Wilcox, do you remember me?'

Herbert Wilcox gave Roger a troubled look, said 'No' quite sharply, buttoned up his flies and hurried out of the urinal. Roger saw the man who could have made his career fleeing away from him in terror. His over-enthusiastic approach had been mis-interpreted by the famous producer/director, and his chance was lost.

Roger secured a walk-on in a 90-minute thriller called *Paper Orchid*, directed for Columbia by Roy Baker, and starring Hugh Williams and Hy Hazel. It was typical of the swiftly-made British programmers popular at this time. The only other film work that he secured in 1949 was a small part as a 'stage-door johnny' in *Trottie True*, a musical set in the London of the 1890s, starring Jean Kent and James Donald, and directed by his old mentor, Brian Desmond Hurst.

The scene in which Roger appeared saw him hanging outside the stage-door waiting for the girls from the show to come out. Miss Kent remembers that Roger was very nervous and kept getting his timing wrong as the door opened, which necessitated some retakes. But she went over to the young bit-player, telling him not to worry, and managed to calm him down so that the scene was finally shot without any problems. It was marvellous for Roger to be working with a famous leading lady who was so considerate towards an actor like himself. It was kindness he would always remember.

Also at this time Roger did a brief stint as a stage manager for the BBC at their studios in Alexandra Palace. Among the artists with whom he came into contact there was a very young Julie Andrews. In the summer of 1949 his agent heard that the management of the little Intimate Theatre in Palmers Green, a suburb of North London, had decided to produce one of Noel Coward's least-known and least-performed plays, entitled *Easy Virtue*. It had been written as a star vehicle for a big leading lady and Broadway's Jane Cowl had created the part both on Broadway and in London in the 1920s. Roger was given a part in the production, playing opposite the young musical comedy actress, Noele Gordon, who was only five years Roger's senior, and had played supporting parts in such enormous West-End hits as *Let's Face It* and *The Lisbon Story*, and had supported Mae West when she brought *Diamond Lil* to the Prince of Wales Theatre in London. Miss Gordon was certainly equipped professionally to be the leading lady at the Intimate Theatre and had already filled this position in a couple of productions at the theatre. Miss Gordon, now one of Britain's most celebrated television stars, recalls that 'this young man, Roger Moore, was cast opposite me at the beginning of his career. I think he appreciated that I wasn't a bitchy leading lady, and that I brought out the best in him, helping him with his performance.' Noele Gordon still remembers how professional she found the young man, and how handsome he was, and that it was unusual to find a man so modest of his obvious good looks, being completely without vanity. They both got on very well and would travel back to Central London together on the late-night Green Line bus from Palmers Green.

It was a friend of Doorn's, who happened to be a photographer, who first asked Roger if he would be interested in doing some modelling. Roger said that he would, and so began an important sideline which enabled him to earn a little money when acting jobs were not available to him. He was to model for knitting patterns; he employed his dazzling smile to illustrate the effects of using Macleans toothpaste, he became the Brylcreem Boy at a time when Doorn was modelling as the Jamaica Rum girl, and appeared as the illustration of the Doctor, in the medical column of *Woman's Own*. He was seen leaning against a piano, glass in hand, in the brochure for the newly-refitted liner *Queen Elizabeth*, and was even the model for the drawings used to illustrate a women's magazine serialisation of David Niven's first book, *Around the Rugged Rocks*. Through his assignments he was able to work with such beautiful and famous models as Audrey Hepburn, Susan Shaw and Fiona Campbell-Walter.

Roger also modelled for Dinah Sheridan's mother, Lisa, who ran a photographic studio with her husband, Jimmy, at 14 Parkway, Welwyn Garden City. Lisa Sheridan concerned herself with posing and lighting of their photographs while her husband looked after the technical side. They were not just any fashion photographers, but a firm whose name 'Studio Lisa' bore the coat of arms of King George VI and the words 'By Appointment to Her Majesty the Queen'. They had been photographing the Royal Family since 1936.

Dinah Sheridan, already an established actress herself, worked as an unpaid model for her mother and remembers Roger at this time, 1949, as a 'beautiful young man'. 'It was essential to him that he made some money, and he came down as a model for my parents.' They specialised in outdoor pictures, which were always natural and informal to show off sweaters and shirts. Often Roger, Lisa and Jimmy would go into the countryside with a picnic lunch and spend the afternoon taking photographs. They had found Roger in a modelling agency's books and once even used both Roger and Doorn together. Lisa needed a boy and girl, and so Roger had said, 'Why not Doorn?'

Roger and Lisa Sheridan became very close. 'Roger liked coming down to be a model because he used to confide in my mother about his terrible worries over his marriage,' recalls Dinah Sheridan. 'She took a maternal interest in Roger; when he was down there for the day she would feed him to make sure that he had a decent meal inside him.' Dinah remembers her mother telling her after a photographic session, 'That poor boy. He really hasn't got enough to pay his train ticket back to King's Cross in London. Would you give him a lift in your car?'

Dinah remembers being embarrassed and shy about driving him as she did not know what to talk to him about, but as always Roger's easy manner kept them chatting as far as the journey to the nearest underground station in London that would get him home. Dinah adds: 'On one occasion, when I had taken him back to London he had gone to his flat and couldn't get in because he had been locked out and he had telephoned Mother to say so. Certainly Mother was quite a confidante to him. She was a wonderfully worldly-wise woman.' She used Roger as often as she could: 'Roger was one of her very favourite models and she was very sorry when he became famous and wasn't available any more. She found it very difficult to get models who were relaxed and good-looking.'

With Doorn and Roger each pursuing careers of their own, they were spending a great deal of time apart, as Doorn's ice-skating was taking her abroad to Spain and Portugal. Roger took over the juvenile lead role of Peter when the play *Miss Mabel* went on tour with its distinguished leading lady, Mary Jerrold, in the summer of 1949. Miss Jerrold had spent most of the war years appearing at the Strand Theatre, London, opposite Dame Lilian Braithwaite in the smash hit American black comedy, *Arsenic and Old Lace*. The thin story line of *Miss Mabel* revolved around a dear old lady who poisons her nasty sister. It was a similar, but not nearly so successful vehicle for Miss Jerrold as *Arsenic and Old Lace*.

In the early part of 1950 Roger had a small part in *The Lady Purrs*, which opened on March 10th at the Embassy, Swiss Cottage, which is now the Central School of Drama. The cast of the play, written by Ted (later Lord) Willis, included the famous West End *farceur*, Charles Heslop, and future leading actors Eleanor Summerfield, Joss Ackland and Dandy Nichols, who was to go on to create the part of Mrs Garnett in *Till Death Us Do Part* on television. The play was presented by Envoy Productions, who were owned by Anthony Hawtrey, a close descendant of the great Sir Charles Hawtrey, the Edwardian actor/manager and one of the first knights of the British theatre. Roger was cast by the play's director, Henry Kendall, himself one of Britain's noted revue comedians, in the small part of 'A Young Man' (who calls himself Julius), billed at the bottom of the programme.

The story of the play was about a cat, let out during a thunderstorm, which turns into a human as a result of the energy of the storm. She re-enters the house as a young girl called Sandra, played by Eleanor Summerfield. Confusion reigns when the mysterious young woman begins letting out all the family secrets she has overheard in feline form. There is another cat in the neighbourhood called Julius, but he is not seen until the final curtain when there is a thunderstorm and Sandra, much to the relief of the family, reverts back to being a cat. Just as the family congratulate themselves that everything is alright again, the window bursts open and in leaps a gorgeous young man, who says, 'I'm Julius. Where is Sandra?' Roger's one line finished the play, after which the curtain came down to a wonderful audience reaction. Because Roger had only one line in the play he spent little time at the theatre, and was able to concentrate on seeking out modelling assignments. Miss Summerfield felt sure that Roger was destined for stardom: 'One look and I felt this is a future film star: physically he was handsome and well-built, he could act and he had such enormous charm too – he lacked nothing.' The play ran for three and a half weeks, but did not transfer to the West End.

The next job that came Roger's way was as understudy to

Geoffrey Toone in *The Little Hut*, the celebrated comedy by Andre Roussin about two men sharing a woman on a desert island. Toone had started his career alongside Errol Flynn at the Malvern Festival in England in 1934 and was to journey likewise to Hollywood, with very little success. The other stars of the production were Robert Morley and his favourite leading lady, Joan Tetzel, who was married to the actor Oscar Homolka, well known for his sinister roles and a force among his co-workers in British and Hollywood films. The play opened at the Lyric Theatre in Shaftesbury Avenue in August 1950 and was to run for 1,261 performances. Roger was also able to earn some extra money as Geoffrey Toone's dresser on the matinees. Part of his duties entailed covering the actor all over with brown greasepaint for his role as 'The Stranger' – a native of the island. For this he received seven shillings and sixpence.

Just prior to the opening of *The Little Hut*, the London production of *Mister Roberts* had opened at the Coliseum. The cast was headed by Tyrone Power, who was returning to the stage for the first time since becoming one of the most popular of all Hollywood stars. Also in the cast was Jackie Cooper, the child actor of the early 1930s who had made a great impact on movie audiences in *The Champ* with Wallace Beery and his then wife, Hildy Parks, later to become the wife of leading Broadway impresario, Alexander Cohen.

Roger heard that they were in need of extras to play members of the ship's crew and so he rushed down St Martin's Lane to the Coliseum. He arrived there, was asked to take off his shirt and was passed as suitable and given a job. Not only did Roger get to play a sailor in *Mister Roberts*, but he also took over as the understudy of American actor Ray Danton, soon to become a popular film actor, who played the part of Wiley. Ray Danton says that the English cast could not socialise with the Americans at this time in London because of rationing and poor pay – and there was no place to go without money. Roger, rather than socialising with the likes of Tyrone Power and Jackie Cooper, would generally mix with the other young actors in the production. Bob Simmons, who would later be the stunt and fight arranger on the James Bond films, was also playing a member of the crew, and he and Roger became great friends. Other friends at this time, all struggling for recognition, were Bryan Forbes, Claire Bloom and Paul Scofield. Their favourite haunt was a coffee shop called Taylor's where the management used to let them put the bills for their food on the slate if they were broke.

As understudy to Ray Danton, Roger presumably only went on once as the actor only missed the last act of one performance. Danton cannot say definitely whether Roger did go on for him because the reason that he missed the last act was that he was burned on stage and rendered unconscious. It is remarkable that Roger was employed at two West End theatres, in two separate productions which were performed eight times a week at exactly the same time. In later years, Roger enjoyed telling the story of his pedalling furiously on his bicycle between the two theatres, which were only a quarter of a mile apart as the crow flies. Had Mr Toone and Mr Danton both been indisposed for the same performance one wonders if both the Lyric and the Coliseum Theatres would have closed down for the night. However, once Roger had checked or been told that Mr Toone was in the theatre, and with Mr Beaumont's kind understanding of the situation, he was virtually free to appear at the Coliseum. It must be said that Hugh ('Binkie') Beaumont, the leading impresario in London, was indeed most generous, and possibly foolhardy in accommodating his young actor in this way by giving him permission to accept both jobs.

Mister Roberts was a great success and ran for six months before Power's studio, Twentieth Century-Fox, persuaded him to step in front of the movie cameras again. As if his juggling of the two jobs were not enough, Roger used his free time during the day taking all the modelling assignments that he could get to bring in more much-needed cash. But even though he kept himself working day and night, he was still only able to make about fifteen pounds a week.

Despite this hectic schedule, Roger still kept his ears to the ground in the hope that he might hear of any other auditions that were going on. In 1951 he heard that Terence Young was going to direct a film about the Guards Armoured Division, which he had also written, to be called *They Were Not Divided*. Terence Young remembers, 'The part we wanted him for was that which was eventually played by Edward Underdown, who was nineteen years older than Roger. He was meant to be the father of two children of about twelve.'

Brian Desmond Hurst was still pushing Roger and advising him on which role to try for. But Terence Young, despite his friendship with Hurst, could not see Roger in the role, and said, 'No, he's too good-looking and much too young for the part.'

This period of frantic activity for Roger was also matched in his personal affairs. His marriage with Doorn was reaching breaking point; much of their time was spent apart from each other and even when they were together Doorn would constantly harangue Roger about his attempts, futile in her eyes, to make a career for himself in acting – regularly undermining his confidence. Their relationship was to become more fraught as at around this time another woman was to become important in the life of Roger Moore.

She was a woman who felt that the young man was a talented actor. At a point in his career when the struggle to make any real progress was so slow, the encouragement of a woman, more experienced in life and already established in the business in which he wanted so much to make a success, must have seemed the kind of breakthrough that Roger had been waiting for. The woman was Dorothy Squires.

Dorothy, christened Edna May Squires, was born in Llanelly, Wales in 1915, the daughter of a steel-rollerman. Dorothy's early life was closely linked with that of a man, eleven years her senior, called Billy Reid. Reid was well known on the variety halls of Great Britain, when he fronted his own accordion band. Then came the fateful meeting with the young Welsh nurse-turned-vocalist named Dorothy Squires. They formed a stage partnership, being billed as 'The Composer and the Voice', in which Dorothy sang songs that Billy had written, while he accompanied her on the piano. They achieved considerable fame during the war years, becoming a top-of-the-bill variety act, and as their professional partnership flourished they also entered into a close personal relationship, and from 1939 were living together as man and wife.

After the war, Billy Reid's success as a composer of popular music reached several peaks. In 1946 the world famous American singing group, the Ink Spots, gave Billy his first million-selling disc with a recording of 'The Gypsy'.

In 1948, American singing star Margaret Whiting recorded 'A Tree in the Meadow', which became the second million-seller for both Whiting and Reid respectively. And in 1953 Billy again achieved a record third million-seller with Eddie Fisher's recording of 'I'm Walking Behind You'. In each case Dorothy Squires had recorded these songs with considerable success in England, and continues to feature them in her solo act to the present day.

As their relationship was nearing its end the couple had all the trappings of success, including a nine-bedroomed house, St Mary's Mount, in Bexley Heath, Kent, and as a team were earning £10,000 a year. But by 1950 their life together had come to a stormy and final conclusion. The break-up followed an embarrassing incident at a theatre in Dorothy's home town of Llanelly, at which the mayor was present. Dorothy's father, outraged at Billy's shocking behaviour towards his daughter, challenged him. Under such pressure their relationship inevitably came to an end and by 1950 they were no longer living together.

The period after the break-up was one of great anguish for Dorothy, who felt emotionally exhausted by the experience she had been through. But in 1952 Roger was invited, by a mutual friend of Doorn and Dorothy, to a party at Dorothy's Bexley mansion. Doorn at the time was skating in Europe, and the way was clear for the unexpected and uninvited events that occurred.

Parties at Dorothy Squires' home usually developed, rather than actually being planned. The people Dorothy invited over used in turn to bring along friends of their own. Amongst the regular guests were Diana Dors and sundry other starlets and British recording personalities of the time. There were not many people in show-business whom Dorothy did not know, and it is hardly surprising that Roger and Dorothy finally met – although, of course, neither could have expected that meeting to have such an effect on each of them. Dorothy was a very attractive woman, about 5' 4" tall, with ash-blonde hair and a good figure. A striking woman to look at, with an extrovert character and natural flamboyance, she was certainly a formidable lady. Generous to her relatives and friends, nevertheless she would not suffer fools, and by the time Roger met her she had settled into a very comfortable position in show-business, with all the trappings of success about her as tangible evidence of her astuteness in the profession. She had a reputation for her colourful language, but it was in truth no worse than that of most people, and in any case she was a woman with enough charm to get away with it.

St Mary's Mount, her home, was a large house dominated by a beautiful sitting room with French windows leading out to the swimming pool, which at the time was enough of a rarity in Britain so that the house, and particularly the pool, were used as settings for several television shows. Behind the pool stretched out an impressive garden with a wood at the bottom. On the ground floor Dorothy stored costumes that she used both for her singing engagements and for the pantomimes that she frequently performed in during the Christmas period. There was also an enormous kitchen and other smaller rooms on the ground floor. The furnishings could be described as 'expensive vicarage', being essentially tasteful but leaning towards comfort rather than elegance, and characterised by expensive coverings and numerous lights and standard lamps. The upstairs rooms were known by their different colours, there being, for instance, a blue room or a green room each decorated with variations on that particular colour. The house was old enough to be allegedly haunted, even, according to some claims, by as illustrious a ghost as Sir Arthur Conan Doyle, the creator of Sherlock Holmes, and it was also possessed of the instantly memorable telephone number of 1066.

In the setting of St Mary's Mount, Roger and Dorothy were immediately drawn to one another. He was fascinated by a different side of the entertainment business from acting or modelling, which the world of variety certainly was. Both were naturally pleased by the interest shown by the other. For Roger the attention of an attractive and successfully well-established entertainer like Dorothy towards a virtually unknown actor like himself was extremely flattering. She, on the other hand, having lived for eleven years with a very ordinary-looking man, was now being courted by a spectacularly handsome one, twelve years younger than herself. Their relationship quickly grew, and with the help of Dorothy, Roger's career began to take some sort of direction.

He went to his old mentor, Brian Desmond Hurst, to seek his advice on what to do about the situation that was developing so rapidly. Hurst says: 'Dorothy helped his career a lot. She helped several other young men too,' adding, with a twinkle in his eye, that like Roger, 'her austerity was not oppressive either'.

The first clue that Doorn had about the relationship that had developed between Roger and Dorothy came on her return from an ice-skating engagement in Spain. She had sent a telegram to Roger informing him of the time she would be arriving at Victoria Station, but, as Doorn recalled in the mid-1970s when she was attempting to write her own account of her life with Roger Moore to be entitled *The Saint That Ain't* (which has not, as yet, been published), when she stepped off the train she was met, not by her husband, but by her father, who greeted her with the news that Roger was having an affair with an older woman.

Doorn claims that she tried to save the marriage, but it had gone beyond the point where anything could be done. She went to the Lyric Theatre where *The Little Hut* was still playing to packed houses, and attempted to see Roger. However, he refused to allow her into his dressing room and so she was forced to wait outside the stage door until the end of the performance, when he left the theatre. As he came out of the stage door she immediately challenged him, asking for explanations. Roger claimed ignorance of the whole matter.

'I don't know what you're talking about,' he said.

Doorn could not contain her anger any longer. She sued for divorce, which brought Roger rushing round to see her in the Streatham council flat they had once shared. He begged her not to divorce him. Doorn relented, but then Roger told her about Dorothy and, Doorn claims, he asked her to wait for him to return to her after his career had been set in motion by Squires. He told Doorn that he loved her, but she refused to believe him, and Roger made his exit out of her life.

Several years later, Roger was to tell his actor friend Robert Brown that the final break with Doorn happened when he came down for breakfast one morning in their flat. The atmosphere was tense between them, and they soon found themselves in the middle of a row. It came to a hasty conclusion when Doorn emptied a pot of freshly made tea over him. Roger said, 'That's it!' and stormed upstairs to get dressed and away. Unfortunately, when he went to collect his clothes he found them all in the bath with the tap running.

Dorothy and Roger marked their first Christmas together by appearing together on a stage, in one of Dorothy's occasional appearances as principal boy in pantomime. In the previous year Dorothy had appeared in *Dick Whittington* at the New Cross Empire, and the venue for Christmas 1952 was another South London theatre, the Empress Brixton, with a production of *Jack and the Beanstalk*. Both these venues were known as number two dates and housed variety bills or light revues for most of the year, with neither theatre being classed as a prestigious engagement. Dorothy was able to secure the part of the King in the pantomime for Roger; the theatrical journal *The Stage* described his performance as 'impressive', although he was not called upon to exert himself in any particular way.

Up to this time, the dame in British pantomime was usually played by a man, but Dorothy's sister-in-law, Joyce Golding, gave a good account of herself in this particular role.

Dorothy's family and friends dominated the production, with her brother Fred and sister Rene also taking part, as well as a nephew who played the piano accompaniment. Fred was a tall, handsome, rather military-looking man who helped behind the scenes while the others joined in on stage. The Squires family was very close, and her brother and sister were always to be found at Dorothy's house.

Roger and Dorothy are remembered as making a lovely couple at the time, with Roger being very attentive towards her and clearly having eyes for no one else. Roger was grateful for the way that he was accepted, and the general view was that he was a nice young man without the conceit which might have been expected from such an incredibly good-looking man. His manner was unassuming, and the essential characteristic that he conveyed was an irrepressible niceness, a quality that helped Roger to project a personality lacking in any real sex appeal. Dorothy was the one with the charisma and dominant personality.

Almost immediately after *Jack and the Beanstalk*, Dorothy embarked on another music hall tour, this time singing in her home country, Wales. Roger, bolstered by his success in the pantomime, felt that it was time to make his debut as a stand-up comic. The location of his baptism was a theatre in Pontypridd in Wales on a very wet night, which caused the theatre to be almost empty. Those who had braved the weather sat scattered about with steam coming off their raincoats and waited to be entertained. In these unfavourable circumstances Roger walked on to the stage dressed in an off-the-peg dinner jacket and looking, by his own admission, like 'a baby-faced ponce lathered in make-up'.

He proceeded to go through a terrible routine about parrots which made no impact whatsoever on the soggy audience, who stared back at him in unsmiling indifference. The more desperate Roger became and the more he tried to be funny, the clearer it became that this audience would never laugh. Fully aware that he had 'died' completely, Roger felt it was time to introduce the next act, which consisted of two fat ladies in tights, and he walked off stage an utter failure. He was taken off the show, having gone through a very humbling experience and one that he would not be keen to repeat, although his fascination for variety performers remained intact and even stronger now that he had had first-hand experience of just how difficult it was to walk on to a stage and win over an audience in the short time allotted to any one act.

Three

As ROGER Moore gathered together the working materials that he usually carried with him and placed them in his hand luggage, the last and most important item was a bulky, well-thumbed, typewritten film script. As he picked it up, the by now familiar title on the cover attracted his eye – *A View To A Kill*. He looked at the script for a moment, hesitating before placing it carefully in the bag. For this screen play had more than usual significance for Roger – momentarily a feeling of sadness and his own mortality swept through his frame. *A View To A Kill* was to be his last appearance as James Bond.

Where did Bond begin? Roger sat down, drawing on his cigar. He could hear his wife Luisa making arrangements to close up their chalet home in Gstaad during their absence – as he thought to himself, 'This really is the end of James Bond for me; no more happy bantering with producer "Cubby" Broccoli for another million or so' – his millions were made. Roger reflected on his world-wide fame and his tremendous good fortune, both personally and financially, as one of the world's top ten film stars and Britain's most highly paid actor.

When did it all start – when did James Bond actually begin? Roger took another draw on his cigar, and his thoughts carried him back to 1953, a year of great significance for his country, marking as it did the beginning of the new Elizabethan era. And a year possibly more significant for Roger than for many of his fellow countrymen, because it was in 1953 that Ian Fleming's novel *Casino Royale* was published, introducing the character of James Bond to an unsuspecting public. Roger's reflections moved to the man who was to give him the break of a lifetime with the role of James Bond – producer Albert R. Broccoli. In 1953, Cubby made the giant step from being a successful Hollywood agent to that of film producer, setting up his first film, *Hell Below Zero*, to star Alan Ladd and to be made in England. Little could Cubby have known how successful the path on which he had set himself was going to be.

Roger thought of that fateful day in 1972 when he was finally told that he was to play James Bond for the first time, in the film version of *Live and Let Die*. He knew that he was right for the part and so, he reflected, did producers Harry Saltzman and Albert R. Broccoli. But it had taken so long to come about – finally to play the part that was to make him one of the big screen's top stars. Now Roger was not nearly as nervous as he had been when he had set off to make *Live and Let Die*; he knew that he had made James Bond his own, and he knew exactly how the public wanted James Bond to be in this, the longest running and most successful film series of all time.

It was time to leave. Roger, resplendent in his usual tasteful but expensive clothes, with all the trappings of luxury that only a millionaire can afford, set out for six months of travel to locations in a rather different style than when he had set out to seek his fortune as an actor in America early in 1953 . . .

Roger's divorce from Doorn came through in March 1953, by which time he and Dorothy had settled in an apartment in Manhattan. Under the divorce settlement Roger was liable to pay Doorn £6 a week maintenance. Dorothy had gone to America to promote her recording of the Billy Reid song, 'I'm Walking Behind You', which had been a big hit for her in England. But, to her great consternation, she found that Eddie Fisher's cover version was more popular in the United States. An additional motive for the trip for Dorothy was the possibility of negotiating with the Andrews Sisters about joining them for a tour as part of the act rather than as a supporting attraction, due to the death of Laverne Andrews. Sadly, this did not come to anything, but at one point it appeared very close to becoming a reality. Roger accompanied her and looked after her in the role of 'manager' while on the lookout for work for himself, as he had the necessary labour permits to work in the United States.

When he took his first walk along Broadway he was stunned by the legendary names blazing out at him from the theatres that he passed. He hoped that one day he might see his own name up in lights outside the front of a theatre. But, at the time, that prospect seemed a long way off, but with this forceful and dominating woman behind him he felt sure that the opportunities that he had been waiting for for so long would start to come his way.

His first break in America was his television debut. An offer came within five days of his arrival in New York from one of MGM's biggest stars, Robert Montgomery, who had gone into television production with a series of plays produced under the banner of his name, 'Robert Montgomery Presents'. Roger was cast as a French diplomat in the United Nations, in a play opposite the late Diana Lynn and Phyllis Kirk, two of Hollywood's brightest and prettiest young actresses.

When the divorce from Doorn had come through, Roger was free to marry the woman with whom he had been living for the past year. On July 6th, 1953 Roger heroically whisked Dorothy Squires across the Hudson to New Jersey and married her. Best man at the ceremony was Joe Latona, of Warren, Latona and Sparks, a comedy knockabout act, who had appeared in the same variety halls as Dorothy in Britain. The day after the wedding Dorothy returned to England – as Mrs Roger Moore.

Roger says, 'There was no honeymoon because Dot had to be back in England next day for a TV spectacular. I stayed on to see what was going to happen next. It was a play on Broadway. It opened on September 17th, 1953 at the Playhouse on West 48th Street, and ran until late that night!'

It was a great disappointment for Roger who, since the middle of August, had spent three weeks working hard at rehearsals for the opening. But this was not as serious a setback for Roger's career as it at first appeared. The play was *A Pin to See the Peepshow* by H. M. Harwood and F. Tennyson Jesse, which had originally been produced at a tiny theatre club in London called the New Boltons. It was a recreation of the Edith Thompson/Frederick Bywaters murder case of 1923. Because of the play's subject matter and the offence it could give to living relatives, it was immediately prohibited from public performance in Britain and censorship limited it to the confines of the theatre club, where it was seen by one Nancy Davids, who wanted to present it in New York. The director of the New Boltons Club, who was also the director of the play, was Peter Cotes, whose real name in fact is Sydney Boulting, being the older brother of the film directing, producing and writing twins, John and Roy Boulting. Mr Cotes was also the man who, the previous year, had directed the first cast of Agatha Christie's *The Mousetrap* at the Ambassador's Theatre, which surprisingly is still running in London after over thirty years.

Roger's part in the production of *A Pin to See the Peepshow* was that of Frederick Bywaters, the lover of Edith Thompson, although for the play the character's name was changed to Leo Carr, and the importance of the part was considerably diminished from the role that Bywaters played in the real-life drama. Roger continues: 'The basic problem was that the producer didn't have enough money to do more than get the curtain up. We had to open "cold" – which means we had no out-of-town tour – and we had none of the block ticket agency bookings because there was no big star name in it.' The part of Julia Almond, based loosely on Edith Thompson, was played by the Canadian-born actress Joan Miller, who had made her first appearance in London at His Majesty's Theatre in September 1934, walking on in a play called *Josephine*. She then went on to understudy the aged Lady Tree as Mistress Quickly in *Henry IV Part I*, before being given the role of May Stokes in *The Golden Arrow* at the Whitehall Theatre in May 1935. It is interesting to note that Miss Miller's understudy in this production was a young girl in her twenties who, after having earned a university honours degree at Birmingham, had decided that she wanted to go on the stage. She was Greer Garson, and within five years Miss Garson had taken over the crown as Queen of Metro-Goldwyn-Mayer in Hollywood, the studio which would claim Roger when he first went West. *The Hollywood Reporter* reviewed the piece and found it 'a glum, hackneyed, cockneyed piece', and the general cheapness of the production was noted: 'The settings by Ariel Balliff are barely more than cut-outs on a raised form . . . Our cousins from across the sea generally have a stylish way with murder, but I'm afraid the conclusion about this one is Dial B for Boredom.' Roger did not go unnoticed, but he was not singled out for praise for his histrionic ability: 'Roger Moore, as the lady's extra-curricular activity, is a devilishly attractive young man.'

Roger continues, on this temporary setback to his career: 'The reviews were so-so. I arrived at the theatre the next night and saw some of the cast hanging about. They showed me the notice of closure and we all went home.' He was now learning about the unfeeling and unfortunate side of the theatrical profession. So much so, in fact, did this affect him that he was only to appear twice more on the stage, and since then he has never loaned his most considerable acting talents to the theatre, which is a loss both to London and to Broadway.

But good fortune followed ill when Hallmark Theatre, a prestigious television series, beckoned. This meant that Roger had to travel to Hollywood for the first time. He was cast in their production of *Black Chiffon*, which the very successful British playwright, Lesley Storm, had written for Dame Flora Robson, giving Dame Flora a remarkable long-running success in both London and New York. Roger also appeared in Hallmark's pro-

56

duction of *Julius Caesar*, and for Goodyear Television Playhouse he supported Jessica Tandy and Gracie Fields in a production of *A Murder is Announced*, in which Britain's renowned singer/comedienne played the part of Miss Marple. Miss Tandy came fresh from creating the role of Blanche Dubois in the Broadway production of Tennessee Williams' *A Streetcar Named Desire* opposite a young Marlon Brando. For a young actor just starting in his profession Roger was indeed fortunate to share screen time with theatrical and film people of such stature, and it is not surprising that with such exposure he did not go unnoticed. It was Roger's fine contributions to these important productions that brought him to the attention of the Metro-Goldwyn-Mayer talent scouts, who suggested that he should take part in a screen test for them, which he made in New York, while en route back to England.

Arriving back in England with Dorothy in late November 1953, the couple received belated personal congratulations from their English friends, who had not seen them together since their marriage. Partly due to their late arrival, so soon before Christmas, Dorothy was forced to forego any thoughts of involving herself in one of her 'family' pantomimes. The family was more scattered than usual: not only had Dorothy been absent for much of the year, but also sister-in-law Joyce had settled in Glasgow for a few months including the Christmas period. But Dorothy did not sit back; she immediately fulfilled an engagement at the New Cross Empire and gave the theatre its best week's business for a considerable time. After Christmas Dorothy was booked for a music hall tour of the whole of England during January, beginning in Hull, while Roger was eagerly anticipating positive results from his MGM screen test. Roger also prepared himself for the part of Stephen Colly in *I Capture the Castle*, which he had managed to secure soon after his return from America and which Murray Macdonald was directing and producing at the Aldwych Theatre, London. It was a romantic comedy by Dodie Smith, the famed playwright of *Dear Octopus*, from her best-selling novel of the same name, published after the war. The story revolves around the Mortmain family who camp out in a ruined castle in Suffolk. The family consists of seventeen-year-old Cassandra, her man-hungry sister Rose, their eccentric father and their step-mother, who is an ex-model. The plot comes to life when two handsome young Americans enter the picture with prospects of love, wealth and happiness. The cast was headed by film-star Richard Greene, who had shared with Roger the distinction of being the Brylcreem Boy in advertisements for the famous hair cream. Roger's part was a relatively small one, and he was required to appear only in the third act. The production was not a happy one and ran for only seven weeks. Three weeks into rehearsals for the play Roger received a telegram from MGM telling him to report to the studio, where they had decided to take up his option after viewing his screen test and offered him a contract. Murray Macdonald kindly arranged for Roger to leave the production early, so that he would be able to report to MGM on April 1st. Robert Brown, his close friend, says that 'whenever the subject of doing a stage play crops up Roger looks back on *I Capture the Castle*, and I don't think he was very happy about it.' Virginia McKenna was in the cast in the key role of Cassandra Mortmain and Brown says, 'I don't think Miss McKenna was one of his favourite ladies.' It is quite obvious that Roger's short experience in *I Capture the Castle* was a further consolidation of his disenchantment with the theatre, although Virginia McKenna remembers him as 'a very nice, genial and helpful chap'.

Roger heaved a sigh of relief as he left the production and headed for the Pacific coast.

Four

AN EXCITED Roger Moore arrived in Hollywood in early 1954 with Dorothy to begin his stay at Metro-Goldwyn-Mayer. Roger's was a short-term contract with the studio, but still long enough for him to be able to prove his worth. He came to a Hollywood that still retained much of the magic of its golden days, with most of the great stars from the thirties and forties still working steadily. At Roger's home studio, Spencer Tracy, Robert Taylor, Lana Turner and Walter Pidgeon were still active. Clark Gable had just completed his last film for MGM, ending a reign as the studio's biggest male star that had started in 1931. Of the newer breed of stars, Roger found himself in the midst of an MGM stock company that included Elizabeth Taylor, Jane Powell, Gene Kelly, Esther Williams, June Allyson, Ann Miller, Glenn Ford, Debbie Reynolds, and fellow countryman Stewart Granger.

Roger was scheduled to start work on April 1st, his first assignment being a supporting part in Elizabeth Taylor's latest film, *The Last Time I Saw Paris*. This was a film adaptation of the 1931 short story by F. Scott Fitzgerald entitled 'Babylon Revisited', with the screenplay written by Julius G. and Philip J. Epstein, who had written the all-time classic, *Casablanca*. The film was to be directed by Richard Brooks, who was later to marry actress Jean Simmons.

The new arrivals searched for an apartment and after a short time found a suitable one in Levering Avenue in Westwood, in the student quarter of the sprawling metropolis of Los Angeles. It was a small but comfortable flat with a balcony; not elaborately furnished, but Roger and Dorothy made up for this by filling the living room with cushions, enabling any guests to sit on the floor. Roger was very low down on the Hollywood social scale and such a bohemian existence was suitable for the social set in which he found himself: the company of similarly lowly actors or writers, many being fellow ex-patriots who naturally tended to gravitate towards each other.

On April 1st, Roger made the journey to Culver City, where the Metro-Goldwyn-Mayer studios were situated. He was confronted with the sight of a vast complex of sandy-coloured buildings, dominated by a huge sign identifying the studios, and dwarfing the squat buildings of the drab streets of Culver City. Roger went first to the Irving Thalberg Building, which lay outside and to the left of the actual studio gates, a solid building with a wide flight of steps leading up to the main entrance. In this building was housed the core of the studio management; producers and directors, and the head of MGM, Dory Schary. At this time it was almost two years since the departure of Louis B. Mayer, one of the undisputed star-makers of all time. He had been replaced as executive producer on June 22nd, 1951 by Schary, the man who had been head of production since 1948. Hollywood was not the flamboyant town it once had been, due to the depression caused by the influx of television, which was stealing away audiences who used to go regularly to the cinema. People were now tending to choose to remain at home, sitting in front of their television sets for entertainment. Gone were the days when studios could afford to hire actors on long-term contracts. Clark Gable's contract had expired in 1954, but, due to the expense of keeping such a highly-paid star under contract – he was earning 520,000 dollars a year – it had not been renewed.

Dory Schary was a man who had no opportunity to revive the fortunes of the ailing studio. In Mayer's time Roger would unquestionably have been star material and would have been guided through a series of films that would have gradually built up his reputation. But such methods of 'star-making' had been considerably curtailed, and success had to be achieved more quickly and with less available opportunities to shine.

It was to Dory Schary's office that Roger made his way on that April day, in a studio that despite the prevailing conditions was still the greatest in Hollywood. Roger later recalled that memorable occasion:

I went into Dory Schary's room and immediately became enveloped in carpet. It was far in excess of anyone's wildest idea of what a Hollywood producer's office is like. For many miles I walked through seas of carpet to reach his desk. Looking back I have this tortuous vision of a tiny Englishman, buried to his neck in carpet, looking up at a huge head behind a massive desk. The head said, 'Welcome to California, Roger.' 'Thank you, sir,' I said. At that time I had a very bad habit of speaking through my teeth. My mouth and jaws locked completely, especially when I was nervous. I learnt that the moment I left

60

the office he picked up a phone and said, 'Teach that sonofabitch to speak English.' Whereupon I was whipped off and dumped in front of diction teachers – with whom I was completely relaxed, so my clenched-teeth problem didn't apply. 'So why are you here?' they asked. 'We're trying to get everyone to speak like you!'

The job of making Roger over was not confined just to his voice. The Moore torso was the object of close scrutiny as well, and it was decided that Roger should build himself up so as to look more athletic. The studio saw Roger as a potential successor to the now faded Errol Flynn or, more close to home, as a rival to MGM's own Stewart Granger, star of *The Prisoner of Zenda* and *Scaramouche*. So Moore was sent to the studio gymnasium and, despite his lack of interest in anything athletic, he did work hard at it for a time.

Once the studio were satisfied with their new contract player's image, Roger began work on *The Last Time I Saw Paris*. For his first screen appearance, he was lucky that the star of the film was the delightful and generous Elizabeth Taylor, who was as pleasant to work with as she was beautiful to look at. At the time she was rapidly reaching the golden years of her brilliant career and Roger, in the supporting role of Paul, was fortunate to be sharing screen time with Miss Taylor.

Roger had several scenes in the film, playing Van Johnson's rival for the affections of Miss Taylor. In one scene he had a short exchange of dialogue with Elizabeth Taylor, followed by a confrontation and fight with Van Johnson, all of this action taking place in a Paris bar. Under Richard Brooks' excellent direction and with Miss Taylor's kindness, Roger made an auspicious debut. He was understandably nervous, and with those working on the film he was quiet and reserved: a natural reaction from a young man working amid the close family atmosphere at MGM, where cast and crew were familiar to each other and Roger a total stranger from England. Roger later recalled this time:

My inexperience on that film must have been a joy for any sadist to behold. On the first day's shooting I was supposed to have a quiet chat with Liz Taylor when Van Johnson comes in drunkenly and seeks to hit me. I had to ward off the blow and bop him instead. I was terrified: here's Van Johnson, great big world-famous movie star – and I'm supposed to hit him: added to which I knew I wasn't all that red hot as an actor. I knew it was all ridiculous, and I knew I didn't believe it was all happening to me anyway.

Roger's nervousness was not helped by Brook's method of direction which had given him a reputation as a shouting director, a situation not improved when on the first day of shooting there was trouble with the censor over Elizabeth Taylor's cleavage. *The Last Time I Saw Paris* was an important film for Elizabeth Taylor and a personal triumph; however, she described it as 'Rather curiously a not so good picture. *The Last Time I Saw Paris* first convinced me I wanted to be an actress instead of yawning my way through parts. That girl was off-beat with mercurial flashes of instability – more than just glib dialogue.'

Elizabeth played the part of Helen Ellsworth in this Technicolor picture. *Babylon Revisited* had been dramatised into a sprawling, colour splashed, drink-by-drink account of a marriage reeling towards a sad conclusion in an entangled Paris following World War II, with the story told in flashback from that point. The Fitzgerald story had been set around the time of World War I, dealing with the 'lost generation' whom Ernest Hemingway had immortalised in one of his greatest books, *The Sun Also Rises*.

Other MGM contract artists in the cast included veteran Walter Pidgeon, Donna Reed, and Van Johnson, whose last film it was under his contract with the studio. Roger felt very insignificant among such illustrious names: 'I was very low on the list of contract performers. Especially being an Englishman. Hollywood was not over enamoured of English actors at that time. Edmund Purdom was starting to play up; Stewart Granger was pretty tough in his attitude towards them. So along came Moore and they were prepared to snap my head off if I got too stroppy.'

But it was not in Roger's character to show temperament, and this, added to his inexperience of a big Hollywood studio, meant that he neither wished to make waves nor even felt that he had any reason to do so. He was well aware that he was in a very fortunate position and that he was by no means inexpendable. Roger was still at heart the poor South London boy, and to be surrounded and working with the screen idols of his youth was an astonishing experience: 'To me, it was absolute magic to wander round and see all these people who I felt I knew. They had all come alive from the screen at the Odeon, Streatham. More telling was that they treated me as an equal. I was psychologically capable of living up to the role of being a film actor. But I had difficulty appreciating that *I* was one of *them*.'

A friendship that began at this time and that was to continue for almost thirty years was one between Roger and Grace Kelly. Upon meeting Grace, Roger experienced a similar reaction to his falling in love with Deborah Kerr while watching her in a studio-constructed railway carriage seven years before. But this time Roger did not have the good fortune to share screen time with the object of his admiration. However, he had the better fortune of becoming friendly with her, and while Grace was working with Roger's boyhood hero Stewart Granger in *Green Fire* and subsequently in *The Swan* with Alec Guinness and Louis Jourdan – another actor who was to become a close friend of the new intern – Roger was to find in Grace Kelly a true and delightful friend, and whether or not they had a romantic interlude, their friendship was to last until the future Princess of Monaco's tragic death. Roger admits that at the time he secretly loved her but his infatuation was so great that he was a rather gauche admirer: 'I was besotted with her. More so than with Deborah Kerr. I recall dinner parties in those days when I sat next to her totally tongue-tied.'

Following the completion of Roger's first role at MGM, the studio gave the young actor his induction into the world of publicity. He was required to tour the West Coast, with the major event being a personal appearance in San Francisco to promote *The Last Time I Saw Paris* and himself. Roger was accompanied by Dorothy, who for the first time experienced the unfamiliar situation of being the secondary centre of attention. But at the moment the novelty of the situation was sufficient to placate Dorothy; nor would a certain amount of fame on Roger's part harm her in America, where any exposure she could get was valuable since she was a comparatively unknown quantity.

The couple returned to Hollywood in time for Roger's next assignment – a supporting part in *Interrupted Melody*, in which he played the brother of the Australian soprano Marjorie Lawrence in MGM's biographical picture about the singer who was stricken with polio at the height of her career. This time Roger shared the screen with Eleanor Parker who played Lawrence. Jack Cummings produced and Curtis Bernhardt directed.

Glenn Ford, who was married to MGM's self-styled 'Garbo of the dance' Eleanor Powell, was making another of his frequent appearances at MGM playing Miss Lawrence's husband. Glenn Ford, although far too big a star to mix socially with the Moores at this time, remembers Roger thus:

When Roger came to Metro-Goldwyn-Mayer he brought a touch of class to the studio when he arrived. We all became a little better because of his presence. Roger Moore made the two separate words 'gentle' and 'man' very clear. His treatment of everybody, in front of the camera and behind, was equally good. He set an example for all of us. I have nothing but respect and shall always remain that way. Socially we are now much closer than we were then.

At the same time Roger was not thought of with any particular kindness by workers on the studio floor, many of whom found him aloof and uninviting, although to be fair to Roger his own shyness could have been misinterpreted.

By this time Roger had settled quite comfortably into Hollywood life, and he and Dorothy had acquired their own circle of friends, including producers Ross Hunter and Jacques Mapes, comedy writer Charlie Isaacs and his charming wife, Jeannie Carson, star of the television series *Hey Jeannie*, and her husband Bill Redmond, and fellow ex-patriots such as Bryan Forbes, who was struggling over at Universal-International where he was under contract. Ross Hunter, the famed Hollywood producer, does not recall the Roger Moore of those days with particular regard. Dorothy was still very obviously the star of the family, and Roger was content to be pushed along by Dorothy's own ambitions for him without troubling himself unduly. It was not that Roger was incapable of pulling himself up, it was rather that he lacked any real motivation. Roger had settled into life as a contract player and as the young husband of an older woman and had no wish to upset his easy lifestyle. The pity was that people who met the couple could see that Roger had far more potential than he would allow himself to exploit. As Ross Hunter remembers, 'Here was not only a terrifically good-looking man but an all-male man, who under the right auspices could become a big, big personality in Hollywood. He had tremendous wit, envious charm, and he was letting his life slip right out the window. People liked him, but Dorothy was really the star of the evening.'

The fact that Roger never managed to get into the more important Hollywood social circles was due partly to his own indolence. A man with his personal gifts should have been able to mix quite easily with a much wider range of Hollywood society. Dorothy, more than anyone, had been the person who had brought Roger to Hollywood but once there their liaison, even though they were married, did not provide a firm base on which to build a notable social network. Dorothy belonged to a very localised form of show business and had very little in common with the side of the film industry found in Hollywood.

With Roger soaking up what attention was directed towards them, Dorothy soon began to find the situation less appealing, as one of the couple's close friends of the time recalls: 'I do think that Dorothy was quite unhappy after a while here in Hollywood because she was a singer songwriter and had been very successful. But over here she was dormant: she wasn't doing anything here but she didn't want to be a housewife. She said, 'In England, by God, I wouldn't be Mrs Roger bloody-Moore.'

Roger's career still appeared, meanwhile, to be progressing well, with another project awaiting him after *Interrupted Melody*. This time it was a swashbuckler called *The King's Thief*, to be directed by the distinguished Robert Z. Leonard in what was to be his last film in a record-breaking thirty-one years exclusively with MGM. A long-haired and bearded Roger Moore played Jack, a highwayman, in only a minor supporting role in spite of the fact that his name was raised on the screen above the supporting cast. The film starred Edmund Purdom, Ann Blyth and a ludicrous George Sanders in a mercifully short piece set during the reign of Charles II. The only redeeming feature for Roger was the participation in the film of David Niven, in what must have been the lowest point in the latter's career, when he was forced to make such token appearances in very inferior productions. It was the first time that Roger and Niven had seen each other since they had met when Roger was a fifteen-year-old trainee animator, and it marked the true beginning of a friendship that was to grow steadily stronger with the passing years and to last until Niven's death. Niven at this time was a rather sad figure, who had fallen victim to high living and appeared to be fading gradually into obscurity, forced to accept unworthy parts in order to keep himself tenuously solvent.

So far Roger had had little opportunity to shine, and time was passing. But his luck did not fail him: halfway through shooting *The King's Thief* he was sent for by Dory Schary, who told him that in his next film he was going to be the star. It really appeared that MGM were indeed grooming their handsome Englishman for stardom. It was the producer of *The King's Thief*, Edwin Knopf, who gave Roger his big chance in what would be his third film for 1955. Knopf's next production was to be *Diane*, another costume film, this time to be directed by David Butler, from a script by the celebrated British writer Christopher Isherwood, based on John Erskine's romance of sixteenth-century France. It was to be photographed in Cinemascope, and for the first time Roger would have his name above the title – partnering a great film star, Lana Turner, in the film that was to end her long career at Metro-Goldwyn-Mayer. Roger was one of the last actors to be groomed for stardom in the fading studio, which was in the midst of an insurmountable recession.

A thirty-six-year-old Turner played Diane de Poitiers, the mistress of Henry II of France, played by Roger. The supporting cast included Sir Cedric Hardwicke, Marisa Pavan, Melville Cooper, and another of Roger's friends, Geoffrey Toone, whom Roger had understudied in *The Little Hut* on the London stage and who now found himself playing support to Roger, a reversal which had taken just three years to come about.

But Roger's good fortune was not without its drawbacks; he was not lucky in having been cast opposite Lana Turner. *Diane* was to be Lana Turner's final film after seventeen years at MGM and clearly she must have wondered what the future held for her. In her autobiography, Miss Turner writes:

> When I finished *Diane* I remember leaving the studio literally without looking back. How strange it was to see those empty streets. They had been my second home – perhaps my most stable home for seventeen years. I remember how it had thrilled me at first when I saw those famous faces, in the golden era of MGM, and how awesome it was to find myself among them . . . Now the glory was gone.

The completion of *Diane* would also mark Roger's last day at MGM, but he did not leave behind him seventeen years of film stardom. His only legacy was having appeared in four motion pictures which at best had been good but in most cases very mediocre. However, he had achieved the accolade of co-starring with one of the Hollywood greats and marked the last in a long line of impressive leading men that included Clark Gable, Robert

Taylor, Spencer Tracy and John Garfield, when at the zenith of their respective careers.

Edmund Purdom had originally been slated for the role of Henry II, but Miss Turner objected to Purdom being cast in the film. However, no such problems faced young Roger, even now remembered by Miss Turner as being a delightful young man with a marvellous sense of humour. Rather ungenerously, however, she does not mention him in her autobiography.

Roger was pleased finally to be starring in a film and to have the star dressing room on *Diane*. He found the experience fun, although he was well aware that his contribution was not as good as he had hoped it might be. His newly acquired elevation in position brought about a more concerned view towards his career, and he began to see clearly his own limitations and to wish to try to break them down, if only he knew how, as he recalled: 'Something was holding me up. I couldn't put my finger on it, but I was still sadly lacking in the right kind of confidence.'

Despite the depressing atmosphere that was wont to pervade the set, the filming was not without its lighter moments. Roger is fond of recalling an incident which occurred in which he had to ride across a cobbled street clad in heavy armour. For some reason the horse reared up and Roger fell heavily to the ground and was knocked unconscious. Members of the crew ran over to him and started to remove the armour in an attempt to revive him. As Roger started to come round he heard Lana Turner saying, 'Is his cock all right?' as he was being helped to a doctor, who, upon examining his badly bruised body, put him in a bath of ice – an experience more agonising than the actual fall.

Roger's own self-awareness meant that he was not completely surprised, although naturally still very disappointed, when MGM did not renew his contract and he found himself the failed star of a very disappointing film.

Roger's professional life seemed to be crumbling, and in tandem with this his private life was showing similar signs of disintegration. Roger and Dorothy's marriage was sprinkled with frequent separations as Dorothy continued to pursue her singing career. Her reputation being very solid in Britain, it was natural that most of her bookings came from there, and fulfilling these meant that she had to leave their home in Hollywood quite frequently for periods lasting usually a few weeks at a time.

Roger's social life did not as a result take on a double-sided nature, whereby his wife's absence enabled him to exploit Hollywood night life to the full. In fact, in Dorothy's absence it was a rare sight to see Roger socialising at all. Ross Hunter recalls: 'Roger was in Hollywood a lot when Dorothy wasn't here and he didn't do very much. He was settled; he was happy with his position. Roger was an enigma to me: he was very happy almost being by himself. In his Hollywood days he was a loner most of the time.'

Hunter remembers the occasion when Roger found that his MGM contract was not being renewed and was impressed with the way he handled himself in the situation, appearing to take it in his stride even though it must have been a traumatic experience for him. Roger took a fatalistic view that since it was inevitable, the best thing to do was to come to terms with it as quickly as possible. His behaviour in this matter indicated to Hunter a strength of character that was not easily apparent but which was clearly a part of Roger's make-up – and an admirable quality in the young man.

Roger could look back on a Hollywood career that appeared to have ended almost before it had started. Free from MGM, he had no imminent offers of work and all dreams of stardom seemed dashed.

Socially too Roger had not made a great impact, not having been able to break away from the lower English set and the lesser levels of the social network, which for an aspiring actor was a hindrance to his meeting those people who could be most useful to him and whose friendship could have given him more weight among the industry heads. But there had been highlights, a particular one being the night when Dorothy and Roger had been invited to the home of Gary Cooper. The great star made them feel immediately at home with his warm gentle manner, and much to Roger's delight a friendship developed which clearly meant a great deal to Roger, who if he had always loved Cooper on the screen in such rousing films as *Beau Geste*, *Sergeant York* and *High Noon*, found that the man lived up to all his expectations. The extent to which Roger was affected by Cooper is indicated by Tony Curtis, who remembers that even fifteen years later, when they were filming *The Persuaders*, the mention of Cooper's name had astonishing results:

He always loved it when I told him he reminded me of Gary Cooper – did he love that! He knew Cooper and he asked me if I knew him and I said, 'Yes, I knew him a lot,' and he said, 'Tell me about him.' He just loved Gary Cooper. He said,

'Don't you think we're somewhat alike?'
I said, 'So much alike it's scarey!'
He said, 'Oh! Really!' He was so pleased.

Early in 1956 Roger Moore left MGM and Hollywood. The actor found himself with no immediate commitments and so decided to make his way back to Britain at a leisurely pace. Noel Coward had recently bought a Thunderbird from actor Robert Wagner, despite not being able to drive himself, and he placed this lovely car in the hands of Moore. Coward wanted to get the car back to England and he suggested that Roger could drive it across America and take the *Queen Mary* from New York, thereby delivering the vehicle safely and at the same time providing the young actor with a marvellous opportunity to see the vast continent of America at comparatively little expense to himself.

Roger drove east, bearing down towards the southern seaboard and visiting such beautiful attractions as New Orleans, before making his way through the Old South and up the East Coast, through Washington and finally up to New York and the waiting transatlantic liner.

The *Queen Mary* docked in Southampton towards the end of the second week in April, and Roger settled back into life with Dorothy at Bexley Heath. But the pattern of their marriage continued to run on its regular course of long separations spotted with brief, and far from idyllic, periods of togetherness. Dorothy's wandering husband had only been home for two days when he was called back to America. This time it was to New York, and the reason was something special: to appear in a two-hour television production of *This Happy Breed*, Noel Coward's drama of the life and loves of a suburban family from 1919 to 1939.

The play launched the CBS 'Playhouse 90' series and was Noel Coward's third television venture, following *Blithe Spirit* with Claudette Colbert, Lauren Bacall and Mildred Natwick, and the first of the trio *Together With Music* with Mary Martin. Coward was to repeat the part of Frank Gibbons which he had created for himself and which he played at the Theatre Royal, Haymarket in London during the war.

The production had been scheduled for early in May, but had been postponed until October. However, it was decided in late March by CBS and the Ford Motor Company, who sponsored the programme, to do the play on May 5th as had originally been intended. Coward unexpectedly found himself facing 'a month of feverish activity' and immediately immersed himself in the matter of casting the production.

The original intention had been to produce the play in Hollywood, from where Coward's previous two television specials had been broadcast. But when the author and star successfully signed Edna Best to play Ethel, arrangements had to be altered. Miss Best had been a noted leading lady in both Britain and America between the two World Wars and had achieved a famous partnership with her then-husband, British actor Herbert Marshall, but by the mid-fifties she was the victim of severely erratic health, as Coward noted in his diary immediately after she had agreed to play the part:

> She has been dreadfully ill with a breakdown for months, but the doctors swear she will be all right for this and that it will be therapeutically the best thing in the world for her. However, she cannot go to Hollywood and so I have finally overridden CBS and Ford and insisted on doing the show from here (New York), which is what I wanted all along.

Cast by Noel Coward himself, Roger received the offer of the third principal part, that of Billy Mitchell (who was played in the film version by John Mills and in the original theatrical production in London by James Donald), and had to leave for New York immediately since rehearsals were due to start on Monday, April 16th. Although it had nothing to do with Coward's casting of Roger in this prestigious production, it is interesting to note that Roger had appeared in a stage version of *This Happy Breed* when he was at RADA. Roger was chosen due to the merits that Coward observed in him as an actor, with the Master perceiving a genuine talent in this handsome young man beyond his obvious attractions.

Roger left for New York determined to fulfil his part in the proceedings to his utmost ability: 'I had been warned that Coward expected actors working with him to know their lines before they turned up for rehearsal. During the flight I made myself word-perfect and I was fully primed by the time of the first run-through.'

Coward lived up to all Roger's expectations of him, and the young actor was able to enjoy 'some marvellous chats' with the great man during the rehearsal period in this his first and only professional engagement with him. Coward offered Roger some

invaluable advice, telling him that he should accept every job that
was offered: 'The moment you are not working, you are not an
actor . . . and if you are offered two jobs at once don't take the
one with the larger part, take the one with the larger money.'

He also told Roger to forget about elaborate diets and provided
a solution that had much more appeal for the young man: 'Eat
and drink what you like until you are overweight. Then starve
yourself until you're back to where you should be.'

After two weeks of rehearsals, the production had already fallen
into shape with everyone being word-perfect, with another week
still to go before the telecast. Coward was particularly pleased
with his leading lady's performance but also had praise for the
others: 'The whole cast is eager to be good . . . They are all
playing true and I am very happy with them.'

As scheduled, the telecast took place on the evening of Saturday, May 5th and, as Coward noted, all went smoothly: 'The
whole cast played beautifully. No one grabbed opportunities or
fluffed or lost their heads and it was an almost perfect production
from every point of view.'

Judging from immediate public response, the telecast was a
huge success and the company were in a jubilant mood during the
cast party at Edna Best's home later that evening. The party went
on beyond five o'clock the next morning, with the other guests
including Gladys Cooper, Cathleen Nesbitt, Julie Andrews, Rex
Harrison and Kay Kendall.

When the notices finally appeared the general consensus was
that it was one of the finest telecasts done up to that time. Noel
Coward and Edna Best received rave reviews, and Coward himself
believed that 'the rapport between us (himself and Miss Best) was
so strong that it gave the play a little personal magic that it has
never had before either on the stage or the screen'. And Roger had
been fortunate to be a part of this unique theatrical experience.

It had been a marvellous opportunity for Roger and provided
him with valuable exposure in one of the most prestigious productions ever produced for television, consolidating his credibility
as a serious actor. Roger and the rest of the cast received good
notices and 'immediate offers of jobs from all over the place', as
the proud author commented. He continued: 'This makes me very
happy because they all worked wonderfully and gave an all in all
team-work performance which was quite remarkable.' Coward
himself jokingly called Roger 'a damned scene-stealer' after reading the reviews.

Roger not only learned a great deal from Noel Coward himself but also had a valuable lesson in professional tact, as he later remembered:

The two producers, Lance Hamilton and Charles Russell, advised me to have my name taken off the credits above the title: 'Have your name under the title,' they said. My contract said my name should be above the title and I didn't see any reason to concede it. They pointed out how foolish I would be to put myself on the same plane as someone like Coward. But if I was under the title the viewers would be pleasantly surprised and the critics would respond. I took their advice and it worked. I had excellent notices.

Roger Moore returned triumphantly to London, having achieved one of his first notable successes and proving that there was more to him than just his incredible good looks.

Despite Roger's success in *This Happy Breed*, his return to England and Bexley Heath was not marked by an overwhelming demand for the young actor's services. Indeed, the only offer that he received was an out-of-town run at the Connaught Theatre in Worthing, Sussex in August 1956. Melville Gillam was the managing director of the Connaught Theatre, a weekly repertory theatre in which a play would have one week of rehearsals and then one week playing in front of the public. Gillam was very keen on putting on a certain number of new plays during the year – as many as fifteen in that period – and he would also invite guest stars who would be certain to enhance the box office takings by their appearance and give the audience something fresh. Emlyn Williams was another actor who appeared there at about the same time.

Richard Buckle, the distinguished ballet critic whom Roger had first met in his pre-RADA days, wrote a play called *The Family Tree* which he submitted to Gillam, who responded to it favourably. Buckle was able to turn the deal into an attractive package by securing Roger, whose name had the advantage of carrying with it his recent association with a major Hollywood studio, in the leading role.

Roger was supported by Elspeth March, the distinguished British character actress and first wife of Roger's boyhood idol, Stewart Granger, and a cast that included the young Daniel Massey, son of the distinguished Canadian actor Raymond Massey and the lovely British star Adrienne Allen and godson of Noel Coward, who was just down from Cambridge and doing his first season. The play, a comedy of manners among the aristocracy, was directed by Peter Wood, now a distinguished director for the National Theatre.

Daniel Massey and Roger shared a dressing room and immediately hit it off – but underneath the easy charm the young Massey could see that Roger was not happy: 'It seemed to me that it was a period of transition for him in his life. Professionally things were becoming a bit purposeless, with a bit of a drift to them.'

Roger's presence among this talented repertory company was regarded as surprising. Here was an actor who seemed as if he should be on the verge of a huge career and instead he was in Worthing for a guest week with the company there. Roger seemed too glamorous a member of the profession to be there, and Daniel Massey was at first wary of how Roger would behave, expecting him to assert his loftier status as was usual – but Massey was pleasantly surprised: 'He was an easy man to know. I was a very young actor and he could have made life very difficult for me – but he didn't; he was enormously sympathetic.'

Roger, in any case, was hardly any more experienced as a stage performer than Massey, who had then just left Cambridge, with *The Family Tree* marking only his fourth or fifth play at Worthing in what was his first professional job. Roger felt his own limitations keenly and their mutual inexperience gave them a bond which prompted a quick and easy friendship during Roger's two-week stay on the south coast.

Both Roger and Elspeth March were at the Connaught only to appear in the Buckle play, with Elspeth playing the autocratic Countess of Avalon in this family comedy, while Daniel played a supercilious young aristocrat and Roger the leading role of a butler-cum-soldier who attempts to discipline Massey's spoilt aristocrat.

The author was in Worthing himself and his eccentric behaviour added occasional moments of off-beat humour.

Elspeth was in Worthing with Jamie and Lindsay, her two children by her marriage to Stewart Granger. The children were on their summer vacation from school and were able to enjoy a seaside break while their mother worked. The children played on the beach during the day and came to the theatre in the evening, where twelve-year-old Jamie earned some extra pocket money by dressing Daniel and Roger for a shilling a performance, while

Lindsay used to sit out front with director Peter Wood. Roger did not actually stay in Worthing, but went backwards and forwards each day to Bexley Heath in Dorothy's chauffeur-driven car.

The play was well received on its first night by an audience that included Viscount Robin Maugham, the author nephew of W. Somerset Maugham, and Gilbert Harding, at that time Britain's most famous television personality. A few days into the run film editor Peter Hunt came down to see the play, a man who was later to direct Roger in two films and also an episode of *The Persuaders*. Elspeth March remembers that the company had hopes of a transfer to London, but it was in truth a weak play, presented mainly on the strength of Buckle's name which was, at the time, very well known.

The play closed after its scheduled run. Dorothy was in the audience to see her husband's performance on one occasion and had been present on occasions during the rehearsal period, but it was clear to other members of the company that the couple were estranged and that matters were becoming difficult. Back in England, Dorothy had regained her former precedence, so that while Roger went through most of 1956 without any work at all, Dorothy had numerous offers of work and even appeared in a starring role in a British B-film musical called *Stars in your Eyes*.

Roger is remembered by his fellow actors at Worthing with great affection. His affable charm won them all round, but Massey for one was aware that the image that Roger projected of himself did not reveal the whole man. 'He had this glamorous screen star image of a man who seemed effortlessly to propel himself through life. But behind all that there must have been a lot of toughness and calculation, because usually instantly likeable or sympathetic people finish way down the line in our business.'

It was tough on Moore to do a play after just one week's rehearsal, because he had not had the experience of the weekly system and the discipline that it entailed. Nevertheless he again gave a very good account of himself – however, this did mark Roger's last appearance in the theatre up to the present time.

It is remarkable to compare Roger the professional actor with how he appeared to people who met him at Bexley Heath during this gloomy year of enforced indolence. Just as Roger, when in work, presented himself as the ideal of the selfless professional, so in his domestic life he was equally adroit at playing kept man to Dorothy, who had so clearly reaffirmed her dominant position. At home Roger could at times cut a ridiculous figure. He is remembered by a showgirl of the time, who was a guest at their house, as being a withdrawn figure wearing cowboy boots and hat, standing in a corner of the room not talking to anyone.

Unemployed for most of the time, Roger accompanied his wife to American bases where she was often performing. He was rarely seen without his hat and boots. He is remembered as once looking very attractive at home wearing a white polo-necked sweater with tailored slacks, but this improved image was short-lived. Just before the party of people that was assembled at St Mary's Mount were about to go out for the evening, Roger excused himself and dashed upstairs. He returned wearing his cowboy boots and hat.

He clearly lacked any real purpose in his life, and so long as his professional and private life continued to run on the paths they were set on he seemed content to drift along. When working, a glimmer of a more admirable Roger was evident but otherwise his dissatisfaction was made clear by his eccentric behaviour and dress, which seemed to be a form of self-laceration.

Luckily for Roger, this dark period finally came to an end. At about the same time that Dorothy's film opened in London, Roger signed a contract with Columbia to star in a television series called *Ivanhoe* in December 1956. Roger's long period of idleness was finally over.

Filming started early the following year, with interior shooting beginning at Elstree Studios. A problem arose when location shooting was required, and due to Britain being in the middle of winter and the landscape being bare and the trees leafless, it was deemed necessary to film the exteriors in California where there were suitable locations on the Columbia ranch.

It was while in Hollywood that Robert Brown, the English character actor, joined the cast, marking the beginning of a long and close friendship between Brown and Roger. On the morning after Brown's arrival in Hollywood, Roger called on Brown at the Knickerbocker Hotel, where Roger himself once stayed, to welcome him. Robert Brown was to play Gurth, Ivanhoe's side-kick, and the only character other than the title part that would run right through the entire series. Knowing this, Roger was determined to establish a rapport and wasted no time in doing so, as Robert Brown recalls: 'He knew that if the series clicked we'd be together all the time. He and Dorothy were marvellous; they just took me over and gave me a wonderful time in Hollywood.'

Brown was able to observe Roger's and Dorothy's marriage from quite close quarters and at this stage he found that essentially the marriage appeared stable, with no sign of the rows that were to come later. Brown is full of praise for Dorothy at this time: 'Dot was great fun and I liked her very much indeed. She was so warm and hospitable and motherly.'

Roger's return to Hollywood was soon over, and the unit returned to continue shooting not at Elstree Studios but at Beaconsfield Studios, in the middle of the Buckinghamshire countryside. With the weather improving the crew were also able to do much of their location work in the muddy fields around the studios. Roger was to spend a year there churning out episodes of *Ivanhoe* until June 1958, making a total of thirty-nine altogether. The series was being made for both British and American television, and became a popular addition to the 'Children's Hour' schedule when it finally started being screened in January 1958.

Roger found the series enormous fun to make at first, with himself and Robert Brown both relishing the physical exertion that many scenes required. As Brown remembers, 'We used to do all our own stunts. Once we had gained the confidence of the stunt boys, Rodge and I used to do weekend exercises and work-out routines down at Bexley. Eventually the stunt men accepted us and allowed us to be members of their fraternity.'

This proved an asset due to the method adopted for filming the action sequences in the series. Brown continues: 'They suddenly decided that they could shoot with three cameras on the one sequence and it would save time. One sequence with the three angles meant they would not have to set it up again and again.'

Obviously with such a method of shooting it was preferable that the two actors did their own stunts, because it would have been impossible to use a double convincingly since with three angles being covered at the same time there would be no way of hiding the fact that the man doing the stunt was not really Roger or Robert Brown.

But Roger's uncharacteristic devotion to physical exertion was not without its hazards. He suffered several injuries, including having his hands slashed, his head struck by a battleaxe – rendering him unconscious – and cracking three ribs. Roger himself injured Peter Diamond, the fencing expert on the series, while filming a combat with broadswords.

Brown noticed that Roger appeared inhibited in his acting at first, a throwback to his days at MGM when he had come in for such criticism about the way that he spoke. Roger tried to combat this by going to a speech therapist who gave him speaking exercises that would help to solve his clenched-teeth habit of speaking. This problem, as Roger viewed it, was a significant reason for his adoption of the pose of being a non-actor, an attitude which even now he is apt to cling on to when his confidence in himself is sagging. Being a leading man who essentially sold his own personality only aggravated the problem, especially as his main aim was to project that he had absolute confidence in himself – something that he felt that he lacked and which therefore prevented him from being able to relax totally in front of the all-seeing eye of the camera. But Brown noticed that when Roger had the chance really to act rather than play a variation on himself, he showed a different side: 'In one episode he had to disguise himself, playing a character part, and he was absolutely brilliant. In other words he is a true actor; when putting on somebody else's mantle and getting inside another kind of character he is marvellous. Whenever he used to put himself down after that I used to think what nonsense he was talking.'

Roger did not have a regular leading lady in the series, with the series rather following the adventures of Ivanhoe with his companion Gurth in a very free adaptation of Sir Walter Scott's novel. A pretty blonde English actress called Leigh Madison appeared in several episodes, but usually each individual episode had its own new characters drawn from the stable of English supporting actors of the time, more or less exhausting the supply by the time that the series finally ended.

When they were filming, Roger would often stay over at the Crown in Penn with Brown and the rest of the crew. Roger and Brown would go over the schedule for the next day, and Roger would look through a list of names that he kept of people who needed help on the series, an early sign of a Roger Moore who would develop into a very professional actor to work with, a reputation that has stood him in good stead right up to the present and a shrewd policy to adopt on the young actor's part. Roger did not hinder the shooting due to lack of preparation, and he had the advantageous gift of an almost photographic memory which made things easier for him. Dorothy would occasionally join Roger for the shooting and together they wrote a song to go with the *Ivanhoe* series. Roger wrote the lyrics and Dorothy the music, intending it to be sung by a baritone over the titles. On the day of the recording, however, it was discovered that they did not have a male singer suitable and so Dorothy immediately offered her services saying, 'I'll give it all the balls I've got!'

With the recording finished she stated, 'My balls touched the ground.' But despite this remarkable achievement their song was not accepted and it was instead a song written by someone that Columbia had already commissioned for the job that was ultimately used.

With Roger hard at work all through the week, the big social occasion for Roger and Dorothy became their Sunday house parties, to which many people would be invited including musician Geoff Love and Jackie Collins and her father Joe Collins, who was a long-time friend of Dorothy's. The couple's near-relations would also be there, including Dorothy's sister-in-law, Joyce Golding, who lived nearby, and George and Lily Moore, who both got on extremely well with Dorothy. There was also a lovely girl called Annie Pratt, who was in charge of the horses on *Ivanhoe* and told the actors how to handle them. Robert Brown remembers a memorable occasion when Roger came to dinner at his Cookham home along with Miss Pratt:

Annie had a marvellous Dobermann which she brought with her to dinner that night. They all left at about half-past eleven and Roger was going to run her back. My wife and I went to bed and then suddenly there was a sound of bashing on the door and I looked out and there was Rodge in his lemon silk drawers . . . What had happened was that they had got into the car and had just gone down the lane when the dog was sick all over him. So he jumped out of the car into the narrow road and took his trousers off. And I had to give him a pair to go home in. Who else could it happen to?

Unfortunately, any enthusiasm for the series that Roger had failed to last until the end of the series. As Roger reached the first anniversary of his involvement in it he fell into a deep depression, feeling that his career had reached a stalemate. Television was still thought of at that time as very much the inferior medium to films, and to become involved in television after a film career was usually taken as an indication that an actor was in decline. With his failure at Metro-Goldwyn-Mayer it appeared that any chance of a film career was over and even in television he felt that he was getting steadily more type-cast as a one-dimensional action hero.

It was at this time that Roger decided to try to provide himself with a role that he felt would suit him and would bring him the success that he craved. He was attracted towards Leslie Charteris's character 'The Saint', feeling that it would be a good departure for him in television, and so he approached the author about buying the rights for himself to do a television series based on the character. But Roger's offer was just another of many that Charteris received which failed to impress the reclusive author, and it seemed that Roger would have no opportunity to play a role that he felt could be so marvellous for him.

Roger's dissatisfaction with *Ivanhoe* was not helped by his failure to find further opportunities for himself. He had by now come to regard all the charging around in armour as foolish and described himself to the press as being like 'a medieval fireman'.

Indirectly, Roger's marriage again came under the scrutiny of the press soon after the New Year when Dorothy was involved in a much-publicised court case with her old friend and mentor, Billy Reid, over the ownership of the house in Bexley, in which Roger and Dorothy were comfortably ensconced. This continued throughout the early part of 1958, and much of the testimony given in court was reported in great detail by the press, who relished Miss Squires' graphic descriptions of her tempestuous life with the portly song writer.

It must have therefore been quite a relief for Roger when he was once again summoned to Hollywood with the chance to star in an important forthcoming production for Warner Brothers. In order to be able to accept the offer, which the desperate actor was very anxious to do, it was necessary to break with Columbia. Fortunately this was easily managed, particularly as the studio had become disenchanted with their young television star, who showed all the signs of developing into a temperamental liability.

Roger finished shooting the last episode of the seemingly inexhaustible *Ivanhoe* in June 1958 and in the following month he flew alone to Hollywood.

Roger Moore arrived in Hollywood well aware of the incredible good fortune which had befallen him. He had felt that with his departure from Metro-Goldwyn-Mayer the doors of Hollywood had been closed to him and even in his most optimistic moods he had never dared to hope that Hollywood would again beckon him – let alone in the shape of a studio that was not lesser than MGM. Warner Brothers, along with MGM, had unrivalled track records as the premier Hollywood studios. The Warner Brothers studios in Burbank were the home of some of the most enduring personalities ever to light up a motion picture screen – names like Bogart, Davis, Cagney and Flynn that even now have lost none of their magic and are still instantly recognisable.

Roger was ushered into this illustrious organisation to play in a film based on Max Reinhardt's stage production of Karl Vollmoeller's play, *The Miracle*, which had originally been mounted in 1911. Set in Spain at the time of the Peninsular War of 1808–1814, it was a particularly turgid, episodic story concerning a postulant nun named Teresa who dreams of finding her own 'knight in shining armour'. A young and handsome officer in the Dragoons, Captain Michael Stuart, passes by the convent with his regiment and stops to water the horses. For both Captain and novice it is love at first sight. Captain Stuart leaves, but soon after is wounded and spends some time recuperating in the convent where their love blooms. But the time comes when he must return to duty and he leaves the convent to return to the wars. The young nun decides to follow her gallant Captain and at this point the 'miracle' occurs – a statue of the Virgin Mary comes to life and takes the form of Teresa while the young girl goes off on her odyssey. The story then sinks into a series of episodes which befall her during her search for the Captain, each one barely connected to the previous one and involving her with various men, from virile gypsies to ageing operatic promoters, and inevitably a matador. Meanwhile, the convent goes to ruin, being afflicted by a drought; Teresa fares no better, leaving a trail of misery in her wake before finally finding Captain Stuart. She decides that she must go back to the convent, and her return brings a much needed rainstorm and the reappearance of the statue of the Virgin Mary on her pedestal.

Roger, of course, played the handsome young Captain Michael Stuart, a nephew of the Duke of Wellington. The part had already been rejected by Dirk Bogarde and Richard Burton – not surprisingly, since it really amounts to little more than a supporting role.

When Roger reported to the studio the director, Irving Rapper, felt that his accent was 'too English' and pronounced and sent him to Jo Graham, the veteran dialogue director at Warners who among others had worked on such classic Errol Flynn pictures as *The Sea Hawk* and *Dodge City*, and was by then a grey-haired man with a hearing-aid. When Graham and Moore met they began chatting to each other and during the course of the conversation Graham asked Roger why he felt so inferior. Their relationship became one of psychiatrist and patient as Graham forced Roger to look at himself and his life. He discovered that Roger had an inferiority complex because of his lack of education, having left school so early, and not having attended college. He was frightened of mis-pronouncing words, which caused him subconsciously to hold back, keeping his jaw shut. Graham made Roger see all that he had going for him – his good looks, his physique – and told him he must have something for a great studio like Warner Brothers to have summoned him all the way from England to be in the film.

Roger has said:

I feel the greatest thing God ever gave me was my meeting with Jo Graham. He opened up roads that I knew were there, but I never had the courage to go through the gates. His logic was impcccable. His understanding of human nature as near total as is likely to be found in any one human being. He was concerned with the valuable side of people's lives more than with their faults and failings. Jo steered me through *The Miracle*. He taught me how to react to relationships and by so doing somehow managed to put my entire life into focus. Nearly all things I was vague about, yet instinctively felt were there, Jo helped me put into little compartments of clarity and hope. He was the guru and I the student at his feet.

Roger was not the first actor to find Jo Graham so personally invaluable. In 1937, young Ronnie Reagan, as the future President of the United States was and is still known to his colleagues in Hollywood, was preparing for his first film, *Love is on the Air* for Warner Brothers. The President remembers:

Love is on the Air got under way after a preliminary reading of the script. I didn't know this reading was not a regular thing, but only the result of the director's concern at being handed a brand-new actor for leading man. It almost resulted in losing the brand-new actor. There I was – faced with my nemesis, reading. It isn't that I flubbed the words, or stumbled and mis-pronounced; I even placed the emphasis on the right syllable. I just lacked personality when I read. The words make sense, but the lines don't sound as if they are coming from a real-live character. There must have been stark panic in cast and crew. A dialogue director named Jo Graham saved me: perhaps because of an intuitive sense regarding my weakness, and perhaps because he too was new in Hollywood from the stage and had a kind heart. He urged the director to wait until the next day and see how I did playing a scene without script in hand. All this, of course, I learned much later.

Judging by the results, from the President of the United States to Flynn and Roger Moore, Jo Graham must be the greatest voice coach of all time and, as with Ronald Reagan, must share a large part of the vocal success of Roger's career.

The part of the Captain in *The Miracle* was very much in the mould of the parts Warners gave to Errol Flynn during his golden days at the studio in the latter half of the 1930s and the early 1940s, though not nearly so rewarding. The dialogue was trite and stiff, and Roger was given little chance to relax and feel at ease with the character, although he did look every inch the dashing Dragoons officer. Despite the coaching from Jo Graham, in the finished film Roger's voice was far too clipped to endear himself to the audience, lacking the warmth and more relaxed quality it was to acquire later.

It is easy to see what Rapper, Blanke and others at Warners saw in the young Roger Moore, and it was an obvious path to follow, putting Roger into the heroic mould of Errol Flynn. Both actors had the same fair good looks – although a moustache suited Flynn better than it would Roger. Both had beautiful voices, although at the time of *The Miracle* Roger had not yet mastered the vocal cadences of Errol Flynn. Both men were tall – 6'2" – and both grew up with incredible good looks, being ardently chased by women: one succumbed to temptation, the other didn't. The supreme grace of Roger Moore's character is in contrast to Errol Flynn's often well-publicised tardy behaviour.

If Roger had been given the same back-up as Flynn, who was given starring roles in superbly-mounted productions, all diverse subjects affording him maximum screen time under superb direction with fine writers and wonderful fellow actors – his career would have been entirely different. Errol Flynn, the supreme film star from the beginning of his career in *Captain Blood*, also had the great good fortune to have as his leading lady in several of his films, Olivia de Havilland, a girl whose enormous talent provided the strong support to enable Flynn to give some marvellous performances.

But for *The Miracle* Roger's co-star was Carroll Baker, who had appeared at the studio in *Giant* with Elizabeth Taylor and

James Dean, and then made her name as Tennessee Williams'
Baby Doll, directed by Elia Kazan. Married to New York director
Jack Garfein, Baker had enjoyed great success early on in her
career with *Baby Doll* and had soon gained a reputation on the
lot. By this time Roger had shared soundstages with such great
actors as Gracie Fields and Jessica Tandy, Elizabeth Taylor, and
the Master himself, Noel Coward. It must have been a traumatic
experience for the even-tempered Moore as Carroll Baker made
it known how much she disliked her co-star.

Charlie Isaacs recalls, 'She wasn't crazy about him and he wasn't
crazy about her. I don't think they seemed too happy with each
other. They were both unhappy with the picture and that was it;
it was a picture that neither one enjoyed doing – that was the root
of it.'

Elspeth March, who had already worked with Roger at the
Connaught, Worthing in *The Family Tree*, was cast as Sister
Dominica in the film and remembers the difficulties caused by
Miss Baker:

What a pain in the neck she was. She was very dismissive of us
all. She had tiffs with everybody and was brusque to people
like Walter Slezak and Katina Paxinou, and she was very
difficult with Irving Rapper, the director. Irving once said to
her rather pathetically: 'But you must have taken direction.
Elia Kazan's direction made you.' But she snapped, 'Elia Kazan
can't direct a love scene!'

Miss March remembers Roger as a great source of relief on the
set of *The Miracle*, breaking the tension caused by Baker. She
was also refreshed to find an actor who had no illusions about
himself or the film. She says, 'The wonderful thing about Roger
is that he is always on to himself. He knew that it was really not
a good picture in spite of the cast. It was a real mish-mash of *The
Miracle* story, and Carroll Baker was terribly miscast.' Although
Warner Brothers had obviously spent money on the production,
nothing could save it from the hackneyed script and uninteresting
story line. The film was quite simply terrible, and Roger's contribution was negligible on screen.

It was not a particularly buoyant period of his life. His career,
although having had the great good fortune to be signed to a
contract with Warner Brothers, was not progressing. The parts
he was being offered were inferior roles in low-grade A-features.

Meanwhile Dorothy had joined her husband in Hollywood, and the couple again settled in the Westwood apartment that they had occupied before. It gave them a welcome opportunity to consolidate friendships from earlier days, and they became particularly close to Mr and Mrs Charlie Isaacs and Ross Hunter and Jaques Mapes. Ross Hunter could see that the Moore marriage was still on its rocky course: 'There was no stability to that marriage whatsoever. It was one-sided. They fought often; it was not a very genial evening spent there when the two of them were at each other's throats.'

Hunter could see that career conflicts were a significant root cause of their arguments. Just as Roger had little pull in Britain, as had been so painfully demonstrated to him upon their return to England after Roger's MGM contract had been dropped, so in Hollywood Dorothy continued to take a back seat to Roger. Publicly, Dorothy would state that this situation suited her, telling the press that, 'Roger's career is the only one that matters now,' but she was never happy just to play housewife to Roger and there were still enough offers of work coming in to convince her that her career was still very much alive if she chose to continue to exploit it. Ross Hunter is sympathetic to the dilemma that faced Dorothy and the resulting friction that it generated: 'I don't blame Dorothy; she was an older woman and a star in her own right in her own country, but over here in Hollywood we talked about Roger. I don't think Roger fought so much because he was a very amiable fellow. He was very easy to get along with, not tending towards temperament.'

Elspeth March was also brought into their social circle and remembers their warm hospitality: 'They had terrific spats and make-ups, but the apartment was a lovely place to go because Dot's such a funny woman. She used to cook up these extraordinary English dishes for all of her American friends; the house was always full of characters. I used to be in and out a lot and they were always so sweet to me.'

Miss March had one very memorable night out with the Moores:

I had just arrived from New York and Roger met me and said, 'Listen – Dorothy's on tonight. We must go and see her. It's her first night.' I remember going with Roger to this cabaret, which turned into an absolute disaster because it was Prom night. It was the end of term with all the young girls in their white dresses and white gloves, and the boys in their best clothes. They didn't want to hear Dorothy Squires sing, they wanted to dance. Dorothy was singing while dinner was being served and there was a great clatter and chatter and Dot lost her temper. There was the most almighty row. Roger just took all the chaos in his stride and laughed.

By now Roger had become used to the traumas and troubles of being married to a variety entertainer. But in this case the audience's behaviour towards the cabaret attraction, Dorothy Squires, was unreasonable to say the least.

Like Ross Hunter, Elspeth March saw that the marriage could not last: 'I think it was absolutely doomed. Dorothy always wanted to be the star in that household and although, as she frequently said, she had invested countless dollars in Roger, she didn't really like him taking top billing. It just wasn't going to work out.'

Roger certainly had his hands full with Dorothy. Her colourful, larger-than-life personality ensured that even when she was not on the stage herself, her volatile temperament would create a performance which would command the attention of all around her. Dorothy was in complete contrast to Roger, who would go out of his way to avoid causing a scene. Ross Hunter remembers an incident at the Macombo Club. She had a violent row with Roger and left the table. Roger didn't say a word.

Robert Brown also remembers Roger telling him of some of the embarrassing incidents that he had to steel himself to cope with in Hollywood: 'He and Dorothy went to a charity function and Kay Starr was appearing. They had a fairly front table and I don't know whether Dot was a little pie-eyed, but she was saying things . . . that didn't go down very well.'

Roger himself was not beyond some more outrageous behaviour when the mood took him. He felt far more at home in Hollywood now and he began to socialise more widely and more enthusiastically than he had done before. Not content simply to stay in the background, he now actually made his own personality felt. Even when Dorothy was with him in Westwood, Roger did not restrict his social activities to those involving his wife. Charlie Isaacs remembers an incident that occurred at this time at his own Westwood home:

One morning I heard a sound at the back of the house and I looked out of the bedroom window. It was just getting light and I saw a figure out on the patio on one of the chaise-longue

85

chairs. I thought, 'What the hell is that?' – until I finally realised that it was Roger wrapped up in a big car coat out there. Apparently he had been out with the boys that night until about two or three in the morning, and he was loaded. He had called Dorothy and had a battle over the phone and decided he would come to my house. Instead of coming to the door he just crept around the side and lay down on a chaise by the pool. He moved around a little later and that awakened me.

Roger had taken to drinking more than usual due to his general unhappiness, and the alcohol served to bring out a more lively Roger than had been previously seen in Hollywood. He made sure that he enjoyed himself despite career and marriage difficulties and his behaviour became unpredictable, as Charlie Isaacs again recalls:

My wife and I were having a barbecue party and we were having some rum drinks and everyone was getting a bit loaded. I happened to remark that the patio furniture should be cleaned soon. Suddenly I heard a noise and I turned around and there was Roger throwing all the furniture into the pool. We got it out subsequently and he apologised later, although he had been so drunk that he couldn't remember doing it.

To the unsettled background of his personal life Roger's career ground on unspectacularly. Next he was cast in *Gold of the Seven Saints*, directed by Gordon Douglas, in which his co-star was Clint Walker, who played the title role in the television series *Cheyenne*. Roger played Shaun Garrett, an Irish cowboy from Dublin; it had been the policy of Warner Brothers to cast British actors in Westerns, excusing their accents by giving them a strong Irish background. The most notable aspect of the production, unhappily for Roger, was that it marked the start of his trouble with kidney stones, which continue to plague him up to the present. Much of the film was shot on location in the stifling heat of the Utah desert, and he suffered from dehydration which was to be a direct cause of his starting to produce stones in his kidneys. Roger recalls:

I lost 10lb making *Seven Saints* in Utah. It was horribly hot, 120 degrees every day. Clint Walker and I staggered about among wild bush and jagged rocks with no trees or shade. We were meant to be two characters who were hot, tired and thirsty. We were. We had to ride across a raging torrent in the Colorado rapids. There was a strong current and a high wind. The director had four launches out of camera range and they caught us in nets and fished us out every time we got separated from our mounts. We did it twenty times before we made the opposite bank.

During this period there was one notable highlight for Roger. He was signed to appear in *The Avon Emeralds* – a twenty-five minute play for the phenomenally successful series *Alfred Hitchcock Presents*. In these television films all manner of famous and future stars were used, and it was a status symbol to be cast in the series. Two other young actors struggling for recognition who had parts in the series at this time were Steve McQueen and Robert Redford. *The Avon Emeralds* was guest-directed by Bretaigne Windust, who had previously been chosen by Bette Davis when she turned producer for her production of *Winter Meeting*, and immediately directed Miss Davis again opposite Robert Montgomery for Warner Brothers in *June Bride*. Mr Windust had also been the first director to bring James Bond to the screen, in a television version of *Casino Royale*, made for the CBS series *Climax Mystery Theatre* and transmitted on October 21st, 1954 with American actor Barry Nelson as James Bond and Peter Lorre as villain Le Chiffre. Roger's leading lady was fellow Britisher Hazel Court, now married to the American director Don Taylor. She recalls that although the play was directed by Bretaigne Windust, Alfred Hitchcock was very much in evidence during the production:

Hitchcock came on the set. At that time we were in awe of Hitch and all of us were scared of him. He always came and supervised and it was a very uncomfortable time because he didn't like actors very much and he really showed it.

Each episode of *Alfred Hitchcock Presents* took two days to rehearse and two days to shoot. We would block it in the morning on the first day and would run through it with our scripts. Hitch would come along and watch it being blocked. He probably made a few suggestions but we would never know. That night you would learn it and the next day we would run through it entirely. We would just go straight through it like a play. It was shot at Universal and at the old CBS studios, where

87

Dick Powell worked. Hitchcock would come and visit when it was being shot.

Hitchcock was so big here that people would love to be on the show; it was always a privilege and a pleasure. Roger was very professional and he always knew his lines – it was a very professional show and you had to be good to get through the two days of rehearsing and the two days shooting. You had to know your job.

This was not the first time that Roger Moore and Hazel Court had been associated with the same project. Hazel had played a supporting role in *Gaiety George* when Roger was just a member of the crowd, and later Hazel was to appear in an episode of *The Saint*.

Roger's last film under his Warner Brothers contract was *The Sins of Rachel Cade*, in which he was reunited with producer Henry Blanke and was directed once again by Gordon Douglas. In this film Roger dropped to third billing to make way for fellow British actor, Peter Finch. Rachel Cade was played by the delightful Angie Dickinson, who was to score a great success as *Police Woman* in the television series in the 1970s. Angie Dickinson's 'sin' in the film was to have an illegitimate son by Roger Moore, playing an American volunteer in the RAF who crash lands in the Belgian Congo, straight into the arms of Miss Dickinson playing a missionary at an outpost there.

Roger's chances of big screen stardom seemed to be fading when Warner Brothers decided to shift their new contract actor away from cinema feature films and on to television, which according to Roger's contract they were quite entitled to do.

It was a sure sign that Jack Warner did not think that Roger was at that point a particularly promising candidate for screen stardom. Whereas in the thirties and forties actors could gradually gain experience and technique by taking large parts in second features or supporting parts in important films, the emphasis had now changed. The production of B-films had declined because television could now supply a similar standard of entertainment; therefore it was on the television side of a film company's interests that contract artists would get their chance to develop. Roger's screen image was a litle too undefined and bland to make him stand out as a memorable leading man.

Roger Moore's first experience of television work with Warners was unfortunately not a happy one for him, either professionally or personally.

He was given the lead in a western series to be called *The Alaskans*, set in the 1898 gold rush, in which he played a fur trapper and con-man, Silky Harris. Roger stipulated that dialogue coach Jo Graham, the man who had given Roger the confidence he had previously so badly lacked, should always be on the set. The schedule was for thirty-six black and white fifty-minute episodes, and it marks the lowest point in Roger's film and television career. Roger had not only suffered the indignity of falling from cinema films to television, at a time when the two worlds of cinema and television were sufficiently divided so that a certain stigma definitely attached itself to such a shift, but he had become involved in what turned out to be one of the worst television series ever made in Hollywood. Indeed, it was so bad that it has never been shown on British television.

The principal director on the series was Leslie Martinson, who remembers Roger affectionately as an outgoing young man with a marvellous sense of humour. Martinson could see a potential in Roger and told him, 'Once we get a little mileage on that handsome face of yours I think you're going to go places.'

But the series was not a happy experience for anyone, including Roger, who himself remembers it as a complete disaster. If the scripts were not bad enough, there was the further aggravation that it was a very uncomfortable series to work on physically. Set in the cold of Alaska, the series was actually filmed under the blazing California sun, requiring the actors to wear heavy furs and attempt to look freezing cold when in fact the temperature was over a hundred degrees.

Roger grew to hate the main street that was the principal set that the studio had mocked up for the adventures. He had endlessly to drive a team of huskies, the only genuine thing in the series, down the street; and they suffered even more than their master, as Roger remembers: 'They were so confused by the phoney scenery that they spent longer than usual relieving themselves up against the false pine trees.' However, for Roger, the faking of Arctic weather was the most agonising physical discomfort during shooting:

They were using aeroplane engines rigged up to simulate snowstorms and gales. The 'snow' was salt and gypsum, and having that blown in your face by wind machines and plane engines is no fun. What was worse, the camera crew had masks to protect them (and they were standing *behind* the camera) and we the actors had to take the full blast. At the end of every day we had our eyes washed out and frequently the eyes were scratched from the gypsum.

Roger found a soul-mate to turn to in the form of his leading lady, a platinum blonde from South Dakota called Dorothy Provine, who was ten years his junior. Up until this time Roger's marriage had run along a relatively trouble-free course. Husband and wife were not frequently seen together socially, but this had always been the case since both were very active with their careers, necessitating them, particularly in Dorothy's case, to commute between Britain and America. Roger's work programme was the less erratic of the two since his commitments as an actor were of longer duration, whereas Dorothy, as a touring singer, had to fulfil short engagements at many different venues.

Despite their frequent separations, their marriage had appeared to be stable and neither had been linked with any other person. Leslie Martinson says, 'He never associated with anyone else. He didn't have a roving eye, which was another of his exemplary qualities.'

But when Roger met Dorothy Provine, he found himself attracted to this pretty young girl in a way that had not happened to him before. He had been used to the admiring looks of pretty girls and had ample opportunities offered to him, but this rather withdrawn young woman was the first real threat to his marriage. Martinson did not view her as the conventional Hollywood actress: 'She was a reserved personality, withdrawn and not available to anyone.'

But Roger brought her out of herself, and their friendship developed steadily until it was not easily hidden from the rest of the crew on *The Alaskans*. However, since neither Roger nor Dorothy Provine were the type to enter into an affair casually it was viewed with much sympathy by their co-workers and director: 'They had a nice relationship. I felt there was a lovely chemistry between them.'

Roger felt almost like an adolescent schoolboy again as he and Miss Provine found a relaxed comfort in each other's company. It was not long before Dorothy Squires began to hear rumours of her husband's interest in another woman. A producer friend of Dorothy's first intimated to her that Roger had become close to his leading lady, and it took her completely by surprise. Never did she imagine that Roger could actually become seriously involved with another woman and she had never felt the need to put on a great show of possessiveness: 'I didn't want to be on his shirt tails. Naturally, I guessed there were always plenty of beautiful girls hanging around his dressing-room but that didn't worry me. Well, I didn't think a man in his job and with his looks could always be faithful. But I told him that as long as I didn't know, things would be all right.'

But Dorothy began to observe her husband's behaviour, and it became all too clear that these were not just idle rumours. Roger's friend Charlie Isaacs was woken up by a phone call from Dorothy at 3 a.m. She told him that she was speaking from a phone booth in Westwood, having run out of their apartment where Roger was asleep. In a state of near-hysteria she said to Isaacs, 'Roger's in love with Dorothy Provine. He mentions her name in his sleep.'

'But your name is Dorothy,' he said.

'No – he calls me Dot,' was her reply.

She decided to confront Roger and find out the truth. Returning home one evening from a cocktail party, Dorothy decided that the moment had come and accused him directly:

'You're in love with somebody else.'

Roger finally admitted it was true and that the lady in question was Dorothy Provine. He had never been the type of man to take advantage of the innumerable possibilities he had with the attractive women who used to throw themselves at him. Isaacs once asked Roger why he didn't make a 'sexual pig' out of himself, given that there was so much opportunity. His answer was, 'I'm cursed with too much will-power.'

On one occasion Roger was driving along the street in his little open top sports car, along with Charlie Isaacs. They stopped the car and a group of young girls started yelling at Roger, 'Hey. I want you. I want you.' They came alongside the car and Roger said to them, 'See me in three years and bring a driver's licence.'

On another occasion Roger was at a party with Isaacs where a woman made an obvious pass at him, but Roger skilfully managed to fend her off. Isaacs went up to him, having observed everything and said, 'You passed her up!'

'I am married, you know,' said Roger.

'But she's chasing you!' retorted Isaacs.

Roger sighed. 'I know – it's wonderful, but you know, a cock is a divining rod that finds trouble for men.'

Their marriage became a source of comment by the press, and one particular incident seemed to confirm that their relationship was souring and that the age disparity had eventually caught up with them. They were involved in a public argument at a Hollywood night club after Dorothy, bolstered by the cocktails she had been drinking, sprang loudly to the defence of Britain and the London Palladium after a comedian had made jokes about both institutions. Dorothy did not stop her attack on the comedian until an embarrassed Roger Moore had to order her to be quiet. Miss Squires later intimated to the press that her behaviour was influenced by a drink which she had innocently believed to be entirely alcohol-free: 'I thought it was a fruit cup, but it had seven different kinds of rum in it.'

This public incident in October 1959 was an obvious indication that life for Dorothy and Roger was not all that it should be. Roger had come as close as he was able to a direct public confrontation with Dorothy. Never being a man to lose his temper easily, he had had to break through some of his natural emotional reserve to cope with the difficult situation which he himself had instigated.

He believed himself to be in love with Dorothy Provine, and while the Hollywood press reported Roger as having said that he and his wife had separated Dorothy stormed back to England, 'understandably furious', as Roger acknowledged, to appear in cabaret and to perform for a week at the Finsbury Park Empire, London's foremost music hall, as she had been contracted to do. She attempted to scotch all rumours of separation, telling English reporters, 'It's such nonsense. He probably meant it as a joke. He often makes silly jokes. His sense of humour is weird. Sometimes I don't understand it myself.'

By the time that Dorothy returned to Hollywood their marriage had begun to return to normal and, with the final episode of *The Alaskans* in the can, Roger and Dorothy Provine gradually drifted apart, but not before Provine had commenced *The Roaring Twenties*, a television series which was to give her a brief taste of stardom. Roger agreed to make a guest star appearance in one episode. Roger's relationship with Dorothy Provine had surprised both husband and wife, neither of whom had expected that Roger's interest in another woman would ever reach the point of actually threatening the stability of their marriage. Dorothy no longer felt the same confidence in her hold over Roger and was aware that if he could err once it was quite possible that it would happen again, and perhaps next time the conclusion would be different.

Meanwhile, career matters took precedence for Roger. His bitter experience of television with the ill-fated *The Alaskans* left him with no enthusiasm for television work and he was keen to return to the cinema, anticipating making another film with Clint Walker.

However, Jack Warner and Bill Orr, who was in charge of Warner Brothers Television, had other plans for their contract actor. One of their most popular television series was *Maverick*, which had turned James Garner into a huge television star. Having done the series for three years, Garner had become tired of the series. James Garner, at this early stage in his career, had already shown his dislike for a long-running series and although he was to remain a big star of the television screen, he showed the same feelings during the hugely successful *Rockford Files*.

Jack Kelly, Garner's co-star in the series and now Mayor of Huntingdon Beach – a suburb of Los Angeles, California – remembers the events leading to Garner's departure vividly:

There was a situation where a writers' strike was called by the Screenwriters Guild in Hollywood and we kept getting scripts in which the writing credit was always 'W. Hermanos' – 'hermanos' is the Spanish word for 'brothers'. We kept getting scripts that were actually written two years before for *The Alaskans* and now we were doing them as a *Maverick*. Everything was being switched around in order to defy the true essence of the writers' strike so that we could get through a period of delivering the numbers of TV segments that Warner Brothers was contractually committed to produce. We finally figured this out and we said, 'Hey, bullshit. You are defying the writers' strike and we don't feel that we can lend ourselves, Jim and I, to perform in this with any old story. They are just re-hashes of material that was already there prior to the strike.'

They changed the title of the script, changed the name of the character and that was the difference in the script. Jim and I both left in the middle of the production under that pretext. We hired one of the outstanding attorneys in Los Angeles and, about two months into this, Jack Warner called me and I went into the studio to talk to him. He said, 'We need you boys back and we are prepared to adjust the agreement to this degree –' He gave me three wheelbarrows full of gold and I said, 'Shit, I'll go back. Who wants a lawsuit?' Then I said, 'What about Jim?' and Warner said, 'Well, we're trying to talk to Jim.'

I went home, called Jim at his house and went up there. I said, 'Hey, are you going to go back too?' He said, 'What the hell are you talking about?' What I really didn't realise was what they were pinning on me – and I went for it.

Jim went on alone with the suit; he said, 'Hey, listen. You have to do what you feel. I'm not going back – screw them! I want out.'

Bill Orr told Roger that he was going to replace Garner as the star of *Maverick* and expected the young actor to fall in with this plan. But Roger had not anticipated doing another television series and had been led to believe that he would be appearing next in a feature film. He could see that *Maverick* was in decline as a series. He knew too that, due to the writers' strike, the scripts for *Maverick* were reaching an all-time low. To do the series would be to take a regressive step in a career which still had such a long way to go.

Roger took himself to Las Vegas. He was able to exercise his craving for all kinds of gambling, spending his time mainly playing blackjack and roulette, while receiving almost daily cables and telephone calls from the studio, all of which he steadfastly ignored. Finally, and not much to his surprise, he received the news that the studio had suspended him. Even Roger was amazed at how truculent and stubborn he could be against these all-powerful men who could either make or break a career which still needed so much nurturing. He was putting his future on the line, but he felt that that was the only way that he could make sure that his acting opportunities did not become limited to second-rate or declining television series, which would type-cast this most English of Englishmen as a cowboy actor.

Roger continued to gamble contentedly in Las Vegas until an unexpected telephone call came. He picked up the telephone expecting to listen to the usual pleas from Bill Orr and, instead found himself talking to the already legendary Jack L. Warner himself, the man who was a walking history of Hollywood with a well-earned reputation as a ruthless businessman. For a young, unimportant actor like Roger, who had no established reputation to back him, it proved too much; he left the gaming tables of Las Vegas and returned to Warner Brothers Studios in Burbank to begin work on *Maverick*. Jack Warner had told Roger that the sponsor for the series would only continue to back the programme if Roger Moore was in it, flattering the young actor's susceptible ego. Expecting that his rebellious young actor was only playing an elaborate game in order to gain more money, it came as a surprise to him when he discovered that the poor quality of the scripts was the actual bone of contention.

The Warner telephone call was an enormous threat to Roger's whole future. He was no Davis, Cagney or de Havilland, and it is a miracle that his career was not ruined by this action. To have been suspended by Warner at this time in his career would most probably have blacked him from working for any other American producer. It was a rash and ill-advised show of contempt for a major studio and Moore was lucky that his good sense prevailed in time, and only just in time, to return to Warner Brothers to carry out the work for which he was employed.

The trouble was that inspiration was severely flagging on the series. By the time that Roger moved into the series well over a hundred of the total of one hundred and thirty-eight episodes that would ultimately be filmed in the series had been made, and all variations possible seemed to have been played out. As a result, the scripts were often clumsy composites of old scripts from *Maverick* and other current series such as *Colt 45* and *Lawman*, as well as even *The Alaskans*.

But the series still had a tremendous hold over the viewing public and it remained almost an institution to watch the latest *Maverick* episode on a Sunday night, which almost knocked out the long-running *Ed Sullivan Show* in the ratings. Martinson used always to watch the show at 8 o'clock with his principal cast members, so that on that night you always knew where to find Roger Moore, Jack Kelly, Richard Long and James Garner (who continued to make occasional appearances in the series in the remaining nineteen episodes that were made after his dramatic exit from the series). When Dorothy Squires was in town she would come along with her husband. Leslie Martinson would fly live lobsters from Maine for these Sunday get-togethers, giving his principals a real clambake. The atmosphere on *Maverick* was almost like a repertory company, providing a closeness which Roger enjoyed and which made working on the series considerably more bearable than it would otherwise have been.

Roger and Jack Kelly consolidated a friendship that had started before *Maverick*, by socialising occasionally, visiting each other's houses and enjoying Hollywood nightlife together. A popular activity was bowling, and Roger and Dorothy used to organise bowling parties to which they would invite several couples. Frequent members of these parties were former stand-up comic Richard Dawson and his then wife, British film actress Diana Dors. Dorothy and Diana Dors had been friends since they had met in Blackpool in 1952, and when in England Roger and Dorothy were often guests at 'The Penthouse', Diana's home in Maidenhead over-looking the river Thames. Dors and Richard Dawson came over to America in the late fifties when Dawson was making cabaret appearances there and immediately joined Roger and Dorothy's circle of close friends. Dickie Dawson was to become one of America's most popular and successful television personalities with the game show *Family Feuds* after the couple had divorced.

Leslie Martinson was again the major director of the series, directing Roger in his first segment, in which he was introduced in the part of Cousin Beau, rather than actually taking over the part of Bret Maverick which had been James Garner's role.

Roger was far from happy, but this did not prevent him from behaving in his usual highly professional manner. He was adored by everybody on the set, actors and technicians alike, and helped to keep an enjoyable creative atmosphere circulating even though most of the people involved in *Maverick* were well aware that the series had reached its lowest ebb. Leslie Martinson was impressed by how adeptly Moore was able to bring a spark of life into even the most dreadful dialogue; he could see that this was one actor who would not just disappear from the acting scene but would develop into a very capable performer: 'The talent was there – he was very natural. With the worst words in the world this actor couldn't be hammy.'

Roger tried to enliven the series by attempting to play up the comic element that he saw as being inherent in *Maverick*. Unable to take the adventures that he found himself in seriously, he could see this approach as being the only one that might give the ailing series a shot in the arm. Unfortunately, not all the directors assigned to the series agreed with their leading man's approach, and the friction that this caused only served to emphasise Roger's disenchantment with his association with Warner Brothers.

Kelly was aware that Roger had not taken his decline into television lightly: 'Roger's heart was always back home and he was champing at the bit to get back to England. He was, to a degree, unhappy with the way his career was going in the United States and in Hollywood.'

Rumours began to circulate about the studio, in the meantime, that a new television series was in the offing, this time to be called *Tenderfoot* and centring on an Englishman who becomes a cowboy. Roger was the natural choice for the leading part, and

As an extra (mid-picture) on stage at the London Coliseum in *Mister Roberts* (1950) with Tyrone Power, Hildy Parks and Jackie Cooper

MGM publicity portrait (1954)

As Henry II with Marisa Pavan in *Diane* (1955)

As Ivanhoe (1957)

As The Saint (1969)

With Tony Curtis in *The Persuaders* (1971)

ABC Television

As Rod Slater in *Gold* (1974)

Michael Klinger

Richard Burton, Roger Moore and Hardy Kruger with their wives (1978)

Euan Lloyd

With Geoffrey, Deborah, Christian and Luisa (1976)

with such prospects ahead of him he could only see stagnation looming in his career if he remained with Warner Brothers. He decided that it would be best, if not imperative, to move on. He asked for his release from his contract and by mutual consent the agreement was terminated.

Roger and Dorothy Moore returned to England, with a bitter Roger determined never to do another television series again.

It is interesting to conjecture whether his career at Warner Brothers would have followed the same path if Roger had not acted as he did over *Maverick*. His behaviour certainly could have brought about the hasty end to his Warner Brothers stay. Just as he had shown a potentially difficult side to Columbia, so the same characteristics were made clear to Jack Warner. To act in such a way is always risky and before doing so you have to evaluate not only your own determination but also your value to the company. Roger very nearly misjudged his worth disastrously, but luckily backed off just in time. Though perhaps only in time to save his immediate career plans; his action more than likely closed off avenues that Warner might have opened to him. He may have had more opportunities to make features, but his punishment became an ever more deadening grind of television work. Their parting may have been by mutual consent, but Roger suffered most. Unlike for Cagney and the others, suspension really would have marked the end for Roger. He acquiesced with Warner, but Warner had his revenge because there was nothing at the end of the line for Moore. The situation had been similar with Columbia; Robert Brown recalls that things might have been otherwise there if Roger had not behaved differently towards the end of filming *Ivanhoe*: 'He had quite a contract with Columbia but that came to nothing. It started with *Ivanhoe* and after that so many films a year – but it was terminated by mutual consent.'

Roger was clearly guilty of major career indiscretions in both cases, particularly with Warner Brothers. At the time Warners were still very much in business – in fact, at this time, probably eclipsing MGM. They were back to making big films with big stars – everything from *Whatever Happened to Baby Jane*, marking the return of Bette Davis and Joan Crawford to the studio, to the three big musicals, *Gypsy*, *The Music Man* and *My Fair Lady*; John Ford was preparing *Cheyenne Autumn* and Jack Lemmon made *Days of Wine and Roses*. It might just have been to Roger's advantage to have hung around the studio. His private life may have benefited from his departure but not his career.

Five

ROGER'S FIRST move upon returning to England was to sign with a new agent. He chose Dennis Van Thal of London Management, which had been known as International Artists, an organisation acquired by Lew and Leslie Grade, the variety agents, through which actors were absorbed into the Grade Organisation. But they were a wholly British agency, with London Management having 'understandings' with several representatives in Europe and the United States. Dennis Van Thal had been an acquaintance of Roger's since the late forties, when he had made a screen test for *The Blue Lagoon* and Van Thal had been one of the casting directors.

It is surprising that Roger should have signed with an agency that could not represent him in America, especially since he had just returned from a seven-year stretch in the film capital of the world. It is a clear indication of Roger's disillusionment with Hollywood that he should have effectively cut off the possibility of lucrative American deals. Hollywood and Roger parted with neither side feeling any regret. Fortune had shone on Roger, giving him the incredible chance of not just one contract with a major Hollywood studio, but two. It is almost unheard of for a young aspiring actor to have had two such companies as Metro-Goldwyn-Mayer and Warner Brothers interested in him, but such was the case with Roger. But to have two such remarkable opportunities and to achieve so little was the awful tragedy of the situation. The fault of this situation must not rest entirely at Roger's feet; he had no agent or manager in Hollywood to guide him in his unsatisfactory relationships with these two studios. Roger Moore returned to Britain with a slightly more enhanced reputation, but he was walking under the cloud of failure. Hollywood had been prepared to take Roger in with welcoming arms, but the young man had not been given the chance to show the spark of greatness, whether in talent or personality, that would mark him out as a natural star like Errol Flynn, Ronald Colman, or other illustrious predecessors from Hollywood's British colony.

Roger was finally to become a star, and then a star of great magnitude, not through an inborn talent for the role but through dogged determination to fulfil that role. Never has Roger been marked for instant stardom and indeed his screen personality has never acquired the strength or magnetism of others who have reached the peak in this extraordinary profession. That Roger was able to continue in his efforts to achieve that ultimate goal is a tribute to the fine professionalism of the man, a reputation that remains untarnished to this day.

Husband and wife arrived in England in the late spring of 1961, with Roger intending to return exclusively to cinema acting. London Management soon found work for their latest acquisition, but it was of the calibre suitable for an actor who had a certain limited fame but little else to recommend him. The only work found was from French and Italian film companies, with their unending appetite for making cut-price epics, exploiting the cheapness of labour in Europe which enabled huge crowd scenes to be filmed which in Hollywood had become an impossible luxury.

Roger read through a pile of these uninspired scripts and picked out the least painful of the bunch. It was a script based on the story of Romulus and Remus, the founding of Rome and the rape of the Sabine women, to be called *Il Ratto delle Sabine*. It was a Franco–Italian production to be made in Cinemascope in Rome and on location in Yugoslavia; Roger would play Romulus. Fortunately for Mr Moore, the film was never released in Britain or the United States.

Having accepted the part, Roger left for Rome in May without Dorothy. The film had a certain distinction because its leading lady was Mylene Demongeot, at that time one of France's most popular film stars, ranking along with Brigitte Bardot. Mylene was a pretty and amusing blonde who, like Bardot – who made *Doctor at Sea* in 1955 – had come to Britain to make a comedy film entitled *Upstairs and Downstairs* in 1959 when she was just twenty-three. But her reputation rested on a film that she had made in 1956 called *Witches of Salem*, for which she received critical acclaim. She was briefly a sex symbol, but she had the advantage of being an infinitely better actress than her rival.

In a small part in the film was a lovely twenty-five-year-old Italian actress called Luisa Mattioli, with striking dark eyes, thick dark hair, and an enchanting smile, already a veteran of twenty-two films.

Both women awaited the arrival of the leading man, Roger Moore. It was a time when Rome had seen the arrival of an increasing number of such Hollywood stars, as the film world expanded and became more international. Sophia Loren, who was only three years older than Luisa Mattioli, had already co-starred with some of Hollywood's greatest stars – Alan Ladd, Clark Gable and Cary Grant – and in 1962 she was to win a Hollywood Oscar as best actress for her performance in *Two Women*. So at this time a Hollywood star, even so English a one as Roger, was an attractive prospect, because he represented a further bridging of the gap between Hollywood and Cinecitta in Rome.

Neither Luisa, the little supporting player, nor Roger, the Hollywood star, could have realised that their lives would be changed so dramatically when they both walked on to the set for their first day's work on this distinctly ordinary film. Roger was not drawn to his beautiful blonde leading lady, as might have been expected, but instead was much taken by the beautiful, dark extra.

The shooting of the film began in earnest on location in Yugoslavia, and it was here that Roger and Luisa first met and were unexpectedly attracted to each other despite obvious language difficulties. Luisa could speak no English at all, and Roger's only exposure to Italian had been way back in his childhood when he lived in Albert Square among a strong Italian community. Fortunately, Roger had always been a quick student when it came to languages, and was soon able to pick up enough conversational Italian.

But their initial attraction was naturally physical and, appraising her, Roger quickly took in Luisa's voluptuous figure and dark, smooth skin. He felt pleased that this young lady was going to be working with him and he felt sure that she was a girl who would be worth getting to know further.

Roger's effect on Luisa was no less dramatic. She was equally attracted to him and immediately singled him out as someone special, while being pleased to see that the attraction was mutual. In the confined world of location shooting it was not long before they were dating and Luisa soon discovered that this handsome young man was in a bad way, drinking too much in order to drown his sorrows over an unsatisfactory marriage and an uninspiring career. Roger was in a frame of mind in which he was open to the attractions of other women and without Dorothy's presence the possibility of a romantic involvement became more tenable. A mutual friend of the couple had warned Dorothy that she should go with her husband to Italy, but she chose to ignore this advice, saying that she had concert commitments in Australia. The friend insisted: 'Go with him! He's very volatile right now. He's a very good-looking man and there's no reason for him to be let loose in Italy because the women are ready, willing, and very able – and he's a good catch, if catch can.'

But Dorothy was still adamant and despite the friend's insistence she never went to Rome. She often recalls that incident now, wondering how things might have been if she had taken that flight to Rome with Roger. But perhaps all her presence would have done would have been merely to delay the inevitable, and to have trailed Roger like a watchdog would have been an undignified way to behave and one that Dorothy could clearly see was unworthy of her. If she was going to lose Roger it would not be through choice, but she was also sensible enough to know that she could not force the issue one way or the other.

Fate took a hand, and while it dealt straight into the hands of Roger and Luisa, it dealt a cruel and hasty blow to poor Dorothy.

With the scene set to their advantage, Roger and Luisa played the dating game, testing each other. He was reminded of the situation that had developed between himself and Dorothy Provine, and he could see a similar relationship recurring. But whether it would end in the same way as with his previous leading lady was another matter.

All Roger knew was that this woman, whom he had only just met, had completely captivated him. While unwilling to believe in such a thing as love at first sight, he did realise that his reaction to Luisa was different from any he had ever experienced with any other woman. He was grateful that circumstances had thrown him together with this stunning girl, with no immediate danger of his wife influencing the situation. Roger was in a foreign world, even more so than in Hollywood, where at least language gave an immediate common bond, but in that different world he felt that this young girl had drawn him into her life, no longer making him feel like an alien abroad.

It was an unusual situation in which their relationship developed. Here was Roger, a married man, with a wife twelve-and-half-years older than him (an age difference that became more painfully apparent as their marriage advanced), from whom he was frequently separated because of work, and Luisa Mattioli, a staunch Roman Catholic, devoted to her family, whose whole upbringing was being challenged by her attraction to this man.

Perhaps what Dorothy had always dreaded was going to happen: Roger had met a much younger girl, ten years younger than himself and twenty-two years younger than his present wife. And beyond a natural physical attraction, which on its own might perhaps be coped with and dissipate itself in a casual affair, Roger also realised that he was already responding to Luisa in a far from casual manner. He welcomed, yet dreaded, the events that might lie ahead.

Luisa was a member of a large, close family consisting of four girls and one boy. Her parents were strict Roman Catholics, and all the children had an ingrained love for the Catholic faith. Luisa had always been a source of great pride to her mother and father, and she had never done anything to shake that pride. But now, for the first time, she found herself forced to challenge everything that she had been brought up to believe because it involved a choice between the man she loved and hurting her beloved family. She made up her mind that she and Roger must stop seeing each other, but found herself unable to enforce this strategy. And it was clear that Roger's ardour was as intense as hers.

On location, with the couple able to spend so much time together, the inevitable happened: Roger and Luisa became lovers. It was not long before the question of their future arose, and they both decided that whatever future lay ahead of them, it would be a future together. Roger decided that he would divorce Dorothy and marry Luisa and raise a family. Ten years later, Roger reflected that the situation might have been different: 'I think it possible, even from this distance, that if Dot and I had had children then I might not have been so determined to do what I did.'

Poor Dorothy had been well aware of Roger's desire for a family and had not been able to have children. But even if Roger and Dorothy had been fortunate enough to have children, Roger certainly found that the intensity of his love for Luisa was beyond even what he had imagined he was capable of feeling, and it is just as likely that nothing, not even children, would have kept Roger and Luisa apart. Luisa herself takes a fatalistic view of their relationship, seeing it as having followed a pattern of such inevitability that neither of them could resist it strongly and that both had ultimately to accept that neither could, or even really wanted, to hinder its progress. Luisa later recalled, 'When I met Roger he was desperate and drunk. He needed someone to love him. We found trust, and we fell in love. Roger wanted a family life. He wanted to become a husband and a father – precisely what an Italian woman looks for in a man.'

Too soon for Roger and Luisa, filming ended on *The Rape of the Sabine Women* and Roger had to return home to a waiting Dorothy, determined to gain his freedom and to marry Luisa. Dorothy found that her husband had returned a different man from the one she had seen off to Rome only a few weeks before. While Roger did not directly admit that he was involved with another woman, it became increasingly obvious to his wife that this must be the case. She began to see less and less of her husband, and when they were together his behaviour was decidedly strange towards her. Dorothy tried to convince herself that his cold attitude towards her was somehow connected with the kidney complaint which had begun to manifest itself and was causing Roger occasional pain.

It was not long before Roger announced to Dorothy that he would be going to Italy again to make another film. It was to be called *No Man's Land* and was another Franco–Italian production produced by Enrico Bomba. The producer knew exactly how to persuade Roger Moore to make another film for him: he ensured that also in the cast was Miss Luisa Mattioli, for whom Roger had asked.

Dorothy was beginning to get used to even more frequent separations from her husband; no direct confrontation had occurred, but Roger was clearly avoiding Dorothy as much as possible. Between the shooting of the two films in Italy, he had to go to Paris to do some dubbing on *The Rape of the Sabine Women*, and he went alone. Meanwhile, at Bexley Heath, Dorothy Squires had discovered the reason for her husband's strange behaviour towards her. While Roger was in Paris, several letters arrived for him from Rome, addressed in a distinctly female hand. When the first arrived Dorothy gave it no thought, but when two more arrived in rapid succession she naturally began to be suspicious.

When Roger returned from Paris the inevitable confrontation occurred, and Roger confessed that he was in love with another woman and wanted to divorce Dorothy. But Dorothy was not willing to give up so easily, and the couple argued continually until Roger finally packed his bags and left the Bexley Heath mansion. He went to stay at Wyx Cottage in Cookham, the home of his friend Robert Brown and his wife Becky, thirty miles west of London.

While staying there, Roger suggested that Brown should travel down to Rome with him, as he thought that there might be a part in *No Man's Land* that his friend might be interested in, and so Brown agreed to accompany him. During this time Roger continued to experience occasional pains and since there was no sign of them abating he went to his doctor, who called for X-rays, the results of which came just before the two friends were to leave on their journey to Rome. The doctor warned Roger that he should not be surprised if the pains became severe, but this did not prompt Roger to cancel his trip, so keen was he to see Luisa again. He was by now totally wrapped up in his love for Luisa.

Bob Brown and Roger left Wyx Cottage in the latter's Alpine Sunbeam and on the first day drove as far as Paris, where they stayed at the Hotel Georges V. On the following day they made good progress, ending an exhausting day of concentrated driving at Lausanne in Switzerland, where they booked into a beautiful lakeside hotel. Roger was eagerly anticipating the sight of Luisa in less than thirty-six hours, and the two men went down to the dining room in a jovial mood. They sat down and ordered *escargots*, with blue trout to follow, a meal that they felt they thoroughly deserved after their long day's driving. The first course of *escargots* was just being set before Roger when the pain hit him.

He had succumbed to the first renal colic pain, as he had been warned by his doctor, and such was the intensity of the pain that Roger collapsed and had to be carried out by the restaurant's shocked waiters. Robert Brown saw his friend comfortably installed in bed and called for a doctor, who upon his arrival gave Roger a shot of morphine to ease the agonising discomfort.

A worried Brown went downstairs and half-heartedly finished his meal, while Roger slept in reasonable comfort in their room. He returned to find Roger still sound asleep. Unable to think of sleep himself after what had happened, Brown nervously paced the room waiting for Roger to wake up. Brown recalls how his long wait finally ended: 'At about half-past two in the morning I was looking out over the lake and suddenly this creature stirred, looked up and said, "Any blue trout left?"'

The two men discussed what they were going to do the next day. Roger was insistent that they should press on to Italy. He slept in reasonable comfort for the rest of the night and awoke feeling well enough to insist that he drove.

Again they drove all day, arriving in Milan that night; but there was a big convention of some kind taking place and they were unable to get a room for the night. Roger just said, 'Right. Let's go!' and they continued on the road to Rome, arriving at Luisa's apartment home there at seven-thirty in the morning, much in need of a bath and a shave. But such minor matters did not detract from Roger and Luisa's joyous reunion.

The first few days in Rome were spent going over the script before shooting began. The couple's happiness was only marred by the fact that Roger's kidney pains kept coming back. On Roger's first Saturday in Rome, the doctor who was treating him decided that an operation was necessary and preparations were made immediately. He was put into a nursing home at Monte Mario, just south of Rome, which was run entirely by nuns. The doctor felt that an exploratory operation should take place at once; however, all was not as straightforward as that. He wanted to perform the operation on the Sunday, but being a Catholic establishment the nuns were not at all keen on opening up the operating theatre on the Sabbath.

A ploy had to be instigated to prompt the nuns into action. Luisa was staying overnight in a room at the nursing home and so as dawn broke the doctor went to Luisa with a plan, which was put into action almost immediately, as Brown remembers:

She had to ring bells frantically and say that Roger had been passing blood and ask what should be done. The doctor was standing by waiting to be called, but the next thing was that the nuns reacted properly, saying, 'Well, where's the evidence?' Luisa said, 'Oh, I flushed it down.' Fortunately the nuns were convinced and opened up the theatre, the doctor was informed, and they performed the operation that morning.

Towards midday Roger was back in his room, and Brown arrived at the nursing home just after twelve to lend Luisa his support. Luisa and Brown were talking amid the peaceful surroundings of the home when the silence was broken. Brown continues:

Suddenly way in the distance we heard this voice speaking in both Italian and English – it was Roger coming round from the anaesthetic and, still senseless, he was telling everybody that all he wanted to do was pee – and certain other things – and, of course, the nuns got the message. One rather large German nun barked something out to one of the others, who left Roger's

105

room and came back with an enormous syringe and walloped him in the buttocks, sending him out like a light.

Unfortunately, all this effort had been to little purpose since the operation had failed: the surgeon had been unable to remove the stone and felt that another operation should take place quickly in order to save Roger's kidney and perhaps even his life. Worried by the failure of the Italian surgeon, Brown and Luisa would not allow the second operation and called Roger's doctor in London to find out what should be done next. His doctor told them to get Roger on to an aeroplane and back to London immediately. Luisa moved heaven and earth to get Roger on to the next flight out of Rome, a feat that she managed after a great deal of effort.

Roger arrived at Heathrow Airport on September 28th and was met not by Dorothy, but by Brown's wife Becky, who drove him to Shooter's Hill Hospital which is near Bexley. Luckily, upon examination of his patient, the doctor did not deem it necessary for Roger to have an operation since he was confident that with the right treatment the stone would pass naturally within a few weeks.

Roger was confined to bed for most of his stay at the hospital, getting up only to do some necessary exercises which were part of the treatment. Meanwhile, Dorothy had found out that Roger was at Shooter's Hill Hospital and she even visited him there. She had managed finally to put all the pieces together and now understood fully Roger's recent strange behaviour. But she still hoped that his kidney complaint was the true cause and that when his health returned he would come back to her.

At this time Dorothy was appearing at The Talk of the Town, London's premier night spot, and on the Saturday that Roger was discharged from the hospital he went to see her after the show. He had already made it clear to her that he was leaving her for Luisa, but Dorothy could not believe it. However, Roger was as good as his word; he left her with a final 'Goodbye' and walked out of the stage door. For Dorothy, hope turned quickly to regret, and as quickly to anger, and she tore off her wedding ring and threw it at the retreating figure of her unfaithful husband. They had been married for just over eight years.

Alone Dorothy tortured herself with comparisons between her own love letters from Roger and the three she had seen from Luisa to Roger. But her solitary anger did not prompt her to destroy the letters; she kept them all, feeling that whatever Roger felt now, they were actual proof of how he had once felt for her and that could not be taken from her.

Before flying back to Rome to complete *No Man's Land*, Luisa sneaked into England, and she and Roger travelled to Ireland, where they enjoyed an undisturbed holiday together around Galway Bay. Fortunately, Roger was not recognised, having not achieved the sort of fame that would carry into the remote Irish countryside. Only Robert Brown knew their whereabouts as they realised their first opportunity to get to know each other fully without the worry hanging over them as to who might see them together.

It was a chance to review their situation. Luisa had been given the opportunity to prove her love for Roger during his illness, and she had come through this test with flying colours. Even now she continued in her nursing of Roger, having been taught how to give the injections which were still necessary to relieve the pain that still plagued him. So here they were, two people from entirely different backgrounds, and if that were not a sufficient hurdle in itself, there was also the problem of Roger's divorce, which was not only going to be difficult to achieve but more than anything else was a continual reminder to Luisa that she was acting in direct conflict with her religion. The couple felt easier now that Roger had made the break with Dorothy; however, they both desperately wanted to marry, and while Dorothy still refused to give Roger his freedom they felt too strongly drawn to each other to face separation, and inevitably Luisa's choice was to become Roger Moore's mistress, as society would label her. Roger already felt more motivation within himself than he had done for many years, and both of them believed that they had everything to gain by their union.

After their idyllic holiday, the couple returned to Rome to complete *No Man's Land*, and for a time Roger was able to work satisfactorily. One day, however, the pain became too severe and during filming he once more collapsed and had to be taken home by car. The intense bleeding that Roger now suffered was a clear indication that he was about to pass the stone, which after an uncomfortable night occurred on the following day. The change in Roger's condition was immediate: he was able to resume work, feeling gradually fitter and more healthy than he had done for many months, and the film was completed with no further problems.

After the completion of *No Man's Land*, Roger had no immediate commitments and so travelled to Barcelona with Luisa, who was contracted to make a film there. They drove down in an Aston Martin borrowed from Roger's friend, actor Edmund Purdom. With Luisa's scenes in that film quickly completed, the couple then headed for Venice.

Roger had to decide where he wanted his career to go next. With the turmoil of his private life dominating events at the time, he had not paid proper attention to his career, but now he could see that the last two films that he had made were yet another regressive step. Neither of the films would get more than a limited release and would not be seen in any English-speaking countries. Roger had still not managed to obtain a part sufficiently suited to his own particular talents as to ensure for him the success that he needed.

However, while on the verge of achieving the stability he wanted so desperately in his personal life, negotiations were going on elsewhere which were to give Roger the security that he needed in his professional life. Robert Baker, an independent producer, was attempting to persuade Leslie Charteris, the creator and writer of the 'Saint' books, to allow him an option on the character and stories as the basis for a television series.

Leslie Charteris had been born in Singapore in 1907, the son of a Chinese surgeon whose surname was Yin and his English wife. He was educated in England, and won a place at King's College, Cambridge. But he was not happy during his time there; a rather shy and lonely young man, it was to the writing of fiction that he turned in order to occupy himself. His interest in writing increased, prompting him to leave Cambridge in order to pursue a literary career. The first 'Saint' book, which introduced the dashing and resourceful Simon Templar to the world, was published in 1929, and marked the beginning of an astonishingly prolific and successful output.

Today, Leslie Charteris is a man in his seventies, tall and broad-shouldered, with a good head of white hair brushed back to reveal a small widow's peak. He has a clipped white moustache, a ruddy complexion, a small almost squat nose which together with his attractively slanted green-brown eyes are the only signs of his Oriental blood, and strong hands with long, bony fingers. He is a man who is no longer at ease socially and is still very much a mysterious, elusive, enigmatic man; he is rarely seen in public and, by his own admission, has not been photographed for fifteen years.

Despite the fact that Roger has said on a number of occasions that he did, Charteris is firm in his recollection that Roger did not approach him, at least not directly, about buying the rights to *The Saint*: 'Roger did not approach me. Bob Baker made the first television deal with Lew Grade. Bob came out to see me in Florida where I lived at that time and we made the deal. Then I saw Lew Grade – then Roger.'

Leslie Charteris was first introduced to Roger at the Associated British Studios at Elstree, when he was starting work on the first series. The two men had lunch, and chatted generally. Charteris has no memory of Roger asking him for advice about the interpretation he should put on the character of Simon Templar: 'I don't think we particularly talked about the character.'

The deal between Charteris and Baker had been set up through John Paddy Carstairs, a friend of both men, who had directed a 'Saint' film in England with George Sanders entitled *The Saint in London* in 1939. Robert Baker and ex-cameraman Monty Berman were, in 1961, partners in a production company called New World. Baker recalls: 'John Paddy Carstairs popped into our office in Jermyn Street, which we shared at the time. We were all talking about possible subjects, and Carstairs was talking about Leslie Charteris, whom he knew very well. I said I thought *The Saint* would make a marvellous television series.'

Carstairs then arranged a meeting between Charteris and the two partners, Robert Baker and Monty Berman. After the initial meeting, Baker went on holiday, leaving his partner to continue negotiations. However, Berman failed to arrive at a deal. Baker continues:

I came back and I renewed the negotiations and succeeded in getting an option on *The Saint* from Leslie Charteris. I took the option to Brian Tessler, who was at Associated Rediffusion Television. I estimated the budget for each episode would be about £15,000, and his reaction was: 'Oh, it's far too much money. We couldn't afford to spend that,' and he turned it down. Then I took the option to Lew Grade. It was a Saturday and I had been invited to a Charity Ball as the guest of Stanley Black, the musical conductor. Lew was at the same table, and after the speeches everyone disappeared from the table, leaving Lew and myself together. I said to Lew, 'I have the rights to *The Saint*.' His reply was, 'Come to my office on Monday morning.'

I went to his office on the Monday morning and showed him the deal that I had laid out, and he said, 'Okay, I want you to take a plane tomorrow and go over to Florida and tie this thing up.' So I went across to Florida where Charteris was living and spent a whole week haggling over a deal. Charteris is not an easy man to do business with but eventually I came back with the rights and arrived back in England just before Christmas 1961.

Charteris admits that he agreed to the deal with Baker because of one thing: 'Money – I have had negotiations with many people at various times but I held out for more money. I always made myself the promise that I wasn't going to sell it short. I knew that one day I would get a deal that was satisfactory. It was my retirement fund. I wanted to get my hands on a lot of money.'

Since Charteris states clearly that previous offers were not good enough, one must assume that if Roger in fact did try to obtain the rights for himself, then the reason that he failed was that he did not offer enough money.

When Baker returned from Florida, the most important matter to be resolved was the question of who was going to play Simon Templar. Lew Grade was anxious to secure Patrick McGoohan for the role; at the time the actor was starring in the tremendously successful *Danger Man* series on television (entitled *Secret Agent* in the United States). But Baker and McGoohan did not see eye to eye on certain matters, and he quickly went out of the running. Charteris remembers the reason: 'He was ruled out because he was very puritanical. He wouldn't have any scenes kissing girls.' This would obviously have been a great handicap for *The Saint*.

Robert Baker takes up the story: 'Then we were going through the list and somebody suggested Roger Moore. We knew his work and it seemed to be fine.'

Roger received the news that Lew Grade wanted him to star as Simon Templar in a television series while he was still in Venice with Luisa. His agent contacted him there, and Roger decided to leave for London immediately to discuss the proposed project. This seemed to be the opportunity that he had been waiting for – and it had come at a perfect time.

Luisa, meanwhile, remained in Italy, finishing off a film commitment. The couple kept in touch by telephone every day, with Roger urging Luisa to come to England, although due to the film that she was involved in this was not immediately possible.

Roger had by now agreed to do *The Saint* and was signed up for an initial twenty-six episodes, with options for more. Lew Grade, as always, held a big press conference and cocktail party to introduce Roger to the press and general public. At the conference Lew stood up and made the announcement:

'I want you to meet Roger Moore, who is going to make a series of that wonderful character, the Saint. There are going to be twenty-six one hour shows . . .'

'Half-hour, Lew,' Roger corrected him.

'One hour, Roger,' Lew replied.

Roger had assumed that like all television series produced in England at that time, including *Danger Man*, the *Saint* episodes would also be half-an-hour each. Roger told Lew, 'My salary's based on a half-hour show. I've signed for the show and I learn it's a one-hour show.' But Roger did not quibble.

Charteris had not been approached for advice about the casting of *The Saint*. Of those who had played Simon Templar for the cinema, Charteris had not been pleased with George Sanders's interpretation: 'I can say, since he is no longer on the scene, that I think George Sanders was terrible.' Charteris's own personal choice for the role when RKO had first bought the rights in the 1930s was either Cary Grant or Ronald Colman: 'Either of them would have been beautiful – but much too expensive. In his prime Cary Grant in particular would have been excellent.' The author was told that Roger Moore would be playing Simon Templar: 'They had already cast him. I wasn't asked. I was very surprised at the casting because I had seen Roger in the television series *Maverick* and from that I didn't really visualise him as the Saint. I told Bob Baker and he said, "He'll be alright!" I said, "Let's hope so."'

With Roger now formally the new Saint, he wasted no time in arranging to be reunited with Luisa, flying out to Italy immediately. Both Roger's and Luisa's parents were sympathetic to their plight and unanimously supported their actions, seeing that the couple were so beautifully matched and so much in love, which made it difficult to condemn their relationship. Roger and Luisa both wanted children and with the threat of drawn-out litigation with Dorothy, they had to decide whether they could safely wait for the divorce before starting a family. They realised that such an action would further ostracise them in society, but what they cared about most of all was each other and their life together. In all probability Roger could not expect to obtain the desired divorce from Dorothy for a number of years, possibly leaving it too late for them to start a family. They deliberated for a long time before making this most enormous of decisions. But finally they decided that they would not and could not be apart any longer. They would live together as man and wife, defying convention and upbringing. And if the divorce took as long as all signs indicated that it would, then they would start their family outside wedlock. With their future decided, they now had to steel themselves to face the consequences of that decision.

Roger returned from Italy to prepare himself for his new series, which was due to start shooting in June 1962, only a month away. The first priority was to find somewhere for himself and Luisa to live. He rented a little house in a tiny cul-de-sac off Hendon Way in Mill Hill, five minutes away from the studios, and eagerly anticipated the arrival of Luisa, who would be joining him as soon as her film commitment was completed.

Once Luisa had arrived soon afterwards and now that the couple were openly living together as man and wife, the first reactions from Dorothy began to become known and were gleefully reported to the press. Roger was portrayed as being caught between two strong women, each wanting to keep him and each ready to put up a fight.

Roger and Luisa tried to settle into as normal an existence as they could. The situation was not easy for either of them, and particularly not for Luisa, who was a foreign girl with still only a poor grasp of English and whose plight was aggravated by the fact that the man she was living with was a public figure. She was entirely dependent on Roger, with no parents or close relations nearby on whom to lean. She faced life in an ordinary suburban world where she stood out as a defiant snub to accepted convention. This was at a time when Roger and Luisa's action was much more shocking than it would be today and Luisa was greeted with whispering and sneers whenever she went into the local Stanmore shops.

The couple were fortunate in that they soon built up a circle of friends. Roger had started filming *The Saint* by now, and one of his first leading ladies was actress Yvonne Romain, who was married to the talented and charming songwriter, Leslie Bricusse. The Bricusses lived in Stanmore proper and as a result of the meeting of Roger and Evie Bricusse, the two couples struck up a friendship which has endured to the present.

The Moores and Bricusses used to meet twice a week at the

112

Kwan Yin, a Chinese restaurant on the roundabout near Hendon Way. The circle gradually expanded, with the regular set including Trevor and Helen Howard, Bryan Forbes and his wife Nanette Newman, and Joan and Jackie Collins.

Although Leslie Bricusse had never met Roger before, it was not the first time that he had seen him. He had recognised Roger previously at one of the latter's last public appearances with Dorothy in the middle of 1961 when Luisa had only just entered on the scene and Roger and Dorothy's marriage was on the verge of collapse. The couple had gone with a group of friends to the opening of the new Leslie Bricusse–Anthony Newley musical *Stop the World I Want to Get Off* at the Queen's Theatre, and Roger became involved in another public incident with Dorothy. Fortunately, this did not prevent Roger and Leslie from becoming close friends.

Roger meanwhile was forging ahead with *The Saint*, gradually gaining confidence in the role. He was determined to succeed in the part, and he worked at it with absolute dedication. He always made sure that he was never late in arriving at Elstree Studios, getting there promptly at 7.30 a.m. in the white Volvo that he drove in the series and had bought from ATV. He would never hold up production; even if he felt ill he would not succumb, preferring to continue working as long as he was able to stand. Roger was still occasionally troubled by kidney stones, but producer Robert Baker testifies that nothing would prevent Roger from working:

If Roger was dying on his feet, he would work. On several occasions I received a telephone call from the studio floor. The assistant director would say, 'I don't think Roger's well – I think you'd better come down.' And I would go down on to the floor and Roger would be there grey beneath his make-up and doubled up. But then he would still go and do a scene and on two or three occasions I made Roger leave the set and sent him home in a car, shooting scenes with a double in the meantime, ensuring that you would never see his face.

Roger's efforts were repaid: the initial series of twenty-six episodes was extended by a further thirteen episodes – and all the time Roger was feeling stronger in the part. Each episode took two weeks to make, working Monday to Friday, and in December 1962 the series began to be broadcast by ATV on Sunday nights.

Critical reaction to Roger's portrayal of Simon Templar was not very favourable initially. Laurence Marks of the *Daily Express* was impressed with neither Roger nor the first episode as a whole:

> Leslie Charteris's hero was tough and ruthless. But Mr Moore looks like a thoroughly scrupulous member of society . . . with his simple, honest L'il Abner face and open smile [he] wouldn't have lasted one chapter among the gangsters [found in the books]. And last Sunday's episode, I'm afraid, was about as exciting as a shipping forecast. It needed more incident and better dialogue to sustain an hour's television.

Reaction in America proved to be even less hopeful; Lew Grade and Robert Baker could not even get the series shown there. When six episodes had been completed, Lew decided that it was time to try to set up an American deal, and so he went over to New York carrying a couple of episodes with him. He had set up an appointment with Mort Werner, the head of NBC (National Broadcasting Corporation, one of the biggest television companies in the United States), for a Saturday morning, when both *Saint* episodes that he had brought with him would be shown.

Lew and Werner sat in a preview theatre together while the episodes were projected for them. The first episode was shown with no comments from Werner and the second one was screened immediately afterwards. It had only been on for just over five minutes when Lew heard the sounds of movement and looked round to see Mort Werner had left his seat and was standing over him. His tone was apologetic as he addressed Grade: 'I'm sorry, Lew. But it's the biggest load of crap I've ever seen.' With that he walked out of the theatre, leaving Lew breathless with surprise.

Unwilling to give up, Lew tried to interest the two other major television networks, CBS and ABC, but could generate no enthusiasm. The only option left was to release *The Saint* on syndication in America – and that is what happened. The difference between a network and a syndication showing was considerable in terms of the size of the audience reached. The three major television networks have hundreds of affiliated stations throughout the entire country, and if a programme is bought for network showing it will go out on all the stations at the same time. Consequently, a network deal means a very substantial payment for the producer of a programme that is picked up by one of the major networks. Syndication is a much more laborious process;

each reasonably-sized town in America has one, and sometimes as many as three, network stations, and also a number of independent stations. With a syndication sale you do not sell directly to the network but instead go to each independent station and individually sell the show there. It obviously involves a lot more footwork than a network sale and a lot more paperwork. Through syndication a series can reach a very large audience, but over a long-term period rather than in one night as on a network. In the United States, *The Saint* was shown on syndication for two years, building up a very substantial audience and developing its own *Saint* enthusiasts and garnering some good reviews.

The situation changed when NBC began having problems with one of their half-past ten night slots. CBS were showing a film at that time each week and whatever NBC showed in opposition failed to capture the audience. A board meeting was called to attempt to resolve this problem and during the discussion someone suggested that they should try *The Saint*, which had proved popular both with the press and audiences alike, and had the further advantage that it could be bought cheaply, so that NBC could not lose on it financially however badly it was received. A deal was made to sell *The Saint* to the network, and on its first showing its viewing figures overtook those for the film on CBS. This was regarded by NBC as a freak event that had occurred only because it was a new show and had attracted high audience curiosity. But this was proved to be no isolated case when *The Saint* proceeded to beat the film each time for the next six weeks.

The experiment had been tried only within the bounds of their New York station, WNBC, but now it was decided that they should try it on either their Chicago or Los Angeles stations, the other two of the three stations covering the entire country between them. Los Angeles was picked for the next area to see *The Saint* and again the reaction was the same, with the show beating the film shown in opposition. The success of *The Saint* was confirmed, and Roger Moore was in an internationally popular series. They were coming to the end of the second series by now and this change in the series' American fortunes was a deciding factor in determining that the next series would be made in colour, at a time when no colour broadcasts were being made by commercial television in Britain. It was a clear move in the campaign for the American market and a shrewd look towards the future.

Roger's fortunes had built up during this period as the series progressed. After the first unfavourable reaction the series had also achieved huge popularity in Britain, and Roger became one of the most familiar and popular actors on British television.

The only factor that marred Roger's new life was that Dorothy still refused to give him a divorce, forcing the couple to make an important decision which could not sensibly be delayed any longer. They had always known that divorce from Dorothy would, in all likelihood, be hard to obtain but now as divorce seemed no closer it was clear that if they waited until they were able to marry before having children, it could be too late. Roger and Luisa had already defied convention by living together, and had been fortunate that this act had not marred Roger's public image, as might easily have happened, particularly as he was increasingly identified with the highly moral Simon Templar. But there was no guarantee that public sympathy would remain with Roger if he and Luisa began to raise a family out of wedlock. Roger had become a hero to millions of young children around the world, and this gave him the added responsibility of presenting himself as a good example to the impressionable young. If public opinion went against Roger and Luisa, it was not inconceivable that Roger might through public pressure lose the role of Simon Templar, just at a point when he had finally found a niche and was steadily building up his position and beginning to amass a personal fortune. But it was a further sign of Roger's new strength that he not only wanted children but would wait no longer. Roger had become much more responsible, a situation forced upon him by circumstances since meeting and falling in love with Luisa. He was the sole bread-winner and the man of the house, a situation which clearly had never existed in his relationship with Dorothy, who was possessed of her own fortune and had never been financially dependent on Roger.

A close friend of Roger's, both in Hollywood and later, views the change in the actor's domestic situation as being the deciding factor in the development of his character and, by association, his career:

What helped his career was the fact that he became a man all of a sudden instead of just a pound of flesh sitting in a chair. When he went to Italy and fell in love with Luisa and did all the things that a normal male should do – became a father, became a family man, a man with responsibilities, a man who had to fight to get where he was going to go and had a goal in mind: because, all of a sudden, while still unmarried, he was having a family. And that is what made his career, the fact that Roger grew up overnight from being just a very lovable, amusing fun guy to a very lovable, amusing serious human being with a purpose in life.

In the early spring of 1963, Roger and Luisa were delighted to learn that Luisa was pregnant and they prepared eagerly for the birth. The situation was made more comfortable for Luisa because she, Evie Bricusse, and Joan Collins were all pregnant at the same time and could bolster each other up during their shared experience. To their friends, Roger and Luisa were as married as anybody else and this ever-present sympathy helped to cushion them.

Roger and Luisa had by this time moved from their little house in Mill Hill into Stanmore itself, settling at No. 57 Gordon Avenue, where they were to live for the rest of Roger's time as 'the Saint'. Their new meeting place with their friends was another restaurant, but this one was owned jointly by Leslie Bricusse and comedian Max Bygraves, who was another Stanmore resident. The restaurant, situated on the village high street, was called 'Maximes', due to Bygraves' influence, and the circle could frequently be found there sitting amid the plush red and purple velvet and gold trimmings eating the best food to be found in that part of suburban London. Roger loved the food and would eat there at every opportunity. Unfortunately, the same enthusiasm was not shared by other local residents, who were put off by its overblown grandeur, which looked distinctly out of place in Stanmore.

As well as developing a close social circle, Roger had quickly built up a family atmosphere on *The Saint* during this time, and this proved invaluable on the long-running series it became. Gone were the signs of temperament which had become increasingly evident as Roger's Hollywood career drew to a close, and Robert Baker remains full of praise for his star:

In all the years we made *The Saint* he wasn't late once in the studio; he was an absolutely total professional. He was a tremendous asset because if you do a thing for a long time it can become awfully boring – but Roger was such fun on the set, and he always knew everyone by their first name and knew all about them. Everybody loved him.

117

The relationship Roger fostered in the studio had tangible results too, enabling production to run smoothly without some of the delays which invariably arise. The unions at that time were very tough, and if the director wanted to work overtime for a short period he had to 'call the quarter', whereby if you had started filming a shot within time you were allowed to run and complete the quarter, thereby gaining an additional fifteen minutes' shooting time. The calling of the quarter was traditionally greeted with groans and threats and problems with the unions, particularly with the electricians, who were the most stubborn and difficult of all the technicians. But on *The Saint* union problems did not arise and, while agreeing to the quarter, the union representative would always be at pains to state the reason for their agreement to continue, saying, 'We're doing it – but not for the guv'nors. We're doing it for you, Roger.'

Devotion to Roger was total, and the harmony he brought to the set was never absent. His frequent practical jokes made the chore of turning out the endless episodes a pleasure. Actress Sylvia Syms appeared in several *Saint* episodes right from its early black-and-white days; she recalls a 'giggling lunatic' who was always laughing and playing practical jokes, but says she could see that Roger was under tremendous pressure and was doing his best to keep the atmosphere as light as possible. But if Roger was prepared to laugh and joke, it was only under certain conditions, as Miss Syms remembers:

> Roger likes to work in a pleasant atmosphere. He's quite prepared to have a joke but you've got to know your lines, you've got to get on and do it – he hates wasted time and respects professionalism. He would not get on with people who wasted time. If it eases the atmosphere, he's the first one to joke, usually sending himself up, if he gets a bit tense or difficult.

It was in 1963 that Roger had his first experience of directing, something he was able to do because he held an ACTT (Association of Cinematograph and Allied Technicians) card, which he had gained when working as a cartoonist at D'Arblay Street during the war. Usually actors are prohibited from directing because they are not members of this union, and it is no easy task to acquire a card. Roger's directional debut was on an episode called 'The Contract', which also featured Dick Hayman; he was to direct eight episodes altogether by the time the series ended in 1968.

Roger was on the set of *The Saint* on October 27th, 1963, when he heard he was about to become a father. He was enormously excited by the news and rushed to Luisa's bedside. Luisa gave birth to a beautiful baby girl, christened Deborah Maria Luisa Moore. Luisa herself had by now legally changed her surname to Moore. The birth had one heartbreaking result for Luisa; she was refused communion by her priest and was unable to take it from then on for as long as her 'sinful' relationship with Roger continued. Such a devastating blow from her beloved Church was very upsetting for her, but she was becoming more stoic in her acceptance of such setbacks, having had to cope with the moral indignation of certain people she came into contact with and at the same time developing a firm faith in the worth and validity of her relationship with Roger.

Roger hoped that, with the birth of a child, Dorothy might be swayed to grant a divorce. Many times it appeared his wish might be granted, but it never came to anything. The law in Britain at that time did not allow the breakdown of a marriage as grounds for divorce; today Roger and Dorothy's marriage would have qualified on these grounds. In those days Dorothy's consent was required and without that there could be no divorce. On one occasion Roger recalled the situation: 'The most uncertain aspect of it was that frequently I was led to believe that a divorce *would* be given to me. After a while I learnt not to rely on these false hopes.'

At one point, Roger became so fed up that he broke the silence which he and Luisa had decided was the best and most dignified way to handle the situation, and talked to the press. The British press had always treated the couple's relationship with tact and had respected their feelings. Anything written of an upsetting nature usually appeared in foreign papers, particularly upsetting Luisa who was unused to such attention. The couple had resolutely refused to give interviews and did not allow pictures to be taken of themselves at home. But after five years of waiting, Roger felt that he should put his side of the story once and for all; it had been a long five years, marked not only by intermittent legal rumblings, but also occasional confrontations. Robert Brown recalls an incident which occurred on one occasion when Roger and Luisa were in bed late at night soon after they had moved into their house in Mill Hill: 'Someone had broken their windows. I don't know what Roger did but I should hope he rang the police.'

119

To keep the public aware of her position as the wronged wife by releasing songs which had clear autobiographical content, Dorothy pictured a woman who had loved and lost. Roger himself was similarly guilty of the desire to express his feelings in music, releasing a single in 1966 entitled 'Where Does Love Go?' in which he recited this well-known song with the support of a screeching female chorus and a mass of violins. Of more interest was the B-side which was a composition by 'Roger and Luisa Moore' entitled 'Tomorrow After Tomorrow', an intense declaration and celebration of their love, with the same dreadful backing as on the other side of the record. Roger gave little to the song, which in any case was marred by its almost total reliance on clichéd phrases strung predictably together.

But now Roger intended to break his silence properly. Luisa had given birth to their second child, a boy called Geoffrey Robert, on July 28th, 1966. Roger's bitterness at the delay to their marriage increased as his family grew up around him, so far unaware of their parents' plight.

The popularity of *The Saint* had by now reached a peak, and on completion of the second series in 1965 a considerable overhaul took place. The second series had consisted of thirty episodes, which meant that a total of sixty-nine black-and-white shows had been made. By now the series had been withdrawn from syndication on American television and was enjoying great success on network television.

At this point, Robert Baker and his partner Monty Berman split up and a new arrangement was formed in which Roger and Robert Baker now became equal partners. Roger's salary had gradually increased during the run of *The Saint*, and he was now able to consider such a venture and take his first steps towards amassing a considerable fortune. The company which the two men bought in order to set this up was named Television Reporters International Ltd.

Baker and Roger went to Lew Grade with a suggestion that the next series of *The Saint* should be made in colour, thereby increasing its marketability in the United States and also at the same time preparing themselves for the near future on British television, which was soon to turn to colour transmission.

Despite occasional outbursts to the press that he was tired of playing the Saint, Roger was very happy to continue in the role. He was well aware that he fitted the part perfectly, and even

Leslie Charteris's initial reservations had entirely disappeared. The author felt that Roger's performance became steadily better, with the actor gradually moving into the character and ultimately representing the best screen Saint that there has ever been or will be. To view Roger as Simon Templar even now, after all that has occurred since, is to realise that the role remains his most successful achievement. Roger plays the part of this wandering righter of wrongs with a hint of detachment which gives a ruthlessness to the character much more effective than it has ever been in his portrayal of Bond. Simon Templar is, as Charteris always described him, 'the Robin Hood of modern crime' and as such becomes a figure tinged with a hint of anachronism.

In a modern world where most people have to struggle through life, ensuring that financial commitments are met and that their families are clothed and fed, here is a man who appears in some location around the world with no other object than to right the wrongs done to others. Like Robin Hood, if he is involved in actions against the law or outside the law, the motive is pure, with no personal gain as his aim. If, in the course of one of his self-appointed missions, he gains money, it is incidental and depends upon the actions of his adversary. Templar is as likely to dispose of a large share of the money in some deserving direction, treating money acquired in this way in much the same way as James Bond, in Ian Fleming's books, who will use such money in the most casual manner because it carries no value for him. There is a form of moral condemnation of what that money represents which makes both men eager to dispose of it.

But more than Bond, Simon Templar has the makings of legend about him. The fact that he is equally well known as 'The Saint' sets him apart from ordinary men. Bond is an underpaid civil servant who enjoys his work, while accepting that it is not particularly lucrative; but Simon Templar does not need to concern himself with such matters. He can appear wherever he wishes and without any need for justification. Wealth enables Templar to do what he wishes, and it so happens that this particular man has chosen the role of a roving defender of the right.

The surname that he carries obviously harks back to the Knights Templar and he can be seen almost as a modern counterpart of the same body of men when viewed in their most simplistic terms. The Order of the Poor Knights of Christ and the Temple of Solomon, as they are strictly known, was founded in 1118, with the declared objective being, as their first chronicler Guillaume de Tyre states, 'as far as their strength permitted, they should keep the roads and highways safe . . . with especial regard for the protection of pilgrims', and they soon came to represent the highest Christian values in man. They were answerable to no secular or ecclesiastical power except the Pope, becoming a law unto themselves by implication. Their wealth became huge due to donations and gains through their services at every political level, from fighting, notably in the various Crusades, to diplomacy, and even led to their involvement in banking development. Their power and wealth ultimately corrupted them, but it is the ideal that they represented that concerned Charteris. Simon Templar may be viewed as an anachronistic figure who, in his way, is keeping the roads and highways safe so far as he is able, and just as the Knights Templar strove to achieve this task outside the law, so does 'The Saint', who holds an anarchist's view of conventional law and order. Throughout the 'Saint' books there are numerous passages which criticise the police and the law, and Chief Inspector Teal, Templar's police counterpart, is made to appear like a bumbling idiot who serves as a convenient butt against which to highlight the Saint's superior skills of deduction.

The Knights Templar were also vowed to chastity, and Charteris endows his character with a similar strain, although he softens it by permitting his hero to have a steady girl friend, called Patricia Holm, who is present not so much to supply a romantic interest as to preclude the possibility of romance when Simon has left her to go on another of his adventures, which provide him with the real thrill of living.

When analysed, Charteris's 'Saint' is not a particularly attractive character, and Roger's performance in the part does hint at this. Simon Templar is very intelligent, socially well-to-do and prospering, handsome, incredibly well-informed, and altogether a paragon of humanity with very little indication of human fallibility. The problem is that Simon knows this and is not averse to extolling his own virtues, in a supposedly humorous but ultimately unattractive way. Even more unfortunate is the fact that Patricia Holm is fully aware that Simon is all these things and is really called on to do little more than look on in wonder while accepting the crumbs of affection that fall from the plate of an almost self-confessed god.

Templar is like a social doctor who, instead of curing disease within a man's body, removes the cancerous elements of society. But like a doctor, Simon does all this with a certain detachment,

122

which Roger successfully brought into his portrayal and which points to his deserved triumph in the role, putting him ahead of all other actors who have attempted the part. 'The Saint' is continually serving the right, but with a curious coldness underneath which both reflects his doctoral approach and also his inherent superiority. The people that Simon helps are like his children and are treated as such; Templar can smile gently at the howling gaffes they make, confident that he would always avoid such pitfalls.

This is not to criticise Charteris's character, but rather to point out certain aspects of the fictional hero that should not go unnoticed. Just as Templar's virtues can be extolled, so he can just as easily be described as a boorish and arrogant snob. Charteris says that the books had to be toned down for television due to their violence, but the character also had to be humanised. The elements of the literary 'Saint's' character are present in Roger's impersonation of him, but in a toned-down manner.

The irony of the situation is that when Roger came to play James Bond the general view taken was that Roger's image would have to be hardened. But when one compares Roger's two performances as Templar and Bond, it is not difficult to see that the reverse has actually taken place. Roger's Bond can threaten death in the most blatant terms, but by the time that Roger entered the Bond circus the humour was much lighter than had previously been the case and the image that this produces reduces the threat that Roger represents when confronted with a dangerous situation or one that requires ruthlessness from him. In contrast, Roger's Simon Templar would threaten more rarely, usually able to dominate a situation with his fists rather than a gun; but even if the Saint rarely kills, the threat is always there because of the way Roger presents the character. Roger has never been harder than as Simon Templar; the humour that he conveys in that role is never much more than a surface humour which by its very shallowness helps to highlight the coldness underneath. But in Bond, Roger's humour seems to spring from a genuine warmth of character with which he has endowed his Bond and which points to a gentleness underneath the blustering surface threats.

Any criticism that Roger can play Bond only in that way is unjustified; it must be regarded as Roger's intention to present the character thus. His performance as Simon Templar shows that he does not always play his roles lightly and that he is capable of slanting a part whichever way he feels is suitable. Roger was sensible in altering the audience's conception of James Bond subtly away from Connery's, and it was a move that has paid him great dividends. He could have played the part like the early Connery Bond, but in truth it would have been too close to his Simon Templar rather than too far from it. By changing Bond's image, Roger was gambling on the fact that this was the only way to make the character his own, a formidable task after Connery's expert performance in the role but one which Roger has achieved triumphantly, with a whole new generation as unwilling to accept Connery as Bond over Roger's interpretation as an earlier one is to view Moore's Bond with any conviction.

Roger and Robert Baker started production of their third series of *The Saint* in 1966 and were to produce forty-three episodes up to 1968, the popularity of the series becoming worldwide with it being broadcast in no less than seventy-two countries at that time – a figure that would ultimately reach eighty. There was another significant alteration in the production of the series that went beyond making the episodes in colour. By the end of the second series all the Charteris plots had been exhausted; up to this point every episode had been based on a Charteris original, but now negotiations had to be made with the author to permit them to continue to use the character in new scripts. Previously, Charteris had acted as consultant, as he admits, although he was not always treated in a manner entirely to his own satisfaction: 'I always saw the scripts and made my comments and criticisms, but they were not always necessarily followed. I had no veto and I can't say I was always pleased with what I saw on the screen.' However, Charteris did permit new scripts to be written for the character, taking a fatalistic view of the matter: 'It was necessary. Television is a monster, like a great big garbage disposal, which it frequently is, and it can eat up a lifetime's output in a matter of seasons. So it was necessary, but I was more critical of their new scripts than I had been of mine.'

Roger embarked on this new series of *The Saint* in September 1966, fresh from an unusual professional experience. He had just completed a brief guest appearance as compère on the popular television variety show, *Sunday Night at the London Palladium*, and had achieved considerable success, being able to draw on the invaluable experience of variety and variety performers that he had gained from his association with Dorothy. It may have been Roger's first major appearance on a variety stage, but he was certainly no stranger to its demands and requirements – and here he was, standing on the stage of one of the greatest variety theatres in the world.

Luck and a shrewd business mind had made Roger one of the most successful television actors, and he now possessed both wealth and fame in generous proportions. His new-found wealth enabled him to enjoy gambling to an even greater extent than before; he had always enjoyed gambling, but now it took on an unhealthy significance for him. Roger was a regular sight at many gaming clubs in London's West End and he always bought a newspaper to study the racing page when on the studio floor:

> It wasn't the winning I enjoyed, it was the masochistic pleasure of losing. I went through a long phase at the studios where every day I tied up the switchboard, ringing several bookmakers at once. The big drain though was chemmy and craps – American dice. I had one good friend, a casino owner who against his own interests put the block on my gambling.

It was almost as if Roger was unable to accept his new-found prosperity entirely and could not appreciate it enough to be able to resist playing with it in this manner, which was a considerable extravagance with two children to bring up and two women hovering about his private life.

At this time, Roger and Robert Baker were developing further plans for the actor's prospering career. Such was Roger's success on television that they felt that the time was ripe for him to launch himself again as a cinema star. The third series of *The Saint* was complete and sales of it worldwide were exceptionally good, with the series being sold to NBC in America alone for £1,800,000. A new series was announced in October 1967, this time for thirty-six one-hour episodes and two special two-hour shows, to be made over the next two years. Roger's commitment to the series was reduced in that the intention was to produce fewer episodes in a year, thereby enabling the actor to fulfil any film contracts that he might have. Indeed, at the same time, it was announced that Roger would be making a film for the cinema, to be called *Crossplot*, a joint venture of Roger's and Bob Baker's, based on an idea of the latter and designed as a comedy-thriller in the vein of so many films of the time.

However, *Crossplot* did not get off the ground as quickly as they had anticipated and Roger spent most of 1968 filming eighteen *Saint* episodes and a special two-part feature-length story called *Vendetta for the Saint*, based on a Charteris plot and including considerable location work in Malta. This was actually released theatrically in Europe, and shown simultaneously on television in Britain and America. Roger did not intend to continue playing Simon Templar for the further eighteen episodes announced. He really did feel now that enough was enough and made it clear that when the cameras stopped rolling, in the middle of August 1968, he intended to walk away from *The Saint*, after six and a half years in the role.

Just as a phase of Roger's professional life was drawing to a close, there were certain indications that the same curious parallel between his private and professional life as had occurred when Roger had started playing Simon Templar would repeat itself when he drew a curtain over that part of his life.

The first moves in what finally resulted in divorce from Dorothy occurred in the most public of circumstances, and the instigator of it was someone totally uninvolved in the situation. The innocent party was actor Kenneth More, one of Roger's closest friends, and the occasion was the evening of the British Film Academy Awards in April 1968. Kenneth More was the commentator for the occasion, which was televised by ITV, and when Roger appeared with Luisa, he jokingly introduced his friend saying, 'Roger is supposed to be the prettiest man in show business. Certainly I think his wife is prettier than he is.' Soon afterwards it was announced in the newspapers that Kenneth More and Granada Television were being sued for libel by Dorothy on account of the actor's remarks on television. As a result, ITV broadcast a public apology to Dorothy.

The whole incident showed just how ridiculous the situation had become. Roger and Luisa were the parents of two children and had been living together for over six years. Pressure had been put on Dorothy by some of their mutual friends to give Roger a divorce, without any success. But with Deborah reaching an age when she was beginning to understand the situation, Dorothy finally decided to act and on August 1st she sued her husband for divorce. The case was listed as undefended at the London Divorce Court and was to be heard later in the year.

Just over a week after this announcement, Roger finished the final shots of his last *Saint* episode. He left the series while it was still hugely popular and indeed, in the previous month, had been given an award by Spanish Television as the most popular foreign actor, as 'El Santo'. His fame was worldwide and very considerable; he was instantly recognisable wherever he went, far more so than any big-screen actor, because he was in people's homes on their television sets every week, in eighty-six different countries. To millions of people his face was as familiar as someone who lived in the same street. His clean-cut features and carefully brushed-back hair were firmly associated with Simon Templar; one of the first things Roger did upon completion of the series was to go to the barber and have his hair cut, making the first move in his attempt to break away from identification with a role which had fitted him so perfectly for so many years.

He did not sit back. He would be starting *Crossplot* within a few weeks and so he took himself down to the Forest Mere Health Hydro to tone himself up before embarking on his first feature film in seven years. The first hydro of its kind, Forest Mere was rigid in its rules, just as, in a different field, the Betty Ford Clinic is in Palm Springs. Two other guests at Forest Mere proved to be fellow actors Hywell Bennett and Noele Gordon; the latter had appeared on stage with Roger in *Easy Virtue* twenty years earlier. Roger's sense of fun did not desert him, and his pranks enlivened the sedate lifestyle of the establishment, as he attempted to put other guests in situations in which they appeared to be breaking the hydro's rules.

It was at this time also that Roger made his first moves into the business world, utilising his familiar personality in what amounted to a public relations exercise. A textile firm, Pearson and Foster, had approached Roger in an attempt to boost their business. Roger was placed on the board of the company in an official capacity of design consultant, at a salary of £10,000 a year, and in the next twelve months, when film commitments permitted, he was to visit agents and potential customers in America, Australia and the Far East. Obviously, the main advantage to Pearson and Foster was the personal appearances that Roger made, the exercise amounting to a good publicity job with a world-famous, instantly recognisable television star being seen to wear Pearson and Foster suits. Roger's role as design consultant was only on the loosest terms, and his own description of what this entailed indicates that the effort required from him was not heavy: he was 'to express ideas which will be translated into designs', which implies that Roger was certainly never expected to put pen to paper, but rather just to verbally indicate a design and get somebody else to attempt to reproduce that idea on paper. If Roger regarded his involvement as a healthy, non-show-business inter-est, it certainly still remained an actor's involvement. Roger was there because of his reputation as an actor and it was really more a respectable form of product endorsement.

For *Crossplot*, Roger attempted to change his facial appearance as drastically as possible for his role as Gary Fenn, an advertising executive innocently caught up in a web of intrigue. The plot clearly borrowed much from Alfred Hitchcock's classic 1959 film, *North by Northwest* starring Cary Grant, but regrettably without any of the skill and assurance so evident in that film. Roger grew some rather undefined sideboards and, instead of combing his hair back, now combed it forward, the result being not particularly flattering to Mr Moore. Roger admitted that *Crossplot* 'was de-signed to get me away from the Saint . . . but not too far. Not at first.'

Roger had two leading ladies in the film: an unknown twenty-three-year-old Belgian actress called Claudie Lange, who bore more than a passing resemblance to Luisa, and Martha Hyer, a blonde American actress married to one of the great film pro-ducers of all time, Hal B. Wallis.

The highlight of the film was a helicopter chase in which Roger and his Belgian leading lady were pursued across the grounds of the Duke of Bedford's Woburn Abbey in their veteran car, having been caught up in a veteran car rally, which was photographed like the worst kind of travelogue.

Crossplot was made on an incredibly low budget of one million dollars, and this is apparent throughout the film. The 'Saint' team at Boreham Wood had simply moved into feature-film production without any refinements being made for the big screen. The result was a clumsily strung together programme, with dreadful back-projection too often evident and some embarrassingly inept matching of newsreel footage and scenes shot for the film, notably at the end of the film in which there is an assassination attempt on a foreign leader during celebrations for the Queen's Birthday at Hyde Park. Filmed sequences are matched with fuzzy newsreel footage of the Hussars firing a twenty-one gun salute, and when villain Francis Matthews is thwarted, by Roger, the actor runs across Hyde Park, chased by newsreel of galloping Hussars with their gun-carriages, and is finally trampled by the horses in a further instance of totally inept back-projection.

It is a further sign of a poor film that when viewed today it appears very dated. The fashions are too outlandish to convince, and by the time the film reached the country's cinema screens it was probably already beginning to look a little faded. *Crossplot* highlights the careless production values of the time when there was little ambition for cheap motion pictures beyond the immediate hope of bringing in a lot of money quickly. 'Swinging London' was already dying by this time, but in *Crossplot* it is presented in all its glory. Roger alone wears sensible, timeless clothing, particularly compared with Francis Matthews' shiny grey suit. It is interesting to note that Bette Davis made a similar observation to her producers at the same studio during this period, while working on *The Anniversary*. She insisted that the exaggerated young female attire be slightly modified so that her film would not appear too dated when reissued in the future.

Crossplot was clearly made without thought, and actually lacks some of the slickness of the later *Saint* episodes, which could more justifiably have been presented in cinemas. The participation of Claudie Lange marked the continuation of a trend peculiar to the low-budget British film, from the fifties to the seventies, in which unknown actresses from the Continent were imported into our studios and allowed enormous chunks of screen time opposite commendable stars such as, in this case, Roger Moore. The unfortunate actors who had to perform opposite these girls were presented with the difficulty of acting opposite such inexperienced actresses with little hope of any creative interaction; even Britain's greatest actors would not necessarily be able to shine in these circumstances. Despite the high failure rate of such combinations, many production companies, to the utter dismay of young British actresses, preferred to import these ladies who were rarely heard of again.

Fortunately, matters were not so bleak in Roger's private life and it would be nice to think that Roger's involvement in *Crossplot* was partly due to his preoccupation with events that were to lead to the final settling of his muddled personal life. At the end of November, while *Crossplot* was in production, the news came through that Roger's divorce had been granted and that, to their bewilderment and absolute joy, Roger and Luisa would be free to wed in the following February.

Reluctantly, Dorothy had surrendered the man whom she had honestly and wholeheartedly loved. She had finally lost the man that she had met as a mere boy, twelve years her junior, and to whom she had remained as true as her word. For there is no question that the young actor, who was, to say the least, undistinguished in his chosen profession, and whose only qualifications were a mere three terms at RADA and walk-ons in half-a-dozen films, desperately wanted and needed a chance to gain a foothold on the ladder of his chosen career. From the beginning, this was no secret between husband and wife, and Dorothy Squires kept her part of the bargain. Just as surely as Brian Desmond Hurst had given Roger the opportunity to take his first steps as an actor, so Dorothy Squires cut away many of the usual falterings and setbacks to give Roger a straightforward journey to the top of his career. Once Roger had met Dorothy, he never had to suffer the indignities of a young actor, or indeed of an actor of any age, waiting by the telephone and grasping at straws in the eternal hope for the next pay cheque. Roger never had to worry again and when he finally decided to leave Dorothy, he was well and truly secure.

When, at the end of 1976, Dorothy Squires announced that she wanted to use excerpts from Roger's passionate love letters to her in her planned autobiography, *Rain, Rain Go Away*, Moore successfully prohibited the use of the letters. For Moore to have brought this case eight years after their divorce is proof enough that he committed great love for Dorothy to paper. Roger's reaction as expressed to the press at the time was curt: 'I don't give a damn. Nothing upsets me . . . I hope it starts her on a career as another Charles Dickens.'

Dorothy now had to learn to live without her handsome, film star husband. She was only fifty-four years old and still an attractive woman with a good figure, who was certainly not short of admirers or suitors. However, she has continually admitted to the pain of losing Roger and has never remarried.

Crossplot opened to hardly any business at all and quite deservedly sank quickly into oblivion. It marked one of the last spy film spin-offs that had been spawned by the incredible success of the James Bond films, which had reached a peak of gigantic proportions in the mid-sixties. But by 1969, the paying public were tired of seeing such pale imitations, and the trend killed itself off with such inferior products as *Crossplot*. This failure also meant the abandonment of Roger and Bob Baker's plans to produce a further three feature films, and so Roger had to look outside his own television empire for his next project.

But before Roger continued with any further film productions, which he intended to do rather than to slink back into television, he and Luisa were able to go through the marriage ceremony that had eluded them for so many years. It took place on April 11th, 1969, at Caxton Hall in London. Roger was forty-one and Luisa nine years younger.

Outside the hall, there was a crowd of six hundred people, mostly women, who had to be restrained by a police cordon due to their enthusiastic attempts to catch a glimpse of the object of their admiration. Roger's name was chanted continually, and cheers greeted his arrival with his best man, Kenneth More, the man who had, perhaps, brought matters to a head with his slip-up at the British Academy Awards ceremony almost exactly a year before.

The wedding ceremony was an emotional experience not only for Roger and Luisa, but also for their many friends who had stood by them in the eight years the couple had had to wait for this day. It proved too much for Luisa, who broke down and was unable to say the last six words of her marriage vows. For almost a minute she was choked with emotion, but after encouragement from the sympathetic superintendent registrar, Mr Donald Boreham, she managed to recite those last important words: 'to be my lawful wedded husband'.

The reception was held at the Royal Garden Hotel in London, where sixty guests gathered to toast Mr and Mrs Roger Moore. Conspicuously absent were their two children, Deborah and Geoffrey, then aged five and two respectively. The couple had felt that the children were too young to understand what was happening, and they remained at their Stanmore home, while Luisa explained to them that she and Roger were just going out to a party.

This deception did not stand up for long. Leslie Bricusse recalls what happened when the new husband and wife returned to their home afterwards: 'Deborah had seen the wedding on the ITN news, and when they came home she went up to Roger and sobbed into his arms. He said, "What's the matter?", to which Deborah replied, "Daddy, you always promised you would marry me!"' But Roger was married for the third and last time, as Luisa emphasised at the reception where she jokingly picked up a knife and told the press, 'I'll kill him if it's not', thereby setting the seal on her public image as the possessive wife almost immediately – an image which remains as strong as ever to this day when Roger and Luisa's marriage remains one of the most public relationships among celebrities. It is almost certain that anyone who has heard of Roger Moore also knows that he has a possessive Italian wife.

Roger has actually flaunted his marriage, building up an image of respectability and of familial happiness which already makes it hard to recall a time when the situation was anything less than blissful. There have been the inevitable rumours about the stability of their marriage, and Luisa has often come in for attack because of her watchfulness over Roger, but the fact is that, from a most unpromising start, Roger and Luisa have established themselves as a very married couple and have proved to an initially disapproving world that theirs was and is an enduring love.

Roger may appear only to tolerate fondly his wife's presence on a film set with him, but the truth is that he wants her there as much as she wishes to be there. It is no secret in the industry that there are always girls available if required and Roger is merely making his position clear in this area, while still retaining his unassailably heterosexual image, which is so important for the roles he frequently plays. As with many things, he puts a humorous complexion on a situation which might otherwise be problematic: Roger is firmly ensconced in the British film industry, where sexual relations are far more open than anywhere else in the world, including Hollywood, whatever its own myth-making may suggest.

The Moore marriage also provides good copy for the newspapers; endless stories are churned out about the incidents, real or imagined, that occur to threaten it, and Luisa's hasty actions to thwart such designs. Their friends tell numerous stories of the verbal and physical onslaught that Roger faces for so much as looking at another woman, and it is hard not to draw the conclusion that Roger enjoys the commotion Luisa causes. The marriage is far from stale; it continues on a seemingly bumpy course which keeps it alive for both partners – and a newspaper-reading public can still read an article on their marriage with interest at a time when it would normally have faded from public view. Instead, with every year Roger Moore gains new stature as a family man, and in a business that rates so many fragmented families, it comes as a refreshing change to see that the Moore tribe remain together in clear and gratifying unity.

After a brief honeymoon with Luisa, followed by a trip to the Cannes TV Festival and then an obligatory visit to Luisa's parents in Italy, who, like Roger's in England, had been so supportive to the couple, Roger soon returned to work.

When he returned to England he was offered the most promising role he had ever been approached to play – that of Harold Pelham,

132

an ordinary middle-class executive who finds his footsteps dogged by an evil *doppelgänger*, who is released from the very respectable Mr Pelham after a near-fatal car accident. This was in *The Man Who Haunted Himself*, based on author Michael Armstrong's story, 'The Case of Mr Pelham', which had already been the inspiration for one of the half-hour episodes of *Alfred Hitchcock Presents*, with Tom Ewell in the title role, and which had now been expanded into a feature-length script by Basil Dearden and Michael Relph. It was to be directed by Dearden, one of the better known directors in the British film industry at that time.

The film was to be made at EMI Elstree where Bryan Forbes, Roger's friend from his army days, had recently taken over as head of production in what was seen as a spearhead in the move to revitalise an ailing British film industry. This was the third film to be made since Forbes had come to Elstree, and it was Basil Dearden himself who recommended that Roger be cast in the role.

Roger wore a moustache for the film, yet again subtly moving away from his clean-shaven 'Saint' image. The film was, unfortunately, not a commercial success, but nonetheless it represents the highest point in Roger's career in terms of performance and it remains a film of which he is especially proud. Its failure at the box office was not entirely self-induced, but partly symptomatic of the state of the British film industry at that time, as Bryan Forbes points out: 'It was a small English film and at that point it was one of the troughs of the English film industry. Whereas in the sixties, British films had been very well received, by 1969/70 we were bad news again and nobody wanted to know. So the film didn't get what I felt were its just deserts.'

The successful team of Dearden and Relph had moved over from their home studio, Ealing, at the invitation of Bryan Forbes, in order to make the film, and it marks one of the unfortunately rare occasions when Roger Moore has been provided with a vehicle worthy of his considerable talent. He shows himself able to sustain a characterisation of a man who is neither flippant, nor an adventurer, nor a lover – in other words, he played an ordinary human being. He demonstrates surprising power, particularly in the domestic scenes in which he rows with his frustrated wife, ably played by Hildegard Neil, reaching just the right pitch to convey a very convincing picture of a marital argument without losing the effect with unnecessary histrionics.

Roger had suffered two box office failures in a row in his initial

133

attempts to turn himself into a cinema star, but fortunately *The Saint* was still being shown and re-shown, providing the viewing public with the Roger that they preferred and the one that had made him a wealthy man.

Now Mr and Mrs Moore felt that it was time to move into their first proper marital home, and they chose the magnificent Sherwood House, situated in sixteen acres of land in Tilehurst Lane, just outside Denham in Buckinghamshire. It had ten bedrooms, a swimming pool, tennis courts, paddocks, a row of garages, and a projection room, and was a clear symbol of the heights of success to which Roger had risen. Only a short walk away were the studios where Roger had made his first faltering steps in the film industry as a young extra in *Caesar and Cleopatra* a quarter of a century before.

It was a home with which the whole family quickly fell in love, particularly Luisa. But if Roger was to maintain such a lifestyle, he would have to ensure that he found another successful venture for himself. He had made his fortune on television and, after abortive attempts to become a film star, it was to this haven that he returned to lick his wounds.

Six

ROGER'S PERSONAL and professional lives up to now had been running parallel to each other with a remarkable consistency, changes in both occurring closely together. During the entire period that Roger and Luisa had been living together, unable to marry, Roger's career had been dominated by *The Saint*, a role that he played for a total of eight years. The couple had met shortly before Roger was offered the part of Simon Templar, and it was not until the time of their marriage at Caxton Hall that he decided to finish with *The Saint* completely.

Roger had previously had reservations about continuing in the series but had always given in; but now he felt that his career would never progress if he continued solely as a television personality, and particularly as one type-cast in a single part. His recent ventures into the world of cinema feature films had been in distinctly domestic products, which never really had any chance of making an impact on the international market. They were rather crudely put together efforts, lacking the gloss of well-mounted film productions that would appeal to a mass audience. His screen presence also left much to be desired when exposed to the larger medium of the cinema screen, where he had so far been unable to demonstrate or reveal a sufficient strength of character or personality to successfully carry a film.

Roger had been considered for the latest James Bond epic, *On Her Majesty's Secret Service*, after it became apparent that Sean Connery meant what he said when he claimed that *You Only Live Twice*, the previous film in the series, was definitely his last outing as the smooth secret agent. The character had blossomed into the biggest cult hero of the sixties, but Roger was not at this time a serious contender for the role because he was already committed to making *Crossplot*. Peter Hunt, the director of *On Her Majesty's Secret Service*, without doubt the most stylish film in the series, recalls the true situation: 'Roger was a great friend of Harry Saltzman's at that time and his name came up within discussion but it was never a serious discussion because he had just done a deal for something else, so his name was null and void.'

In any case, Roger did not fit in with what the producers and director wanted to see in a new James Bond. Peter Hunt again recalls the events that led up to the casting of the coveted part:

A great deal of time, days and perhaps weeks, were spent in discussing the sort of character that we would get as a new Bond. These discussions were between United Artists, Broccoli, Saltzman, myself, and everyone involved because we said, 'Okay, maybe now this is the opportunity to get a younger, more modern man. Perhaps he should have longer hair or be more hippy?' But it was eventually resolved that we would try as hard as we could to find a physical replica of Sean Connery – and that was what we looked for and that is how we came up with Lazenby. So, on those terms, Roger would not have fitted the bill; there is no way he would have at that time, on those terms.

So former car salesman and model George Lazenby, from Australia, whose main claim to fame was as the crate-carrying 'Big Fry' man on a chocolate bar television commercial, took over the role for one attempt. He left the series after just one film, leaving the role again unfilled.

Meanwhile, having finally turned his back on *The Saint*, Roger was once again open to offers. His dreams of a big screen career were not bearing fruit and with *On Her Majesty's Secret Service* finished, Roger became a stronger contender for the James Bond role in the next one, *Diamonds Are Forever*. But the offer was not concrete enough and he was obliged to keep his options open. The producers were immersed in protracted discussions with Sean Connery, whom the public associated so indelibly with the role and who, after Lazenby's comparative failure, seemed an even more necessary ingredient for success than they had previously wished to acknowledge. Neither Roger nor any other actor could rely on getting the part so long as Connery stood hesitantly in the wings.

Time marched on, and in July 1969, the press announced that Roger would be starring in another television series, despite the actor's habitual announcement that he had finished with television series for good.

But the inducements were high, especially following the expense of obtaining the divorce from Dorothy. For the new series, Roger was to get an initial large contract with options for more. He was reported as saying that Lew Grade had had a hard time persuading him to agree to do another television series, but that he discovered that Lew had already set up the deal in the States on the strength of the Roger Moore name; the whole package had already been sold, and Lew appealed to the reluctant Roger's patriotism, telling him that Britain needed the foreign currency that worldwide sales of the series would generate. Lew Grade cajoled Roger into submission and the actor admitted to the press that he had 'consented for Queen and Country'.

However Roger had been aware that plans were afoot to produce another series built around him. He had discussed it with his friend and business associate, Robert Baker, who had been toying with a similar idea for over a year. He and Roger had talked about it when they were still making *The Saint*. Towards the end of the series they had decided to experiment with an episode of *The Saint*, using it as a 'pilot' by making it in the style of the planned series.

The concept was to have two characters, one English and the other American, both wealthy, who team up and work together on the basis of a friendly rivalry. The experiment proved that the formula worked well and, as a result, it was decided to expand the idea into a television series which, if it proved as successful as *The Saint* had been, would keep Roger busy for about the next five years.

With a new wife and two children to support, Roger needed to replenish his finances, and the firm offer of a television series, giving him a steady income, was very tempting. But Roger, understandably, still had his mind set on film stardom, and stipulated in the new contract that he should be allowed to make at least one film a year. He was determined to break away from the limitations of being a television personality, albeit one of the most highly paid and successful in the world, but he could not afford to bide his time waiting to be offered the role of James Bond. Since all practical considerations favoured his involvement in this new television venture, Roger sensibly agreed to star in it.

Robert Baker had gone straight to Lew Grade and explained the project, just as he had done when he had picked up the option on the 'Saint' books from Leslie Charteris. The idea of another television series with a hot property like Roger Moore appealed to Lew, who was particularly attracted towards getting a big American star name to play opposite Roger.

Since the American character was to be a rich oil man, the role was originally sketched out as a Texan. They initially approached

Glenn Ford and then Rock Hudson for the role, but neither actor was available. Robert Baker decided to fly over to New York for a meeting with the television networks and while there he obtained from them a list of acceptable American actors. The list included Tony Curtis, whom Roger had already suggested as a possible co-star. But the networks, knowing Curtis to have turned down similar offers from television, were convinced that he would not do it.

Tony Curtis's name, however, was the one that stuck and when Bob Baker reported the outcome of the network meeting to Lew Grade, he immediately retorted, 'What do you mean, he won't do it? Curtis's agent, George Chasin, is an old chum of mine. I'll phone him up right away!' Never a man to waste time on words, Lew telephoned Chasin in Los Angeles.

'I want Tony Curtis to do a television series with Roger Moore,' he told him. He then arranged to meet Chasin two days later in the film capital.

As agreed, Lew arrived in Los Angeles and met both agent and client in a suite in the Beverly Hills Hotel. Tony Curtis remembers asking the recently knighted Sir Lew Grade during negotiations, 'If I work for you, what do I call you?', to which Sir Lew replied, 'You can call me anything if you'll take the job!'

Tony Curtis liked the concept of the series, and a deal was made; Lew Grade left Los Angeles having gained Curtis's signature and completed his team. It was no mean feat to gain the participation of Tony Curtis, who had been a cinema star of great stature and was still a big box office draw.

Born Bernard Schwarz and brought up in Manhattan and the Bronx, Tony Curtis belonged to the last generation of studio-manufactured stars. He had progressed from small parts in the late forties and early fifties, including a role in the classic western *Winchester '73* with James Stewart, to leading roles in sword and sandal epics for Universal-International like *The Prince Who Was a Thief* and swashbucklers like *The Black Shield of Falworth*. By the time he played Houdini in the film of the same name, with his then-wife, actress Janet Leigh, he was one of the biggest stars in Hollywood, enjoying huge world-wide popularity. He proved himself to be a talented actor, graduating quickly from the rather vacuous Universal-International family fare into more challenging roles, and reaching new peaks in such films as *Spartacus*, opposite Laurence Olivier, the classic comedy, *Some Like It Hot* with Marilyn Monroe, and *The Sweet Smell of Success*. His popularity had continued throughout the sixties, but by the end of that decade he had gone through a run of unmemorable films. Tony Curtis himself says: 'It was a perfect time for me, and Roger instinctively knew it. I was dissatisfied with the type of films I was making at that time; I wasn't choosing properly.'

Soon after the two stars had signed up, *The Friendly Persuaders*, as the project was initially titled, was announced at the Monte Carlo Television Festival. It was heralded as the most expensive television series ever to be produced, with a planned budget of £2,500,000. Sir Lew Grade also reported that he had pre-sold the first twenty-four fifty-minute episodes to ABC Television in the United States for 3¼ million pounds and that filming was scheduled to start in the middle of May. Roger, who attended the Festival with Luisa, could ponder the· fact that his share of the profits would make him the first British actor to become a millionaire through television. At this point in his career, despite the failure of either *Crossplot* or *The Man Who Haunted Himself* to make any noticeable impact at the box office, Roger was still very much in demand. In the previous January he had even been asked to host his own 'chat' show by the BBC but, sensibly, he had turned it down.

The BBC bent over backwards to get me and offered me a great deal of money. The series would not have interfered with my other work. I turned it down because I am essentially an actor and when I act I use only a tiny part of my own personality. A TV show is much more demanding and if you are going to appear as yourself you must give viewers everything you've got, every aspect of your personality, and at this stage I don't want to become a TV personality.

Diplomatically, Roger hid the real reason for refusal. To become a mere television personality as opposed to a television actor would have killed the credibility he possessed as an actor, and this would have become more accentuated the more successful Roger had become as a chat show host, with the result that audiences would no longer accept him as an actor playing anyone other than himself playing a part.

In March Roger, accompanied by Robert Baker and the story editor, Terry Nation, flew to Los Angeles to meet forty-four-year-old Tony Curtis in order to discuss the project in detail. This marked the first significant teaming of a major Hollywood film star with a British television star, and although the two men came from similar backgrounds, they were as unalike as two men in the same profession could be.

Roger and Tony were not total strangers to one another, having previously met socially both in England and in Hollywood. Tony Curtis remembers their initial reaction to each other:

Both being handsome men we were immediately attracted to each other because we saw in looking at each other that there was no possible way that we would ever be in conflict with each other. We were equal on that level and that pleased me and I think it pleased Roger. Our relationship at that point was no relationship, we were just acquaintances.

Roger was well aware of Curtis's stature as a great Hollywood star and was not slow to acknowledge this, as Curtis admits:

When we first met he admired me; he has always admired me in that sense because he always felt that I had that international quality that comes out of Hollywood and is very hard to get at from any other country – it must be generated here. The first thing he said to me was, 'Tony, I've never seen such penetrating eyes on a man or a girl, anywhere in my life.' He said this in no uncertain terms.

Naturally the question of billing arose and, since this was the first time that a top-line Hollywood star had agreed to do a British television series, the form agreed on was, not surprisingly: 'CURTIS + MOORE – THE PERSUADERS', in respect to Curtis's standing as a major star.

When Roger arrived with Bob Baker and Terry Nation in Los Angeles, he felt pleased and excited about the prospect of working alongside Curtis, and since his own company, Tribune, was making *The Persuaders* for ITC (Independent Television Corporation), he had a vested interest in keeping his co-star happy.

Before Roger went to Curtis's home, he was warned of the actor's much-publicised role as spokesman for the American Cancer Society, both on radio and in television commercials, his association with the words 'I quit,' having stopped smoking cigars, cigarettes, and pipe tobacco. Curtis had been very keen to talk about his anti-smoking campaign, telling the press that since giving up the habit he had become less argumentative and more sexy. However, the media were ever ready to undermine his new 'Mr Clean' image, and there were constant stories of alleged 'sightings' of Mr Curtis having a quick drag on the rooftops of the television studios or in the toilets between takes on the commercials.

To avoid upsetting Curtis, Roger was determined not to smoke – very difficult for a man who had been an habitual chain-smoker since his youth. At first Roger's resolve held fast, but as the discussions with their future star progressed, both Roger and Terry Nation became desperate for a cigarette. Finally, Roger took one out, asking Curtis if he objected to their smoking.

'No, no, really I don't mind at all. It's your life,' Curtis replied, adding, 'Where's that ashtray we used to have?'

An elaborate search was put on for the lone ashtray, which was somewhere in one of the rooms of his large home. The ashtray found, it was placed next to Roger who began to light up. Meanwhile, all the windows in the room were opened and the fans set in motion so that no sooner had Roger exhaled the cigarette smoke, than it was quickly whisked outside where it could disperse safely and do no harm. When Roger had finished the cigarette Curtis also felt obliged to alert him, 'That's another minute and a half out of your life.' And as he, Robert Baker, and Terry Nation left, Curtis handed Roger a book on the dangers of smoking and lung cancer. But the meeting had been a success, even to the point that by the time that Curtis and Moore next saw one another Roger was no longer smoking cigarettes.

Roger stayed in Los Angeles only for a couple of days before catching a flight to the Bahamas, where Luisa and the children had begun the holiday that Roger had arranged to continue with them. After the hectic activity of the past few days he was content to head straight for the beach and relax in the sunshine with his family. However, Roger's time of relaxation was short-lived; at the end of the first day, as he was walking back to their hotel from the beach he suddenly started shaking. Assuming that he had a virus, Roger put himself to bed and within a couple of days felt well again. Once more he headed for the beach, his holiday now hopefully back on course. But, 'Suddenly I coughed, and noticed there was blood. I didn't say anything to Luisa but I spent the whole day at it, disappearing into the water and coughing up blood.'

That night he took a sleeping pill to get some rest, but it was of no use. He lay awake all night worrying over this frightening

141

development. First thing in the morning he arranged to see a doctor, although to avoid alarming Luisa, who was still unaware of what her husband was going through, he arranged to meet him at another hotel.

On the pretext of getting the Sunday papers, he went over to the other hotel, where the doctor awaited him. He examined Roger and diagnosed a sinus infection, prescribing the necessary antibiotics to clear it up. Roger, however, was convinced that he had lung cancer, even though the doctor tried to reassure him that it was certainly not so on every occasion, while he continued to see Roger daily in order to check on his condition.

The shock of the incidents of that week convinced Roger that he should give up smoking completely. Only a month later, however, he was to begin smoking cigars as a less dangerous alternative, so developing a habit to which he is now strongly addicted.

Roger was back in England when, at the end of April 1969, Tony Curtis arrived at London's Heathrow Airport, ready to start work on the new series. As the actor walked through customs he was stopped by officials and searched. He was found to be in possession of cannabis and was immediately taken to West Drayton police station and charged.

Meanwhile Roger was in hospital, having had more ill luck with his health – a recurrence of trouble with the painful kidney stones from which he suffered. Unable to pass the stones naturally, he was forced to go into hospital for an operation to remove them. Producer Robert Baker was also flat on his back in another hospital suffering from a slipped disc. He heard the news of what had happened to Curtis from John Lee Goodman, another director of Tribune, who had gone to Heathrow to meet Tony and his young wife, Lesley, only to find himself confronted by the awful situation.

Baker then telephoned Roger in hospital and told him what had happened. Roger muttered, 'Right,' and immediately got in touch with his own lawyer, who arranged counsel for Curtis. He was released on bail, pending a court appearance next day at Uxbridge, Middlesex. Tony Curtis remembers the incident:

It was nothing. I had enough makings for one or two marijuana cigarettes and when I went to court I just stood up and said, 'I'm a stranger in a strange country. I don't drink, occasionally

I smoke some marijuana and if that is an offence I apologize, I am certainly not loaded with drugs, as you can see.'

The magistrates went out and huddled together. They came back and said, 'Fifty pounds.'

I said, 'Well, I don't have any money on me,' and everyone laughed. I hadn't made any currency change yet. So my barrister stood up and said, 'I will take care of Mr Curtis's obligation.'

So that is where the newspapers got the headline 'BROKE AND BUSTED'. It was inoffensive, there was nothing obscene or nerve-racking about it. It had nothing to do with the future or the past. In fact it helped us because it made you aware we were doing the show called *The Persuaders* with Roger.

Roger's response to the incident was suitably humorous, but with a clearly caustic edge to it. Curtis continues:

Roger was in the hospital and he took every one of the headlines and put them together in a book and he wrote on it, 'Dear Bernie Sneaks Into London', and in it were the headlines from everything: 'TONY CURTIS BROKE AND BUSTED!' – every piece of information that was printed he put in this book. My God, was he cute!

The whole incident could have been disastrous for the imminent series because the contract with the American network, ABC, had a morality clause and these events might have been construed as being in breach of that clause. But fortunately the storm passed, the only result being that it caused the American Cancer Society and Tony Curtis a great deal of embarrassment, and the Society to withdraw his anti-smoking commercials from circulation.

With Roger out of hospital and Tony out of trouble, filming began on *The Persuaders* a few days later. Initial work for the series was done on location in the South of France and Italy. To give the first episode an air of gloss and sophistication, Roger's director from *The Man Who Haunted Himself*, Basil Dearden, was brought in. Tragically it was Dearden's final directorial effort; he was killed in a car accident soon afterwards.

Roger Moore played Lord Brett Sinclair, an English aristocrat who, wealthy but bored, teams up with an American, Danny Wilde, who has fought his way up from the slums of New York to become an equally wealthy man, and who also craves adventure and excitement.

Tony Curtis very quickly saw into Roger's character and his reaction to the part that he played in the series:

I saw in Roger things that he did not even see in himself. Roger as Lord Sinclair: that is his fantasy. His father was a cop; he was brought up in little better than a poor environment. So was I. Roger had that illusion of the Lord concept, which in England is very important because of the caste system. There is a tremendous system in England from bottom to top, and in the manner by which your speech indicates and dictates what quality of life you come from in England. And it is not possible for any Englishman to acquire or even imitate the aristocratic pronunciation; there isn't an actor alive who can do it. Either you are born of the cloth or you're not.

And for me the charming thing about Roger is and was that that cloth was his way of life, he loved it. And that is what he aspired to; he would order a bottle of champagne and it was a bottle of 'shampoo' – 'Shall we have some shampoo?'

Brett Sinclair was a sliver of someone Roger loved and wanted to be. That's what makes us actors, wanting to be what we are not. I would not say these things about Roger if I did not like the man and I say these things with love and affection; for these are the things that I see in the man and I feel that whoever gets to know Roger should know of this very delicate and intricate person who is there, who isn't the aristocrat sitting in the stern of a yacht – because he isn't that. As famous as he will ever be, as rich as he will ever be, and whatever he will be able to acquire and have, will never truly satisfy him, as it doesn't satisfy me and many people of my ilk; because that is what we are striving for – satisfaction. We are not striving for fame and fortune, we are striving to fill up an emptiness in us and by acting it is easy, because when you do that work it is fulfilled. It is when you are not doing the work that you have that gnawing feeling of abandonment and that feeling of not being. Roger and I have had twenty-five different lifetimes; when you are doing this work you are doing it and when a guy holds a gun on you, that's a gun, and when you kiss a woman in the movies you are kissing a woman. It is not a fantasy – that's reality. And Roger and I have had extraordinary different experiences in our lives.

Curtis also had his own very definite view of his own role in the series and was not entirely satisfied with the way that the part had been written:

It was written by English people so they didn't understand the American genre and the American attitude about living life. I ad-libbed all through the series because when the material was originally conceived it was conceived perhaps that I was Roger's major-domo; his servant or his dresser. Well, I wouldn't play that because it was not part of the fabric of the man I was. So constantly pushing Roger, challenging him as an American tough-guy against this very aristocratic English gentleman was a wonderful combination. It wasn't appreciated at the beginning; Lew Grade wanted me to always dress in suits – I wouldn't. I constantly wore a short jacket; I just mixed up my clothing. Finally he went and made me some suits, but the suits didn't make that much difference. I was still that kind of maverick and Lord Sinclair somewhat accepted me as his crazy friend and would introduce me to his very aristocratic friends as his friend. So in one way he disapproved of me, in another he approved of me – you can see how life, reality and fantasy, particularly in our profession, intermingle.

Curtis felt that both of them came as close as they have ever done to showing their true characters with their acting in *The Persuaders*: 'Do you want to know what Roger and I are? Look at *The Persuaders*, look at every one of those episodes and you will see what the relationship is and you will truly see what we are.'

With filming under way, Roger and Tony were brought together to begin an on-screen partnership that would involve them in fourteen months of working closely and intensely together, with barely any separations in that time. Following the incident at Heathrow Airport, Roger was understandably cautious with his co-star at the outset, as Curtis recalls:

Right at the beginning he wasn't quite sure what to expect from me and rightly so. I am intense in scenes, so I don't take things lightly, and it took Roger a little while to understand my mechanism. Once he understood that, then the relationship was perfect – our working relationship. I'm not interested in our personal relationship; we had a job to make huge chunks of money. You can't be worried about loving or hating each other.

Most journalists were eager to uncover any signs of dissension between the two actors. When asked about working with Curtis, Roger was as diplomatic as ever: 'We've become great pals – so have our wives. He and I have no secrets from one another. It's almost like a happy marriage.'

But behind the scenes, the situation quickly looked as if it would explode. While on location something occurred which seemed to forewarn of worse to come, as Curtis again remembers, this time an incident involving Joan Collins, a close personal friend from Roger's earlier days:

We started to do all the exteriors in the South of France and Joan Collins was going to be one of our guest stars. She was in the first or second episode and I had never worked with her, and she and I had to drive up in a van. Roger and I had been working by then and we started out very low-key, so that we would be able to pace ourselves through this long, arduous series.

And Joan was very nervous, saying, 'Oh God! Will they love me? I don't know what to do! Do I look all right?'

I said, 'You look great.'

She said, 'Oh God! I can't do the shot.'

Finally, I just said, 'Joan, would you stop acting like a ——.' I have never said that word before, never to anyone except to her and she said, 'What did you say to me?'

I said, 'I'm sorry.'

She leaned out of the window of this little van and said, 'Do you know what he called me?' The crew was there, Roger was standing there, and Bob Baker, and she's screaming, 'He called me a ——!'

Roger almost fell out of his suit. Joan leaped out of the van and went to her dressing room.

I said to Roger, 'I'm sorry, Roger, but I couldn't stand it. I mean, she was just such a pain in the ass.'

He said, 'Well, I know what to do.'

So I ran to a flower shop close by, bought two dozen big roses and went to her dressing room. I said, 'Joan, forgive me. Please. There was no intent meant by it. I don't say it maliciously or viciously, just that we're working hard and please forgive me.'

She said, 'Well, all right,' and she came back and we worked and we did the show. And we left, I felt, in a wonderful and a good relationship. If Joan still takes umbrage from that, that's her problem not mine.

And when that happened Roger said, 'Oh, Jesus God, do I have my hands full with this crazy bum' – because that's the way it went from then on.

Tony Curtis is quick to take the entire blame on his shoulders for all the troubles that arose during the making of the series, feeling that the relationship between Roger and himself was potentially very firm and steady right from the beginning:

> I could tell instantly that Roger and I had no conflict. We never did during the making of *The Persuaders*. I'm a bit of a madman and there were times when I would, for no reason at all, find some problem. But the problem was within myself and I know myself well enough to accept that responsibility. People around me will misunderstand it; they will mistake it for whatever they wish when in reality it is a psychic pain. I will not compromise my feelings. And anything I say is never a criticism, it is always an observation; so if they had made paper walls and they said, 'You'll have to come through the door slowly,' I would say, 'It's not possible. Danny Wilde does not come through a door slowly. He comes through and bangs it.' And the set would quiver; so they would have to fix it. So they thought it was an ego problem, when in reality it wasn't – it was the character speaking.

Socially, the two actors tended to go their own way. Tony had his own circle of friends and Roger had his. Whilst in the South of France, Roger took advantage of the fact that his close friend David Niven lived nearby in a luxurious house on Cap Ferrat. Roger used to visit Niven frequently, often dining out with him, and they were joined sometimes by Luisa, who was with Roger during the first part of the location shooting. Curtis and Moore only met occasionally socially, and that was usually at parties.

Having finished the European location work, which consisted of Roger sweeping round the roads of Europe in an Aston Martin and Tony in a Ferrari, the film unit returned to England at the end of the summer to begin shooting interiors at Pinewood Studios.

Tony obviously felt that the series was shaping up extremely well and, anticipating a hit, he bought a 120,000-dollar house at No. 49 Chester Square in London. The producers ensured that

Curtis had every comfort, as he remembers: 'They were kind enough to give me a beautiful four-door Bentley, with a wonderful young man, Bob Hobbs, as driver, who drove me morning and night to and from Pinewood.' It was while Tony and his wife were living there that Lesley Curtis gave birth to a son, whom they called Nicholas. He was born in London on December 31st, 1969, just three hours before midnight. All Tony's children visited him at some time when he was in London – Alexandra, Allegra, Kelly and Jamie.

Roger and Luisa mixed occasionally with Tony and Lesley, and they got to know Roger's children, Deborah and Geoffrey. The Moores sometimes visited Chester Square and the Curtis family visited Sherwood House in Denham. Of Roger's wife, Tony says: 'Luisa was a charming woman. I liked her very much; I still do. She was always so open and gracious with me.'

During the filming of the series, Curtis claims that some of his behaviour was deliberately provoking in order to bring out certain results on the screen and that both men learned considerably from each other:

If I didn't learn it, I observed from Roger an ability to take things as they come and not provoke them, because they will happen eventually – that I never knew. What Roger learnt from me was to never take anything for granted. I pushed him all through the series. At the beginning it threw him a bit off guard but he got back on his feet immediately. I did that deliberately because it provoked him and it provoked me. So that when you see these films they are unique and different – you never saw two men work so in tandem with each other; whether we liked each other or not was immaterial. On the set, above and beyond anything else, we respected each other. He loved and admired me on the set. Personally, to each his own – and I don't question that. I just know that those twenty-four fifty-minute films we made were unique and different.

Roger's relationship with his co-star was complicated by the fact that he had two different roles in the production – that of star and that of producer. It helped to colour Roger's behaviour on the production, as Curtis observed: 'Roger was always like the host with the show because it was his company that was producing it. I would say he was the largest independent owner of it; Roger and his company owned it with Bob Baker and Sir Lew owned the rest of it.' Roger's dual role also caused Curtis to view the actor and the producer as two different men:

There were times when I insisted on certain things going a certain way. It never interfered with Roger's and my work; he as the producer – I have no truck with the producer – but the actor, he and I together, never had a problem. He, as the producer, had extra pressure. That was the unfortunate thing for Roger, because he was not only the actor, but he was producing it and he was obligated to bring them in within a certain time. I had no such obligations, I just had an obligation to give the best work I could. And perhaps that created some tension between us, but I just remember the really wonderful experience in getting to know a truly interesting man.

It is clear that the two men were capable of enjoying a very close professional relationship as two performers.' Peter Hunt directed one episode and found the experience enjoyable:

I did a *Persuaders* episode which worked out very well. They sent it out with two others as a film. As regards Curtis and Moore that was fire and water. It was very bristly at times, although I didn't find that when I was working. I found Tony Curtis very good too – a very professional man.

Fortunately, in my episode, Roger and Tony only had a couple of scenes together but it wasn't really a sequence that involved the two of them playing together too much so I did not have to deal with any discontent. And I'm sure that on the floor they didn't take it to that point; I think this was a personal relationship problem.

There were times at Pinewood when the two actors behaved in the most amiable way towards each other, as Curtis recalls: 'We had dressing rooms alongside of each other with huge closet space, and they built us a sauna. Between shots we would run in and out of each other's rooms – we were like room-mates.'

Both found acting together a very rewarding, constructive experience, discovering that their acting styles blended together perfectly, as Curtis again remembers:

We would make up dialogue and he would accept it, which is why I knew it was okay. One day Roger came in dressed in velvet because he was a Member of Parliament and I said to him, 'Where are you going?'

He said, 'Well, today is the Investiture and I have to go to Parliament, we members of the aristocracy.'

And Laurence Naismith, who was in the scene, said, 'When you've finished, I've got a new job for the two of you, so what do you want to do?' by which he meant, 'Do you want to do that first or do you want to hear what the caper is going to be?'

But when he said, 'What do you want to do?', I ran over to Roger, grabbed the crown he was wearing, put my arm in his arm, and said, 'We want to get married.'

They left that in the show; it was just an ad-lib. Now Roger, when those things happened, began to see exactly what the relationship was going to be. He once showed me his crypt, because members of the Sinclair family were being killed like in that movie *Kind Hearts and Coronets*. Inside the crypt there were slabs and then there were some open spots and he said, 'Daniel,' and he pointed to the third one along on the top, 'that will be my resting place.'

And I said, 'Well, you'll certainly have a wonderful view.'

These were the kind of jokes that I ad-libbed, and we came up with them together. Roger had the perfect partner in me. He did not dare at the beginning do that because the structure of the material was such that it demanded certain intent. But after he started working with me he saw that he could do it. There were some of our episodes that were completely improvised; what was the intent of the scene, what information had to be passed on so that the next scene would make sense, one of us had to find out. We had sixty seconds to get you that information, so up to that point we could do a scene like Laurel and Hardy. We could do anything until we got to that point, and so that is what we did. We broke down these scenes and analytically laid them out. Similarly, we had stunts that he and I did together; we never hurt each other, we always worked it out carefully.

Both were spontaneous and it worked beautifully, but the director made sure that Roger had the key plot lines in his speeches to ensure that the thread of the story was always apparent. It would be left to Roger to get the story back on its track, while Tony would go off at a tangent until Roger brought him back to reality.

As well as designing his own clothes for the series, Roger also took advantage of his ACTT card and directed two episodes himself, in one of which seven-year-old Deborah played a schoolgirl. Five-year-old Geoffrey never got the chance to appear in any of the episodes, but there was the consolation that his picture was seen every week in the opening titles, posing as Lord Brett Sinclair in his early school days, backed by the pounding theme written for the series by John Barry, who had written most of the music for the James Bond films up to that time.

Tony Curtis is full of praise for Roger as a director:

I loved him as a director; he was outstanding, because to be directed by Roger is not to be directed – it was, 'Tony, what do you think?', 'Where shall you say that line?', 'Why don't you come in this way?' It was a collaboration, which is what direction is. Any time a director makes you feel that it isn't that, then he is not a good director: his ego is being provocative. If there was a scene that didn't play right I would question it. Roger would stand right next to me and we would go over it until we resolved what I felt was not proper or in order.

With *The Persuaders* Curtis was convinced of the value of television and found that he liked the format of a television series: 'I rather like the fifty-minute timing. It was wonderful to know you were going to make a movie that was going to last fifty minutes on the nose and not a minute longer. It took ten days to make, which is twice as long as it took to make in Hollywood. That is why there is so much quality in the show.'

The shooting schedule was tough on both actors, and both were near to exhaustion as the shooting drew gradually to a close. Tony Curtis remembers that both were on call almost the whole time:

I worked 190 days in succession and we would spell each other once in a while. We never had any time off, Roger and I. We were always in every episode. Once in a while he would get a few days off or I would get a few days off.

I remember when we were doing about the eighteenth episode, and neither of us had any idea how hard we were working physically. We had to do a sequence where we were both running in a forest. We were running, and all of a sudden my legs gave out from under me; they just collapsed and I fell

151

down. Roger stopped and shouted 'Cut!' He came back and he looked at me with such concern and said, 'Are you all right?'

I said, 'I don't know, Roger. My legs just stopped.'

And he sat down next to me and said, 'You know, I think we're both tired.'

I said, 'I think we are.'

We got up and we did it again. A little moment like that meant a lot to me because I could see that we were like *The Defiant Ones*, chained together like Sidney Poitier and I; perhaps at the beginning not trusting each other, but as the chain became stronger and stronger, so we could rely on each other in our work. I never upstaged him, never tried to hog a scene – that's not in my soul and I think he saw that. We both did. I learned a lot in that series and I know Roger did, whether each one of us will admit it or not.

With the filming finally over, both men could finally truly relax and take stock of the events of the past fourteen months. Tony Curtis sums up their partnership:

In the time that Roger and I were together there was not a cross word, not any contention between us. If, by my behaviour, it in some way provoked Roger it was never done with intent – it was done out of my own personal madness and my own inability to accept what that situation was. And if Roger was there, or Bob Baker, or the director – well 'fuck 'em, feed 'em fish' – that's the man I am. Roger and I never picked fights with each other. Roger never provoked me. There was nothing in his behaviour from the minute I met him that I could ever take umbrage with and I know there must have been many things that I did which provoked him. But to dear Roger it was never done with intent, never done with malice; it was done out of my own madness.

There were rumours that another series of *The Persuaders* might be a possibility but Roger made it clear that he was not interested. Tony Curtis, however, was reported to be quite keen on doing another season – but it was not to be. The series over, Curtis and Moore parted ways and to this day have not renewed contact with each other, as Curtis regretfully admits:

I won't call and he won't call me, but we will meet somewhere along the line – eventually. But there is no reason. After that intense fourteen months of being together, day in and day out, getting pissed off at each other, not showing it, not wanting to upset each other, wanting to get our work done. That is the kind of professionals we were and are. Never a cross word between us, whatever we felt; always on time – never held up the company.

We spent fourteen months together. We haven't seen each other since. That means we truly love each other because Roger and I cannot have a passing relationship. It was intense, working hard – or it wasn't.

Tony Curtis still waits for that telephone call from Roger, but still, fifteen years later, the telephone does not ring.

With *The Persuaders* finished late in June 1971, Roger announced that he would begin preparations for another television series – but this time a factual one. Whatever it was going to be, one thing was plain – Roger did not want to do another series of *The Persuaders*.

Initial sales on *The Persuaders* were very promising, and it was not overly optimistic to hope that the series could rival the success of *The Saint*. Within days of the completion of shooting, it could be announced that the series had been sold to every country in the world except Russia, China and Albania, which meant that it had already beaten *The Saint* on that score. It had paid for itself and also earned considerable profit before it had ever been shown.

The series was to be premiered on British television on September 17th, and a day later in America, and Roger spent the preceding months helping to publicise the show in both countries. First, however, he allowed himself a much needed two-week holiday after the emotionally draining experience that *The Persuaders* had proved to be.

But Roger's travels were not merely the result of his acting interests. He had also become a director of the perfume company Fabergé, where Cary Grant was already on the board. His involvement with the textile company, Pearson and Foster, had come to an end. In his capacity as design consultant and director, Roger had been paid £10,000 a year by the firm which meant that he made personal appearances on behalf of the company and allowed his name to be associated with their product – he was usually seen in a Pearson and Foster suit, which benefited from Roger's ability to wear clothes to good effect. The company marketed a range of clothes under the 'Saint' label to emphasise further Roger's involvement, but after a year the novelty of these added features proved to have played itself out.

The directorship with Fabergé was along similar lines, Roger's main task being to appear as himself at various functions. The extent of his fame at this point is indicated by the fact that he was chosen to be a representative along with such a great star as Cary Grant.

But despite publicity to the contrary, it would be wrong to believe that such a position put Roger in the role of high-powered businessman. Roger was there for what he represented and was, like Grant, indicative of the character of the man who had brought him into the company – George Barrie. Roger also managed to get a position for Ross Hunter, his friend of long-standing, who does not remember the association with much affection: 'It was the saddest day of my life. George Barrie is a man who is very rich but lacks taste.'

Ross Hunter was hired as chairman of Fabergé's recently established film production company, but soon departed due to a conflict of personalities.

Roger became involved in the film production side of Fabergé and was one of the people responsible for the production of the very successful romantic comedy, *A Touch of Class*, which starred Glenda Jackson and George Segal. The pity is that Roger was not able to cast himself in the male lead, which would certainly have given him an excellent opportunity to display his talent as a light comedian, a facet of Roger's acting which always appears to be on the point of blossoming but which even now remains unfulfilled. Indeed, it is in *The Persuaders* that this lighter touch is most to the fore, and the result is very pleasing. Sadly, Roger has never tried since to build on the potential that he has in this field, with the exception of the singularly dreadful picture, *That Lucky Touch* in 1974, which is a very strong contender for being the worst film that Roger has ever made.

Meanwhile, the fate of *The Persuaders* was not all that had been anticipated. The series proved to be hugely popular in Europe, with both Roger and Tony being named Best Actor of the Year in France, while in Spain the series was voted the Best Foreign Telecast, and in Germany, the Best Dubbed Programme. But in America it died a death to such an extent that it was eventually taken off after only twenty of the total of twenty-four episodes had been screened, due to the battering that it received in the ratings war with the rival series *Mission Impossible*, a more straightforward and imaginative series than the Curtis/Moore collaboration proved to be.

The failure of *The Persuaders* in America is in many ways understandable. The episodes were for the most part uncommonly mediocre and the whole weight of the series fell upon the shoulders of Roger and Tony Curtis. Both performers acquitted themselves very well and it was their personalities that made the series watchable. With his involvement in the show, Roger had gained one massive advantage, a plus that most other stars experience near the beginning of their professional careers. This was that he had to work opposite Tony Curtis, a veteran who had gained enormous success on the screen and had himself worked with actors of the stature of Laurence Olivier, Cary Grant, Burt Lancaster and Jack Lemmon, to name but four, as well as with exceptionally talented directors like Billy Wilder, Stanley Kubrick, and Sir Carol Reed. To say that Roger held his own opposite Curtis is complimentary and meant to be so. It was an experience that the forty-three-year-old actor desperately needed and he proved himself to be capable of benefiting from it. Curtis in his turn was wholly entertaining, bringing his great gifts as a screen actor to the series. Roger Moore had not previously worked opposite a great actor before and, in fact, has not done so since, with the exceptions of Gregory Peck and Richard Burton, when both were far from their respective professional peaks.

In *The Persuaders* Roger gives the best account of himself on screen in light comedy, and it is in no small measure due to the fact that he had Curtis to play against and had to match up to him. Considering that Roger had no previous experience with an actor of that calibre this was certainly a challenge. If the production of the series was at times fraught, the benefits to Roger were inestimable and indeed perhaps such tension causes a more creative atmosphere than can ever be achieved on the kind of relaxed set that Roger favours.

Seven

In 1961 two men were determined to buy the rights to film the James Bond thrillers from their author, Ian Fleming. Their names were Albert R. Broccoli and Harry Saltzman.

Albert Romolo Broccoli was born in Astoria, Long Island, New York State in 1909, of Italian immigrant stock. His early years were marked by struggle; his father, a civil engineer by trade, was forced to work as a bricklayer in New York City in order to feed his family. As soon as he was old enough Albert worked for an uncle, Pasquale de Cicco, who owned a twenty-five acre truck gardening farm on which he cultivated vegetables for the New York market, including the broccoli which he had introduced to America and to which he had given its distinctive name. Albert's duties were to wash, crate and then take the vegetables to the Harlem markets on a horse-drawn cart. Eventually he tired of this, and went to work for a cousin, Augustine D'Orta, as manager of the Long Island Casket Co., which made coffins. However, after a vacation spent in Hollywood in 1933, he decided that his future lay in the film industry and, with this in mind, he left his job and travelled West.

Albert sold Christmas trees from a streetcorner caravan in Los Angeles, worked as a salesman for hairnets in San Francisco, and took a job in a Beverly Hills jewellers before finally getting his first foothold in the film industry, working in the mail room at Twentieth Century-Fox studios. He progressed steadily until, in 1941, he became assistant director to Howard Hawks on Howard Hughes' production of *The Outlaw*, starring Jane Russell. The shooting lasted nine months, during which time he also doubled as Miss Russell's bodyguard. At the outbreak of war, Broccoli enlisted in the US Navy. He served four years and was discharged with the rank of Lieutenant in the Special Services.

The war over, and still determined on a career in show business, Broccoli went to work for Charles Feldman, one of Hollywood's top agents. Although subsequently he became a successful agent, Broccoli's true interests at that time were in film production. However, he found it impossible to establish himself as an inde-pedent producer in Hollywood and, in 1951, he decided to move to England, where he co-founded Warwick Films with Irving Allen and, enlisting the services of a former client, actor Alan Ladd, he started to produce his own films. With Ladd he was to make *Hell Below Zero*, *The Black Knight* and *The Red Beret*; other productions included *Fire Down Below* with Rita Hayworth, Robert Mitchum and Jack Lemmon, *The Cockleshell Heroes* with Jose Ferrer, and *The Trials of Oscar Wilde* with Peter Finch. In 1960 Broccoli and Allen split up, and with his share of the business Broccoli began his attempt to bring James Bond to the screen.

Harry Saltzman, born in St John, New Brunswick, Canada, in 1915, had begun his show business career by working in vaudeville and a travelling circus around the United States and Canada, and later went to Europe, becoming a theatrical entrepreneur in France. At the outbreak of war he enlisted in the French Army and in 1945, with peace once again in Europe, he worked for UNESCO. He eventually returned to the world of show business and set up Woodfall Films with Tony Richardson, producing notable films such as *Look Back in Anger* with Richard Burton, *The Entertainer* with Laurence Olivier, and *Saturday Night and Sunday Morning* with Albert Finney. When he split up with Richardson he decided to try to secure the rights to film James Bond, paying Ian Fleming fifty thousand dollars for a six-month option on the stories – with the exception of *Casino Royale*, Fleming's first Bond novel, which the author had already sold to producer Gregory Ratoff in 1955.

To his surprise, Saltzman was unable to interest any of the big film companies in the project. With twenty-eight days left before his option was due to expire, he heard that independent producer Albert R. Broccoli was interested in a fifty-fifty partnership to produce Bond for the cinema. Rather than see his option expire with nothing to show for it, Saltzman reluctantly agreed to pool his resources with Broccoli. As the latter recalls:

> When I tried to buy the rights to the James Bond stories I found out that there was someone who had a hold on them for twenty-eight days – and it was Harry Saltzman. So I made a deal with Saltzman and we became partners. I think my entering into the picture brought it together, because I was in contact with Arthur Krim of United Artists. When we had the property I called Arthur and he said, 'Come to New York, and we'll talk about it.' And that's where it all started.

157

The meeting between United Artists' President, Arthur Krim, and partners Saltzman and Broccoli took place in New York on June 20th, 1961; they asked for a budget of one million dollars for the first film, but United Artists knocked it down to 800,000 dollars. Author Ian Fleming was to receive 100,000 dollars per picture, plus 5% of the producer's profits. The stage was finally set to bring secret service agent, James Bond 007, to the screen.

The first production was to have been *Thunderball*, but the rights to the story became the subject of a legal battle between Ian Fleming and Kevin McClory. The complicated court case, and the long wait for its outcome, threatened to delay production and, with this in mind, it was decided to film *Dr No* instead. Initially Bryan Forbes and Guy Green were approached to direct the film, but both men rejected the offer, and so Broccoli and Saltzman approached Terence Young in New York. Young had worked for Broccoli as a director for Warwick Films, but at this time he was trying to set up the film version of a story called *The Jackals*, by the French thriller writer, Frederick Guard. The film was to be made by Paramount as a starring vehicle for the glamorous Ava Gardner, whose co-stars were to be Curt Jurgens and Roger Moore. Terence Young had Roger in mind for the film when he read the script and had asked him to send some pictures of himself; Roger complied, sending photographs from *Diane* in which he was dressed in armour. Young remembers: 'Roger was to play a young doctor – marvellously good-looking – who, on his first job meets this "femme fatale" played by Ava Gardner. He was also meant to be quite a bit younger than her, and so he would have been absolutely perfect.'

Problems arose between Paramount and Miss Gardner and the project collapsed – so Roger Moore was left to make low-budget films in Italy. Terence Young was luckier; while he was fighting to save his film, he received the telegram from Broccoli asking him to direct the James Bond picture. Only too happy to be given the excuse to extricate himself from what had become an impossible situation, Young cabled his acceptance.

Meanwhile, the search for an actor to play Bond was in full swing. Initially Roger Moore was in the running, but there were certain reservations, as Broccoli recalls: 'When we made the deal with Fleming we considered quite a few people, and Roger was one of them, although at the time he had signed to do *The Saint*. He was one we would have liked to have had, who could have been up for it; the only thing was he did look a bit young – more than young, in fact, he looked very boyish and we were looking for somebody older.'

By the time Terence Young became involved in the pre-production of *Dr No*, Roger was no longer among the actors thought to be most suitable for the role. Young says, 'I was given five names: Sean Connery, Patrick McGoohan, James Mason, Cary Grant and a stunt man, Bob Simmons.' Cary Grant was approached in Hollywood, but would only agree to make one picture; then James Mason was contacted in Switzerland, but he would commit himself only to making two. This was a stumbling block, since Saltzman and Broccoli were hoping they might be lucky enough to make four James Bond films before the series died out. Patrick McGoohan, when approached, rejected the part on moral grounds.

Needless to say, Sean Connery got the part and was flown out to Jamaica for location shooting, which began on January 16th, 1962. The film was completed at Pinewood Studios on March 30th, and premiered at the London Pavillion, off Piccadilly Circus, on October 6th. It marked the start of a world-wide success which would make Saltzman and Broccoli rich beyond their wildest dreams, and push Sean Connery to international stardom over-night.

After the formation of Eon Productions in 1961, Albert R. Broccoli devoted the whole of his energy to the making of the James Bond films. The only exception was his 1968 production of *Chitty Chitty Bang Bang*, adapted from Ian Fleming's children's book of the same title about a flying car. Harry Saltzman, on the other hand, produced a considerable number of other films, including three 'Harry Palmer' films and the mammoth *Battle of Britain*, made in 1969. Saltzman had always been on the lookout for other projects; immediately after *Dr No* he had produced a comedy with Bob Hope and Anita Ekberg entitled *Call Me Bwana*. The next two Bond productions were *From Russia With Love* and *Goldfinger*, but by the time the third film in the series had been made Saltzman's interest was noticeably waning. It was not helped by the death of Ian Fleming on August 12th, 1964, shortly before the release of *Goldfinger*. Despite this, he went on with Broccoli to make *Thunderball* and *You Only Live Twice* with Connery, followed by *On Her Majesty's Secret Service*, when George Lazenby stepped into the role, and then *Diamonds Are Forever*, when Connery returned for what he vowed would be his final appearance as James Bond.

Connery's stubborn refusal to make any more Bond films meant that a replacement had to be found – and this time Roger Moore was free of any binding commitments which prevented him from taking over. But the situation was not so simple since United Artists had other ideas, as Broccoli recalls:

Since we had an American distributor, they were looking for American actors to play the role. I couldn't see it, even though they had suggested Burt Reynolds, and I kept saying, 'The man has to be British.' My partner, Harry Saltzman, liked Roger Moore but he preferred a couple of other people. But Harry agreed with me that Roger was right and we put up a fight for him.

The pressure from the American distributors was considerable and, determined to see an American actor in the part, they recommended Paul Newman and Steve McQueen as other possibilities. Understandably they were cautious about going with a new face as Bond after the disappointment of George Lazenby. For *Diamonds Are Forever* they had had the luxury of Sean Connery's return to the part, which had ensured high box-office takings.

Although Roger Moore was known in the United States because of *The Saint* television series, this in itself worked against him to some extent so far as the distributors were concerned. One of his agents, Dennis Selinger, feels that it was a disadvantage to be so familiar to television audiences:

Roger was one of the biggest television stars in the world, to the extent that when I would go out for an evening with him and Sean Connery, more often than not people would go up to Roger first, being so immediately recognisable because he was in your home every week on television. This very often made people hold back in the film area; the film world is always rather suspicious and careful of using television people, as they say that the public has seen too much of them and that consequently they are not box office. So it was much more difficult to get Roger the film roles at that time.

Luckily for Roger, producer Albert Broccoli felt sure that he was the right man for the job, as he says: 'Roger was my choice and United Artists were very surprised when he became successful

As Sebastian Oldsmith in *Shout at the Devil* (1976)

Michael Klinger

With Richard Kiel ('Jaws') in *The Spy Who Loved Me* (1977)

Richard Burton, Stewart Granger and Roger Moore off the set of *The Wild Geese* (1978)   Euan Lloyd

Line-up for *The Sea Wolves* (1980) including Trevor Howard, David Niven and Gregory Peck

MGM publicity portrait (1954)
MGM/UA Entertainment Co.

As Mr Pelham in *The Man Who Haunted Himself* (1970)
Thorn EMI Screen Entertainment

As Shawn Fynn in *The Wild Geese* (1978)
Euan Lloyd

As Rufus Excalibur ffolkes in *North Sea Hijack* (1980)
Universal City Studios

Filming *A View To A Kill* in 1984

Live and Let Die (1973)

Publicity still (1983)

At the Academy Award ceremony (1983)
Academy of Motion Picture Arts and Sciences. 'Oscar' © AMPAS

As Dr Judd Stevens in *The Naked Face* (1984)
Cannon Films Inc.

During filming of *A View To A Kill*, 1984, with producer 'Cubby' Broccoli, Christopher Walken and director John Glen
© 1985 Danjaq SA

As guest star on *The Muppet Show (1980)*

as Bond. I had to struggle to get him accepted, but I believed that he was the one who could play the part.'

There was a great deal of speculation as to whether Roger would take over as Bond. Sean Connery had made it quite clear that he was finished with the part and even tipped Roger as his likely successor. The prediction gained credence when Roger was seen in the company of Sean Connery at the press preview of *Diamonds Are Forever* in London. The producers were still hoping that Connery might be wooed back, but they had to be prepared with a ready replacement. David Hedison, who played Felix Leiter in *Live and Let Die*, says: 'I was originally there to do *Live and Let Die*, but Roger was not set for it; it was supposed to be Sean. Although Sean said he wasn't going to do it they felt that they could woo him back with money.'

Speculation ended on August 1st, 1972 at a press conference at the Dorchester Hotel in London, when a long-haired Roger Moore smiled happily over a cigar and a vodka Martini as it was officially announced that a worthy successor to Sean Connery had been found. Rumours fled around that Roger would have to dye his fair hair to play the world's most famous secret agent, but whatever the truth behind such rumours he was certainly obliged to have his hair cut short; he was also told to lose the weight he had gained while making *The Persuaders*. Prior to the start of shooting, Roger and Luisa went to Rome to visit her family, while Roger concentrated on losing weight and getting back into condition. He said at the time, 'I practically knock myself out doing exercises to get the old heart going. By about 9.30 in the morning I feel I've done a full day's work.'

Early in October Roger was flown to New York, and thence to New Orleans, to begin the shooting of *Live and Let Die*, and on Friday, October 13th the cameras at last began turning with Roger Moore in the role he had wanted for so long.

Roger Moore was catapulted into the world of James Bond and immediately began to understand why Sean Connery had found the life so tiring. As Connery had often found himself in the ridiculous situation of having to excuse himself from interviewers and press photographers in order to go to work, so Roger found that the pressures from the world media were considerable. If he had a moment free there would always be a press man lurking nearby, eager to pounce, while television crews from all over the world would follow him around all day to get shots of the new James Bond to relay across the globe. There was an inexhaustible number of people all wanting exclusive interviews but, as Sean Connery had found to his irritation, in spite of the diversity of interviewers from countries as far apart as Japan and Germany, they all wanted to know one thing. In Roger's case the question was, 'How will your Bond be different to that of Sean Connery?'

Roger answered this question a thousand times until he hardly knew what he was saying in reply. Apart from the world's press, the locations would also attract hundreds of sightseers who would stand around watching the filming, and he found himself signing autographs continually.

But this was the life that Roger Moore had always wanted – this is what it meant to be on top. In 1956, in an article for the English magazine *Plays and Players*, Roger wrote: 'When I was a drama student, I once passed Anton Walbrook strolling conspicuously along Charing Cross Road. How wonderful it must be, I thought, to be so easily recognised in the busiest street – even when wearing large dark glasses. I just couldn't wait to be in the same happy position myself.'

The Saint had made Roger Moore a household name, but playing James Bond put him firmly in the big league; his life-style was to change completely, and he would become one of the most recognisable faces in the world. People would seek out his company, women would throw themselves at him, he would be followed wherever he went and would even be approached when eating in restaurants – his life would never be the same again.

Roger's liking of the attention is not only personal vanity, but the cool-headed knowledge that the more people he gives interviews to, the more autographs he signs, the more the media and the public take up his time, the more lasting will be his fame and his fortune. Roger is one of the lucky stars, in that he enjoys his position; other stars of equal importance in the cinema seem to take a masochistic pleasure in being disagreeable to the media and their public, which seems to result in their being in a constant state of misery over their success. This in turn, gradually but very assuredly, communicates itself to their audience and, notwithstanding his or her undoubted talent, their star wanes in front of them.

Production of *Live and Let Die* was not without its troubles for the new James Bond. Before one shot had been filmed, Roger was injured while rehearsing for the spectacular speedboat chase in the film, when the engine of his craft cut out as he was taking a sharp corner at sixty miles an hour. The boat smashed into a large corrugated iron shed on the bank of the Louisiana swamp and Roger, pulled out of the wreckage, was rushed to hospital in New Orleans. He suffered a fractured tooth, a paralysed leg and an aching shoulder but, although he was limping quite badly when he walked, the shooting schedule was not upset, since he was required only to sit in a speedboat for his first few days' work on the film.

Soon afterwards, when the unit had moved to Lake Front Airport, New Orleans, for a sequence where Bond steals a small aeroplane to escape the villain's henchmen, his kidney stone problems re-surfaced. In the middle of shooting a scene in a car, Roger was suddenly gripped by the terrible pains that he knew so well; he collapsed in agony and was taken to a nearby hospital.

Jane Seymour, who played 'Solitaire' in the film, had arrived late the night before, after a hectic journey from England, for her first scene as a James Bond heroine. She says:

> I well remember Roger's kidney stone because it was my first day's shooting. I arrived in New Orleans so nervous, and I had one line to say which was, 'My only regret is I won't be there to see it' – and it didn't make any sense. Before I got to say the line they put me in this enormous trailer. I was sitting there for hour upon hour, and in the end, after three hours I thought, 'This is ridiculous. No one here.' I looked out and everyone had gone. Roger had collapsed from a kidney stone, and they had taken him straight to hospital in his motor-home. They had all left and forgotten about me, and I was left alone there in the aerodrome. After that Roger came back to work very quickly.

Everyone working on the film knew that, if the series were to continue, Roger had to be acceptable to the public as James Bond. Miss Seymour says:

> I think Roger was very nervous because it was his first one, and everyone was very nervous about him being James Bond too. A great deal of the reason why the director, Guy Hamilton, spent no time at all with me was that he was very concerned about Roger being just right. They were very anxious that he shouldn't use the mannerisms he had in *The Saint*, like lifting one eyebrow. I always remember them doing another take to make sure that he didn't come across as the 'Saint' again.

163

Despite the enormous amount of pressure he was under, Roger hid any anxieties that he might have felt, and he is remembered fondly by his co-workers on the film as being perpetually in a good humour, cracking jokes, handing out cigars and patiently listening to their problems. Miss Seymour observed: 'Roger always, on the surface, treats things lightheartedly. One thing I learnt was that the most important thing to him is that everyone around him likes him a lot – especially the crew. If he can make sure that the crew are happy and everyone's happy around him, then he works really well.'

Roger was fortunate in having a number of close friends working with him on the film, including Bob Simmons, the stunt and fight arranger, who had known Roger since they had both played sailors in the London stage production of *Mister Roberts* in 1950, and particularly David Hedison, a friend for the past ten years. Hedison says that he 'couldn't have been more thrilled' when he was told that Roger was to take over as Bond in place of Connery.

Hedison had started his acting career under the name of Al Hedison, and had originally been signed to a long-term contract with Twentieth Century-Fox in the late 1950s, starring most notably in the horror film, *The Fly*. He was clearly intended to continue the mould of darkly handsome leading men at Fox, which had started with Tyrone Power in the 1930s and continued with contract players like John Payne, George Montgomery and Richard Greene. Al Hedison was a very good-looking young man, but with the breakdown of the studio contract system, he lost the support which might have brought him success in films.

By the time Roger and Hedison first met in September 1963, in Cairo, where both men were attending an International Television Festival, he had changed his name to David Hedison. They liked each other immediately and, along with American actor Robert Conrad, spent an enjoyable three days socialising, after which Roger had to return to England to continue filming *The Saint*. Hedison stayed on in Cairo a few more days, not having any pressing commitments, and when he finally headed for home travelled via Moscow and London. Arriving in London, he called his agent and discovered that Roger, aware that David would be passing through, had secured for him a part in an episode of *The Saint*. Hedison accepted at once, and enjoyed the experience of working with Roger immensely. While working in England Hedison was offered one of the leading parts in a projected television series to be called *Voyage to the Bottom of the Sea*.

After some hesitation he accepted the part, on Roger's advice, and was to have a very successful run with the series until 1968.

When David worked with Roger on *The Saint* he did not get the opportunity to meet Luisa as she was in hospital, awaiting the birth of Deborah. They would not meet until seven years later, by which time David was married to a half-English/half-Italian girl named Bridget. Roger and David were reunited in Fortnum and Mason, the store in Piccadilly, London, when they ran into each other quite by chance. Since their first meeting they had kept only spasmodic contact, but from this point on friendship blossomed between both men and their wives, as Hedison remembers: 'It was from December 1970 that we really started getting close and cemented our relationship. Luisa met my wife, Bridget, who is half-Italian, and they would speak to each other in Italian and got on very well.'

David and Bridget had decided to live in England for a couple of years, and Roger and Luisa soon became their closest friends; the two couples were always travelling between Denham and Islington, North London, where the Hedisons lived. Although David had gained the part of Felix Leiter in *Live and Let Die*, Roger wasted no time in attempting to ensure further work for his friend. He himself had been setting up a project with Fabergé, entitled *Getting Rid of Mr Straker*, in which he was to star; he offered David a part in it. (It was intended to be a comedy about an inept secret agent, but when Roger subsequently signed to play James Bond the project was wisely abandoned.) To the present day, Roger will use his influence to get David on a film, as Hedison himself explains: 'Roger will talk to the director and say, "I would like David to be in this film. There's a part he could play." Roger's got a lot of power.'

Both men benefit from working together, and for Roger, with the weight of a film on his shoulders, it is comforting to have a close friend with him. Hedison says, 'Since we are friends it's really lovely being on the set together. I'll go into his trailer and we'll sit down and have lunch, and this and that. It's nice – a pleasant experience.'

One surprising outcome of the growing friendship between the Moores and the Hedisons occurred when David received a telephone call from Dorothy Squires: 'I was quite amazed because I had never met her. She was perfectly charming and asked how we were enjoying England, and invited Bridget and me to go to the races with her. I said, "Yes, well, one day that would be lovely," and then she picked a particular day. I said we couldn't manage that day and that was the end of it. I told Roger. He didn't say anything.'

If Dorothy hoped to cultivate the friendship, she did not get the opportunity. Today the bond between them is as strong as ever, as Hedison unhesitatingly asserts: 'I would kill for Roger. I regard him as the best friend I have.'

For the location filming of *Live and Let Die*, Luisa accompanied her husband; she spent much of her time taking pictures of Roger which she later sold to newspapers and magazines, as well as incorporating some into the paperback book of Roger's account, in diary-form, of the filming of his first James Bond film, which was published in 1973. In the coming years Luisa would frequently be seen on the set of her husband's films taking pictures of him, commissioned by magazines all over the world. With her husband having taken on the mantle of James Bond, Luisa knew that she would have to be doubly vigilant to combat the numerous predatory females who would flirt with him. Jane Seymour remembers a particularly stunned Luisa watching helplessly as a girl made an exhibition of herself over Roger.

Unlike any other film that Roger had worked on previously, there had been a great deal of travelling from one location to another. The company spent about a month in and around the New Orleans area and then flew to Jamaica for five weeks' location work, returning to England for Christmas to work on the interiors at Pinewood. When they got back to England Luisa went to see her doctor, and was delighted to be able to tell Roger that she was pregnant once again. In the early part of the New Year shooting was completed at Pinewood Studios, after which Roger flew to New York to wrap up the film, shooting scenes in Harlem under the watchful guard of six armed black policemen.

Because of the vast amount of location filming abroad for the Bond films, and the majority of the other productions on which Roger was to work in the future, he was able to spend increasingly less time at their home in Buckinghamshire. Work on *The Saint* and *The Persuaders* had been predominantly based at Elstree and Pinewood Studios, or nearby locations, and had permitted him to live a relatively settled life in Denham village. However, the fame that James Bond would bring him was to change this way of life completely and would eventually result in a heart-breaking decision to sell the house in Denham when Roger, like many other actors before him, decided to become a tax exile.

The next ten years were to be a period of almost non-stop film making for Roger, with very little time for anything else. No sooner had he finished one film than he would go straight into production of another. His children would receive their education at schools all over the world, studying in California and eventually at the exclusive Swiss school, Le Rosey, where their fellow-pupils would be the sons and daughters of royalty, politicians, millionaire business tycoons, aristocrats, and other rich film actors. The settled home life that Roger and Luisa, and their children, had enjoyed so much at Sherwood House was fast disappearing.

From now on Roger would, more often than not, be living out of a suitcase or in a specially-rented house – in whatever country he was working. The increasing demands on his time, for publicity tours all over the world to promote his new films, changed his life completely, as he became a member of the jet-set. It would be some time before his lifestyle became more settled once again.

The shooting of *Live and Let Die* over, Roger and Luisa flew from New York to Los Angeles where they stayed at 'Cubby' Broccoli's house in Beverly Hills, which he had kindly put at their disposal for the duration of their visit. Roger had been asked to present the Oscar for Best Actor at the Academy Award Ceremony to be held at the Dorothy Chandler Pavilion of the Los Angeles Music Center on March 27th, 1973. As expected, *The Godfather* and *Cabaret* dominated the awards. In the Best Actor category the favourite to win was Marlon Brando, nominated for his performance in *The Godfather*. Brando had, for the first time since he had won the Academy Award for *On The Waterfront* in 1954, accepted the Academy's invitation, amidst much publicity, to attend the ceremony.

On the night of the awards it came as no surprise when Roger opened the envelope and announced Brando as the winner, but those present were both disappointed and horrified when a young woman dressed as an Indian girl approached the podium after the announcement was made. She put her hand up and Roger, thinking that she was saying 'How', did the same, only to be totally ignored by the young lady as she tried to deliver a statement prepared by Brando, which had nothing to do with the activities of the evening. His primary objections to accepting the award were the industry's treatment of Indians in films and on television. Roger could only stand by helplessly, clutching the unwanted Oscar in his hands. The Indian girl, who called herself 'Sacheen Littlefeather', was later identified as an actress named Maria Cruz.

167

After Miss 'Littlefeather' had been virtually barracked from the stage, all Roger could do was to pick up Brando's unclaimed statuette and take it with him as he retired from the stage.

Together with Merle Oberon who was also taking part in the ceremonies, he had learned at rehearsals the previous day of the sudden death, in Jamaica, of Noel Coward, which brought a particular sadness to several of Noel's other friends who were taking part in the ceremony, including Julie Andrews, Greer Garson, Laurence Harvey and Frank Sinatra – all close friends and admirers of 'The Master'. Within the same twenty-four hours Roger had further cause to mourn – the death of Hugh 'Binkie' Beaumont, the man who had given him his first West End opportunities.

In January 1973, when he was working on the Bond film at Pinewood Studios, Roger had been nominated as the new Chairman of the Stars Organisation for Spastics. The retiring Chairman, Dickie Henderson, the well-known British comedian whose career had started as a child actor in Hollywood, had himself chosen Roger as his successor, after consultation with the President of the Organisation and one or two honorary officials. Roger gladly accepted. He had supported the charity in an unofficial capacity for a number of years, by attending functions they had organised.

The SOS was founded in 1955 when a group of show business personalities met to organise a Ball in aid of the Spastics Society. The charity flourished and in 1973, when Roger became Chairman, they had already built two centres for the care of spastic adults and children: one in Brighton and another in Colchester. His chairmanship was very successful, running for nearly three years, the standard term of office, and was completed in November 1975.

With the weight of his connections in both the film and the business world, Roger was able to achieve a great deal for the SOS. Mrs Sheila Rawstorne, the charity's chief administrator, is full of praise for Roger's work on their behalf: 'Roger took us into the world of glamorous show business. He opened up a whole new world for us with his contacts. SOS had been very successful, but with Roger we went into the big time.'

Although Roger no longer played such an active role in the affairs of Fabergé, he kept the connection open. In an interview in 1974 he said, 'Fabergé are very good. I don't work for them full time any more, but in exchange for getting their product into my films they support charities I am involved with.'

As Chairman of SOS, Roger had to organise committee meetings at the Organisation's London headquarters, just off Regent's Park. These were usually held every six weeks, depending on his other engagements. After the meetings, at which they would discuss the latest fund-raising schemes and the finances of their centres, they would adjourn for lunch. Mrs Rawstorne remembers one of the committee lunches when Roger ate only a small piece of fish, as he was dieting in preparation for a new Bond film. She says that he had dieted so much that his clothes no longer fitted and appeared to hang on him, and he was ruefully eyeing everybody else's plates which were full of food.

If at any time Roger was not available in person to deal with a problem which arose, they were always able to reach him through his secretary, and he would devote his attention to finding a solution as soon as he could. Also, if he was unable to attend one of their functions, he would always ensure that someone of a similar status would be present at the event to give it credibility.

It was during Roger's chairmanship that the SOS were able to build their third centre, called 'Good Neighbours House' – a residential centre for adults, in Camberwell, South London, and of particular interest to Roger, as he had been brought up nearby. Because of the high rate of inflation in Britain then, the estimates for the building costs kept escalating, and there were doubts as to whether the project should be undertaken, but the plan was finally approved after Roger said to them, 'If you don't build now, you never will.'

Roger turned over the first sod at the proposed site for the centre and, the gamble taken, he worked tirelessly to try to ensure that there were sufficient funds. The massive expenses did put the SOS temporarily in debt, but Roger organised a number of lucrative fund-raising events, including the premières of his own films which brought in a considerable amount of money. Perhaps the most glittering occasion was a Charity Ball in Leeds, held in October 1974 in conjunction with the Variety Club, which netted the SOS £10,000. Fabergé had sponsored the event, which was attended by HRH the Duchess of Kent, Roger's fellow board member, Cary Grant, Douglas Fairbanks Jnr and David Niven. Roger also participated in, and organised, other events such as fashion shows, fêtes, and dinners. At one such dinner Mrs Rawstorne remembers that they had hired a cabaret of Greek musicians. Later in the evening, as some of the guests began entering into the spirit of things, they started throwing plates and glasses around the room. Luisa, who always accompanied her husband to these events, was caught in the line of fire and was hit by some breaking china; her leg was also splattered with glass. Wearing a lovely evening dress for the occasion, she was furious as people rushed to help her.

Roger also lent his name to a series of children's adventure books, the royalties from which went to the SOS and the Police Widows' Fund. Mrs Rawstorne says: 'It was really Roger who got us out of financial difficulty.'

Roger's work for the organisation spanned the period of his first two Bond films but despite his increasingly busy schedule he always found time to fulfil his duties as chairman. In November 1975 he invited his good friend, Sir John Mills, to be the next chairman. Mills, who was not at all prepared for this honour, recalls:

Roger suggested me to succeed him as chairman of the SOS without my knowing. At the beginning I was shocked because there is a great deal of work to be done and it is a hard graft as it is an up-and-going charity. The chairman has to travel all over England attending different functions and has to write endless letters. But I was pleased and very glad at the end of my chairmanship that I had done it.

Roger Moore's James Bond was revealed to the world on July 5th, 1973, when *Live and Let Die* had its Royal Charity Premiere at the Odeon, Leicester Square in London, in the presence of HRH the Princess Anne. The proceeds were donated to the National Playing Fields Association, a favourite charity of the Duke of Edinburgh. Roger, as the newly-appointed chairman of the SOS also arranged for them to be involved in the event, securing for them 25% of the profits, which amounted to £15,000.

The publicity for *Live and Let Die* emphasised the supposedly tougher image of Roger Moore as James Bond, compared with his interpretation of Simon Templar: 'The look is meaner, the hair is clipped shorter, the build is more slender, but the character is unmistakable. James Bond 007 is back in town. And he is back with a bang! Roger Moore IS James Bond.'

The film's plot involves Bond's investigations into the murders of a number of agents in New Orleans and the Caribbean, which eventually leads him to Mr Big, played by Hollywood's Yaphet Kotto, who, behind the shield of the voodoo cult, masterminds a plan to flood the world market with heroin grown on his Caribbean island. To establish a lucrative monopoly for himself, he initially intends to distribute the drug free of charge, thereby putting all other dealers out of business while increasing the number of addicts at the same time. The highlight of the film was the extended speedboat chase around the Louisiana bayous.

Most critics reacted favourably towards Roger in the film, and good box office takings seemed to indicate that the public had accepted him. However, this would not be proven until his second Bond film which would show whether he had been able to retain the audience after their initial curiosity to see a new face in the role.

The film was the first in which Bond did not appear in the pre-credits sequence, which instead of showing the tail-end of one of his missions, is used to introduce the murders that he will be called on to solve. Director Guy Hamilton said that this was a deliberate ploy to build up to Roger's first appearance when he is seen, after the main titles, in his London flat, in bed with a voluptuous Italian agent. It was felt that, to avoid the many connotations with previous Bond films that a briefing in M's office would bring forth, it would be better if 'M' and Miss Moneypenny, because of the nature of the emergency, went to Bond's own flat to prepare him for his mission. This would give Bond a different background as his flat had never really been seen, except very briefly in *Dr No*, in the other films in the series.

For his first performance as James Bond, Roger did remarkably well. The light-hearted quips were in evidence in this early effort, although not delivered in the confident manner he was soon to attain, after he had begun to relax in the role. With hindsight, one can see that the pressure of taking on the part did tend to hold Roger back from letting his own personality come through fully. At this time he was still trying to find his own interpretation – not an enviable task considering the public's affection for Sean Connery as Bond.

Roger had been fortunate that he was not the first actor to play the role in the footsteps of Sean Connery; the unfortunate George Lazenby had that impossible task. It is interesting to conjecture what the public and critical reaction to Roger would have been if he had made *On Her Majesty's Secret Service* instead of George Lazenby. When Roger took over the part Lazenby had already borne the brunt of public reaction against a different actor taking Connery's place.

Great stress was laid on the fact that Roger Moore, with his clipped, well-bred accent was much more in tune with author Ian Fleming's own conception of the character, as a drop-out from Eton, much more concerned about his clothes and his food than Connery ever appeared to be. In the books, Fleming intended the character to be a relatively anonymous and colourless but attractive man to whom things happen. His very name was chosen to be as ordinary as possible.

In the film Roger was a very youthful-looking secret agent, looking nowhere near his forty-five years. His Bond was a carefully groomed spy, hair immaculately styled and seldom out of place and clothes distinctly modern; his was a man who was much more likely to follow fashion trends, wearing carefully selected ties, slacks, and safari suits. Roger has always taken a particular interest in how he dresses on-screen, and in his first exercise in 'Bondage' the clothes clearly followed his own blatantly trendy tastes – and James Bond was never trendy.

Roger's approach to the character matched the way in which the series was proceeding. Since *Diamonds Are Forever* there had been a notable change in direction – in the hands of director Guy Hamilton, the easy route was taken and the films became parodies of themselves. When dealing with the outrageous plot-lines of the Bond films, with their larger-than-life villains obsessed with world domination, the real skill is to be able to present it all without giving the audience the opportunity to become aware of its implausibility. In the books Ian Fleming used detailed technical descriptions and identifiable props and backdrops to convince his readers that what they read could actually happen, without stretching the imagination beyond the bounds of credibility. For this to work on film a different approach is necessary in order to carry the audience along. Since the early Bond films this had been done by injecting a sense of humour, but not so much that the film itself becomes ridiculous. The dry asides of Connery's Bond provided the necessary humorous element, showing that he wasn't taking it seriously even though everyone else around him did. Through his cynical charm he achieved a rapport with the audience, allowing them either not to notice, or to excuse, the ridiculousness of the plots. Much of the enjoyment of the films is derived from watching Bond's handling of a situation – he becomes a rebel, but a respectable one, because although he may be able to see through to the tawdriness of a 'sophisticated' world, he is not averse to exploiting its benefits at the same time.

Moore was a victim of the manner in which the films had begun to develop; he also helped to consolidate it. With Guy Hamilton the humour becomes the most important element: he is clearly a director suited to bring out the talents of Roger Moore to advantage, as Roger fits more easily into his view of Bond's world than Connery ever could. The light touch of the director is complemented by Roger's similarly lightweight image, and rather than toughening his image Hamilton actually indulges his star by allowing Roger Moore to play a character who very closely resembles the public image he presents. James Bond would never have smoked foot-long cigars if Roger Moore had not done so first. While Guy Hamilton may have made things easy for Roger to assume the mantle, he did not challenge the actor by forcing him to develop a character beyond his own.

Although claims of large budgets have been made concerning Roger's first two Bond films, it is apparent that the financial investment was not as wholehearted as it should have been. Gone were the elaborate sets; more emphasis was put on real-life locations in order to give the films the aura of expensive big-screen entertainment. On the technical side, Moore's first two efforts were not filmed in widescreen Panavision, but rather in conventional screen size – a peculiar move since the last Bond film to utilise the old-fashioned format was *Goldfinger* in 1964, before Panavision had become widely used. It was strange to be presented with a square-shaped image when the epic scope of wide-screen Panavision had become an accepted element of the Bond films.

The main value of Roger's first two Bond films was to consolidate public acceptance of him in the part. It is significant that these two films marked the final collaboration in the always uneasy and volatile partnership of producers Harry Saltzman and Albert R. Broccoli. Saltzman, eager to get away from a series in which he had lost all interest, was prepared to sell his share in Eon Productions, leaving Broccoli to continue as sole producer.

Eight

ROGER SPENT the time immediately after the release of his first James Bond film helping to publicise the film all over the world, giving interviews and making public appearances. Although he had always appreciated the value of publicising the films in which he appeared, Roger was anxious to fulfil his commitments as Luisa's third pregnancy was well advanced, and the couple wanted to be together at home in Denham when the baby was due. All went smoothly and, on August 18th, 1973, Luisa gave birth to a healthy boy, whom they named Christian David Michael Moore. Roger was now the proud father of two boys and one girl.

While he was looking for a suitable film project to fill the time before the production of his next Bond epic, Roger took time out to record a song for a Burt Bacharach television special, to be called *Bacharach 74*, which was due to be broadcast when he would be filming *The Man with the Golden Gun* in the Far East. For the show, Roger was dressed as a toothless old tramp with a monocle and a moustache, who sits on a park bench singing 'Raindrops Keep Falling On My Head', one of Bacharach's own compositions.

Roger found that being the screen's James Bond opened doors which had previously been closed to him, both socially and professionally, and he was at last being considered for parts in major film productions. Producer Michael Klinger offered him the part of Rod Slater in his intended production of *Gold*, adapted from a novel by Wilbur Smith, to be directed by Peter Hunt, who had worked as an editor on the early Bond films before successfully turning director for *On Her Majesty's Secret Service*. In the film Roger was co-starred with Susannah York and veteran Hollywood actor and Academy Award winner, Ray Milland. Roger was very happy working with Miss York, whom he found very professional, something he always appreciates, and a friendship developed. He was also proud to be working with an actor of the calibre of Ray Milland, as he had had little chance of working with international names in his more recent career.

The role of Rod Slater was that of a tough manager working in the gold mines of South Africa who, while having an affair with the wife of his boss, played by Bradford Dillman, thwarts her husband's plan to flood the mine in order to upset the world's gold standard. In the autumn of 1973 Roger, accompanied by Luisa and their three children, flew to Johannesburg to begin location shooting for the film. The actors and technicians were luxuriously quartered at the President Hotel in the city, and from there travelled to locations in the surrounding area. Roger, along with director Peter Hunt and other members of the cast and crew, actually filmed deep down in the stifling heat of a gold mine in Buffelfontein. Hunt recalls: 'We had to drop down two miles which was horrendous. It was great to start with, and I got tremendously enthusiastic about the mine, but after ten days down there it got very claustrophobic.'

For the climax of the film it was necessary to flood the mine, and initially it was the intention of the company to film the scenes on the South African location. A mock-up of a section of the mine was built above ground but it proved impossible to contain the water, and it was decided to complete the sequence at Pinewood Studios, when they were back in England in the New Year. This was not the only problem which arose during the production of *Gold*, as a row broke out with the technicians' union, ACTT, in England, who threatened to black the film on its release in Britain since they felt it was wrong for British crew members to work in a country that supported apartheid. The union suggested that a mine in Wales could quite easily double for the South African location, but the cast and crew fully supported producer Michael Klinger, who stubbornly continued filming in Africa, despite the union's threats to prevent the film from being shown in Britain. Roger Moore and other members of the cast and crew stated quite clearly to the press that their filming in South Africa was in no way intended to show support of apartheid, which they abhorred, but was in the interests of making the film as realistic as possible.

During their stay in Johannesburg, Roger attended the Christmas premiere of *Live and Let Die*, although he found the film to be cut by about twenty minutes as the love scenes between him and the black actress, Gloria Hendry, had been excised by the censor. By the time the unit returned to England the union trouble was settling down, and there was to be no action taken by them when the film was finally released. Roger was at Pinewood until early March, working on the sequence where he fights to prevent the mine from flooding.

Gold had been made on a very modest budget of one million pounds and, being a solid and unpretentious action film, it was very popular and did well at the box office. It was good for Roger to be associated with a film which had the earmarks of a quality production and at the same time reinforced his image as a tough adventure hero. Roger gave a strong, authoritative performance, although it was a pity that the script did not give him the chance to act with Sir John Gielgud, cast as Farrell, the evil brain behind the plot to sabotage the mine.

The film was completed in good time to allow Roger to prepare himself for his second James Bond film. Before flying to the Far East, where shooting was to begin in Hong Kong and Bangkok, he first travelled to Los Angeles, where once again he had been asked to appear at the Academy Award ceremony. With his friend David Niven also presenting an award, he was able to enjoy the occasion, especially as there was no repeat of the embarrassing incident of the previous year.

Broccoli and Saltzman had been eager to start work on Roger's next Bond film, so as to lose no time in establishing their new star in the role. Just over a year after Roger had completed *Live and Let Die*, he found himself filming in the Far East for *The Man with the Golden Gun* – an interesting experience which he described in an interview at the time:

We were shooting in the Gulf of Siam and you could tell whether it was high or low tide by how fat or thin the dead dog in the river was. I fell in a couple of times. We all did. In the morning you could see the women cleaning their teeth in the river, washing their hair, disappearing right into the water to do the other thing. The hum off the river in the morning was amazing.

Made at the height of the Kung Fu craze the film, not surprisingly, had a martial arts sequence integrated into the plot. Roger reportedly studied Mongolian Kung Fu for two months prior to filming and earned himself a green belt in karate after taking only thirteen lessons instead of forty, which his instructor had said was the normal number needed to reach such a high standard. Viewing the film, it is difficult to see why Roger's extensive training had been necessary, as in the Kung Fu fight sequence he does little more than grimace and kick his opponent in the face. Bob Simmons, the fight arranger on the Bond films, asserts:

Roger doesn't put extensive training into everything. The fight is worked out maybe two days before, or even on the day. What happens is that ten minutes before we're going to do something, I say to Roger:

'I've got an idea. We'll do this . . .'

And he says, 'Yes. OK, let's do it.'

In any case, Bob Simmons is very careful not to allow Roger to perform any stunt that might cause him an injury and hold up production. He states:

If I have a fight sequence with a big fall, then I don't want him to do it because there's a chance that he's going to hurt himself. It's so easy to use a double anyway, because all you've got to do is use a double for the fall and put Roger in a close-up at the end of the fall, and so it's unnecessary to risk a good artist. Of course, he's so keen that he wants to do everything, and I have to say, 'No, you're not doing that, Rodge. All you have to do is a start and a finish – in between, it's a body.'

It would seem unlikely that a man who is reputed not to be particularly well co-ordinated should find a natural ability in martial arts fighting. Roger himself has candidly admitted in interviews that he needs a double when he is called upon to run on-camera, due to his being slightly flat-footed and knock-kneed. If he were a small man it would be less noticeable, but as he is 6'2" tall it tends to be emphasised, and was particularly apparent when Roger handled his own jogging scenes in *That Lucky Touch*, the film he made immediately after *The Man with the Golden Gun*.

In private life Roger enjoys many sports, being particularly keen on skiing, swimming and tennis. David Wardlow, a chief executive of MGM/UA and Roger's one-time agent, frequently plays tennis with him when he is in Hollywood, and corroborates this: 'Roger loves to play tennis, but he plays poorly. He is a bit of a "klutz". It really is quite remarkable when you think of the public's perception of Roger Moore. They think of him as an athletic and fluid person when, in reality, he steps on his feet.'

Nevertheless, this does not prevent Roger from enjoying sports, as he has never been driven by an obsessive desire to win, and claims that this is due to his not being naturally competitive. He plays sports as much to keep himself in good physical shape at all times, so that winning does not mean everything to him. He says, 'I find I don't function properly until I have exercised. I like feeling fit. It is the best feeling in the world.'

Roger has often been asked how he manages to remain so youthful and healthy compared with most other actors of his generation. Once, in a flippant mood, he said that it was through 'never drinking out of a dirty glass' but, in reality, he is very serious about fitness and puts himself through a strenuous work-out each morning, doing push-ups, sit-ups and various other stretching exercises. He once confessed to the bizarre and, from the sound of it, very dangerous habit of hanging upside down like a bat from the banisters at the top of the stairs in his villa at St Paul de Vence, on the French Riviera.

Principal photography on *The Man with the Golden Gun* was completed at the end of August 1974, after twenty weeks of filming, and the film had its Royal Charity Premiere at the Odeon, Leicester Square in London on December 19th, in the presence of HRH Prince Philip, Duke of Edinburgh. Again, part of the proceeds were given to the Stars Organisation for Spastics, amounting to £10,000. Three months before, in September, the premiere of *Gold* had earned them £12,500, all of which was put towards the high building costs of 'Good Neighbours House', the organisation's projected new centre in Camberwell.

The plot of *The Man with the Golden Gun* concerned Bond's efforts to trace Francisco Scaramanga, a hired assassin who charges one million dollars for killing his victims and who appears to have been employed to dispose of James Bond himself. Flying to the Orient, Bond ultimately confronts 'the man with the golden gun' and, in a very tame duel on Scaramanga's private island, succeeds in outwitting and killing him. The most spectacular action set-piece involved Bond driving a car across a broken-down bridge, cork-screwing in mid-air from one side to the other.

In the film, which had the distinction of being the first James Bond film to be shown in Moscow, Roger was much more assured and relaxed in the part, and gave a subtler performance. Under Guy Hamilton's direction, once again, there was a definite move towards a greater toughening of Roger's image, particularly in the scenes when he ruthlessly extracts information from Scaramanga's mistress, played by Swedish model Maud Adams.

The relationship between Bond and Scaramanga was initially intended to be an up-dated equivalent of that between Alan Ladd and Jack Palance in the classic 1953 western, *Shane*, building

178

up to the duel as the climax of the film. Inspired by this idea, the part of Scaramanga was originally offered to Jack Palance, although it was finally played by Christopher Lee. As a villain, Christopher Lee was a marked improvement, compared with the unimpressive Mr Big, as played by Yaphet Kotto, in *Live and Let Die*, although like all Bond's adversaries, he was certainly no great villain in the tradition of Conrad Veidt or Basil Rathbone, the prime exponents in this field in films of the thirties and forties. They had the ability to portray villainy with a charm that never dissipated their essential menace, but added to it. It is a sad comment on today's films that hardly any actors seem able to match their skill in such parts, and the few exceptions are sadly under-used in this field. Laurence Olivier's portrayal of Szell in *Marathon Man* is a lesson in ultimate screen villainy which deserves a place alongside those of Hollywood's great screen villains. Only Robert Shaw as Red Grant in *From Russia With Love* has so far provided James Bond with a worthy adversary, and this omission has continued to remain one of the most unfortunate faults in the series.

Despite Roger's better performance as Bond, the films were slipping into a very pedestrian formula and had lost their ability to surprise and excite their audiences, as they had done in the past. This was reflected in the lukewarm critical reaction to the film and its less successful performance at the box office, particularly in America. The series appeared to have run its course, destined to peter out in a series of meaningless adventures. The confidence of the 1960s was no longer evident – the films had become too much of a national institution, relying on the glories of the past to lure their audiences into the cinemas. It was after finishing this film that Saltzman took the opportunity to pull out of his partnership with Broccoli, being only too happy to rid himself of future involvement in the series. Roger had been contracted to star in three Bond pictures, but after only two it seemed that his longed-for dream might turn sour. Fortunately for him, 'Cubby' Broccoli still retained his enthusiasm and confidence in the future, and was determined to put James Bond on top again.

In the middle of 1974 Roger had read the script for a projected comedy entitled *Heaven Save Us from Our Friends*, based on an idea by Moss Hart. He considered it to be one of the funniest scripts to have come his way in years and eagerly agreed to producer Dimitri de Grunwald's suggestion that he should star in it. In July de Grunwald approached Sir Peter Hall, the eminent

179

director of Britain's National Theatre, and asked him to direct the film. Hall was told that the film would star Roger Moore and Sophia Loren. He agreed to look at the script and thought it was quite funny, but he had certain reservations in his mind about the project and knew that if he accepted the offer he would be doing so purely on the strength of the financial inducements.

Negotiations continued into the next month when Sir Peter Hall, together with de Grunwald, Roger, Luisa, Dennis Selinger and Carlo Ponti, representing his wife, Sophia Loren, had dinner at the Ritz Hotel in Piccadilly. However, both Sir Peter and Miss Loren backed out of the planned film, which was eventually directed by Christopher Miles with Susannah York in the female lead, thus reuniting Roger with his co-star from *Gold*. Sophia Loren and Peter Hall's professional judgment proved correct as the film, retitled *That Lucky Touch* during production, was not the sophisticated 'screwball' comedy that Roger had thought it to be, and the completed film was unworthy of the talent involved.

The story centres on the romance between Michael Scott, a rather ineffectual arms dealer, with Julia Richardson, an unattractively aggressive correspondent for the *Washington Post*. Julia is repulsed both by Michael's profession and by his romantic approach towards her, and much of the film's running time is spent showing his vain attempts to break down her resistance. Rather improbably, she is finally won over by his charm, which enables them to unite at the end of the film. Supported by an international cast that included Shelley Winters, Lee J. Cobb and Donald Sinden, and made partly on location in Brussels, the film can only be described as a sorry effort.

As it was made during the winter of 1974/5 and filmed for the most part at Pinewood Studios, Roger was able to spend more time with his family. Although baby Christian had accompanied him when he was making *The Man with the Golden Gun* in the Far East, he had been separated from Deborah and Geoffrey, who remained at school in England. They kept in contact with their father by telephone, while Luisa travelled backwards and forwards all the time, checking on both halves of her family.

When one views *That Lucky Touch* one is amazed that Roger was not more careful in the selection of his work away from the Bond films, since a production of such poor quality, lacking the polish that a cinema audience expects, might have done his career irreparable harm, especially at a time when he was still trying to establish himself as the screen's James Bond. The film presented him as a ridiculous, rather than humorous, figure, lacking any real charm and, not surprisingly it was a box-office and critical failure.

In March 1975 Roger was again in South Africa with director Peter Hunt and producer Michael Klinger, making another film version of a Wilbur Smith novel. Klinger, who had taken out options on several Wilbur Smith books, thought that *Shout at the Devil* had all the makings of a great adventure film, and was determined that it should be his next production. From the start he wanted Roger Moore and Lee Marvin for the two lead characters, and he had secured Roger's agreement in the previous July. Roger was to play an English adventurer, Sebastian Oldsmith, opposite Lee Marvin as Flynn O'Flynn, a drunken ivory poacher, in this adventure yarn set in Portuguese East Africa prior to, and during, the first months of World War I. Marvin, a supporting player in Hollywood for many years, had come to prominence in *Cat Ballou* starring Jane Fonda, which won him a very surprising Oscar, particularly as he was in contest with Olivier, Burton and Steiger, actors of supremely greater quality in performances commensurate with their great names.

The fifteen-week shooting schedule took place entirely on location in South Africa and Malta. During the time that they spent in Africa, Roger, Luisa and the crew stayed at Port St John on the Indian Ocean, a small holiday resort between Durban and Cape Town, which had originally been a half-French/half-British colony. When the unit moved to Malta, Roger and Luisa lived in a specially-rented house.

Roger and Lee Marvin got on tremendously well, helped in part by their mutual fondness for Jack Daniels whiskey, and this great rapport came through in their work together on the screen. Director Peter Hunt recalls: 'They were very funny together and liked each other a great deal. They would socialise and get drunk together in the evenings, although they never had thick heads in the morning.'

In the April of the following year, at the London première of the film, Roger was most effusive in his praise for Marvin, and told the press: 'I love this gentleman. Thanks to him I have given my best performance ever. I can only be as good as the other guy. Working with Lee Marvin hauls you up, forces you to try to reach his level.'

Jean Kent, reunited with the young bit-player she had helped when making *Trottie True* more than twenty-five years earlier, had a small part in this film, and she remarks on Roger's determination to remain pleasant with the people with whom he works: 'Roger gets on with everybody – he makes a point of it. He has natural good manners and he intends to get on with everybody.'

Once completed, although the rough-cut of the film was very much liked by those who saw it, it was thought that cinemas would be reluctant to book the film because of its long running-time, which would limit the number of daily performances. Michael Klinger had seen the story as encompassing a broad canvas and wanted to make a lengthy film, and it was scripted, devised and shot on that basis. Faced with the possibility that the film might lose bookings if it were not cut to a more acceptable length, there was no option but to edit it severely. Hunt claims that about fifty minutes were excised – and the film suffered as a consequence.

After finishing *Shout at the Devil* in June, Roger, with Luisa and their three children, flew to Rome, where they visited her family. Spending so much of his time abroad, with his salary climbing higher, Roger was beginning to show signs of discontent with the heavy taxation in Britain. He denied that he intended to follow the many other actors who had gone into self-imposed tax exile, because he was loathe to part with the family home in Denham. The summer of 1975 marked a break in Deborah and Geoffrey's education in England, as at the start of the new school year in September they were to be sent to school in Los Angeles. It was only a matter of time before Roger would change his mind and seriously consider leaving England.

While in Rome he was approached to make a thriller in Italy and, towards the end of the year, found himself at the De Paolis Incir Studios in Rome making a film entitled *Gli Esecutori* for producers Manolo Bolognini and Luigi Borghese. Apart from American actor Stacy Keach, who played Roger's side-kick Charlie in the film, the cast was made up entirely of Italian actors, unknown outside their own country. They would later have their voices dubbed into English when the film was released in Britain in 1976 under the title *The Sicilian Cross*.

Filmed partly on location in both San Francisco and Italy, Roger was cast as Ulysses, a half-Sicilian educated at an English law school who becomes a corrupt San Francisco lawyer working for the 'Mob'. The screenplay, credited to no less than six writers, was incoherent in its handling of the attempt of a Mafia boss to leave 'the family', having become tired of the life he has been leading. The story is a mish-mash of car chases, murders, family vendettas, drug smuggling, religion and soft-focus flashbacks – all of which defy logical explanation. The film looked no more than it was – a low-budget feature cashing in on the name of Roger Moore to give it a push into the international market.

Roger undoubtedly saw the film as giving him a chance to play a less sympathetic character, to divest himself of the heroic image with which the public associated him, but once again his enthusiasm for a change of pace for its own sake blinded his better judgment. The film can only have done him harm, severely damaging his credibility as a leading man for top-quality productions. For Roger to have accepted the film in the first place defies comprehension; he was fortunate that he had already contracted to make *The Spy Who Loved Me*, which would erase the memory of *The Sicilian Cross*.

It is not surprising that 'Cubby' Broccoli has expressed concern over the choice of films that his James Bond actors have appeared in. He must have had a very poor opinion of Roger's professional judgment at this time, for since making *The Man with the Golden Gun* Roger had managed to become involved in two very mediocre productions: *The Sicilian Cross* and *That Lucky Touch*. Broccoli says:

> There were pictures made by Roger that were quite awful, and I think it does reflect on the success of the Bond picture if the public are turned off by some of the pictures that are made – but we have no control over that. It always does worry us. That's why we hope that the pictures that are made by the people who do Bond are good and that they are successful.

Next Roger agreed to play Arthur Conan Doyle's legendary sleuth in a two-hour NBC-TV production, *Sherlock Holmes in New York*, set at the turn of the century. Roger was adequate in the role, but came nowhere near the definitive performance of Basil Rathbone. His best moments were when he had to don various disguises, most notably when he impersonated the great Bandinia, an eccentric Italian escapologist with rangy, long hair, a drooping moustache, a built-up nose and a wild Italian accent. He clearly enjoyed submerging his own character in this way, and threw himself into equally vivid portrayals of a New York cab driver and a religious fanatic with a beard and flowing robes.

Throughout his career Roger has displayed a remarkable gift for mimicry, although this facet of his talent has been sadly under-used. In *The Persuaders* he was given his best opportunity in an episode based loosely on the classic film comedy, *Kind Hearts and Coronets*, which had starred Sir Alec Guinness. In the episode Roger impersonated various members of the Sinclair family, both male and female, demonstrating yet again his genuine gift for comedy, which makes one regret that he has not been able to find a film script of this kind to do justice to his ability.

In the Sherlock Holmes TV-movie his Dr Watson was played by Patrick MacNee, with fellow cast members including the film director John Huston as his arch-enemy, Moriarty, and Charlotte Rampling as Irene Adler, who enlists the help of the famous detective when her son Scott is kidnapped. Nine-year-old Geoffrey Moore, sharing his father's dressing room, made a brief appearance as the young boy who is rescued by Holmes.

In April 1976 Roger returned to England to attend the premiere of *Shout at the Devil*, but he stayed only a few days before flying back to Los Angeles. Because he had rarely been on British soil in the past couple of years he was treated as a tax exile, but he knew that when he returned again in the summer to start work on *The Spy Who Loved Me*, which entailed a much longer stay in the country, he would be presented with a heavy tax demand. Prior to re-entering Britain he went to Rome for a holiday and to visit his in-laws, accompanied by Luisa and the children.

Trouble appeared on the horizon in April 1976 when Roger's first wife, Doorn Van Steyn, now living in Washington with her third husband and working as a freelance photo-journalist, suddenly hit the headlines with the announcement that she was planning a book entitled *Roger and Doorn – The Saint that Ain't*, in which she would reveal the truth about his days as a struggling young actor.

Her book has not been published.

Nine

THERE WAS a gap of almost three years between the release of Roger's last James Bond film, *The Man with the Golden Gun*, and *The Spy Who Loved Me* – the longest lapse of time between films since the series started. This was due partly to the change in the production set-up after Harry Saltzman had sold his interest in the series to the distributors, United Artists, and partly to delays which had prevented an earlier starting date. Because of the mention of SPECTRE, the fictional organisation developed jointly by Ian Fleming and Kevin McClory, in the original shooting script, it was decided to rewrite the offending parts. Years before, Kevin McClory had gained certain rights to the James Bond character through his involvement in the fashioning of a film script with Ian Fleming, utilising the Bond character in the days before Saltzman and Broccoli had turned him into one of the most lucrative cinema attractions in the world. Fleming had published his book *Thunderball*, basing it on the script that both men had worked on, without acknowledging McClory's participation. McClory took Fleming to court and, after a long legal battle, the court awarded him limited rights to the Bond character. These rights meant that McClory was invited by Saltzman and Broccoli to act as producer on the film version of *Thunderball* in 1965; they also paved the way for Sean Connery's return as James Bond in *Never Say Never Again* in 1983, which was a re-make of the former film. McClory's conflict with Eon over SPECTRE was part of a long series of legal battles between the two parties over Broccoli's quite understandable attempts to ensure that the Bond film rights remained solely his concern.

Production on *The Spy Who Loved Me* began on August 31st, 1976 at Pinewood Studios where they worked for four weeks before moving out to the island of Sardinia, where a spectacular car chase was filmed. By October the unit was filming in Egypt among the Great Pyramids of Gizah, on the Nile and in the city of Cairo. Production was made doubly arduous due to the excessive heat and the often poor conditions, although director Lewis Gilbert remembers that Roger managed to keep them all laughing, even when they were filming around the Pyramids at

185

four o'clock in the morning, surrounded by 'smells like you never smelt before'. With much relief all round, shooting was resumed at Pinewood in November, where the largest sound stage in the world had been built to recreate the interior of an oil tanker, used by the villain in the film to hijack nuclear submarines. After an eighteen-week shooting schedule the First Unit completed work on the film at the end of December.

The Spy Who Loved Me was a high point in Roger Moore's film career, putting the James Bond films right on top again, making a fortune for all concerned, and establishing once again a distinctive style of entertainment which the public was eager to see. Right from the opening scenes the film exudes confidence and Roger Moore is in total command of the role, looking marvellous and delivering his lines immaculately. From the pre-credit sequence when Bond skis off a mountain top to elude his pursuers, to a very inventive car chase in which Bond's Lotus Esprit becomes amphibious, and concluding with a pitched battle inside the giant oil tanker, the action is deftly handled and excitingly staged. There are many echoes of the past, including Bond's gadget-ridden Lotus Esprit which harks back to the Aston Martin in *Goldfinger*, the ski-chase reminiscent of *On Her Majesty's Secret Service*, and the battle in the tanker which is presented on the mammoth scale of the climax inside the volcano in *You Only Live Twice* – but the whole treatment is fresh and very entertaining.

Involving James Bond's attempt to stop millionaire Carl Stromberg's plan to destroy the nations of the world and create a new civilisation under the sea, the story has 007 working alongside his female Russian counterpart, Major Amasova, played by Barbara Bach. The male–female rivalry is exploited to the full, giving Roger the opportunity to play off his leading lady, in a manner reminiscent of the inter-play so successfully achieved with Tony Curtis in *The Persuaders*. Although Curt Jurgens' portrayal of the villain, Carl Stromberg, was not particularly striking, he was allied to a very effective 7' 2" henchman named Jaws, who killed his victims by biting through their jugular veins with his metal teeth. Bond was once again pitted against an adversary who appeared to be indestructible, dumbly enjoying the violence of his profession, as Oddjob had done in *Goldfinger*.

By the middle of the 1970s the world had changed a great deal from the previous decade, when the world of James Bond could be taken more seriously. In the 1960s, a decade which saw the building of the Berlin Wall, the Cuban Missile Crisis and the

Vietnam War, the world was insecure, with the Cold War still very much a reality. By the 1970s the James Bond of that period was no longer relevant, and desperately needed new life pumped into it, to re-establish its former glory. At a time of more cordial relations with the Soviet Union it was topical to have James Bond working alongside an attractive Russian agent, against a common enemy.

Lewis Gilbert, who had previously directed Sean Connery in *You Only Live Twice* in 1967, felt that the character of Bond should be brought more into line with Roger Moore's own personality:

Roger is a totally different person to Sean – as a type and as an actor. When Sean Connery killed someone in a Bond film you really believed it, but with Roger, somehow, because of his sense of humour, you didn't quite believe it. So I went more for Roger's humour, because Roger is a wonderful light comedian, which is very rare today. So we changed the character of Bond so that it could fit Roger.

When asked what had influenced his interpretation of Bond, Roger said, 'I always played it with a certain reluctance to kill because my only key to playing Bond from the books was the beginning of one of Fleming's stories where it said that Bond was on his way back from Mexico, where he had eliminated somebody. He didn't like killing particularly, but he took a pride in doing his job well. That's my key to it: I don't like killing.'

He has also said, 'I play it differently to Sean: a little lighter, a little more tongue-in-cheek. Maybe if Sean had continued after the first six, he'd have sent it up a bit more too.'

Lewis Gilbert appreciated the challenge for Roger of playing James Bond after Sean Connery:

It was a very difficult thing for Roger to take over that role, and I'm not sure that he was particularly successful in the first two, *Live and Let Die* and *The Man With The Golden Gun*. In fact, *The Man With The Golden Gun* was right down in America and didn't do very well, but *The Spy Who Loved Me* was right up, because then he ceased to be Sean Connery. If I had anything to do with it, I think that my contribution was that it was quite wrong for Roger to continue to be Sean, because he wasn't Sean, and now I think Roger is more acceptable than Sean around the world because new generations have come up that didn't know Sean, but who know Roger, and to them he is James Bond now.

Broccoli too was under pressure to show that he could make Bond work his way, without his partner of the past twelve years, as Lewis Gilbert recalls: 'For Cubby it was a huge undertaking in the sense that he had to prove something. He was on his own, and if the film were a disaster people would say that he couldn't do it without Harry Saltzman. I think Cubby was conscious of that and worked very hard on the film, probably more than he did on other films.'

The hard work that Broccoli put into making the film paid off, as the film received very good notices everywhere in the world and was an enormous hit at the box-office. Of his Bond films, it remains Roger Moore's own personal favourite, as he felt 'Its story worked the best, and I think it had the right degree of humour.'

Broccoli said at around this time: 'When Connery quit we were sure that there would be no more Bonds. But the public would not let us stop making them. The demand was greater than ever. And with Roger taking over the role in such style, we have gone from strength to strength.'

After the phenomenal worldwide success of *The Spy Who Loved Me*, 'Cubby' Broccoli was eager to sign Roger to another three-picture deal, but Roger's shrewd business sense told him that it would be preferable to negotiate the terms for one film at a time. Roger was in even greater demand for big-screen adventure films, having firmly established himself as one of the major film stars in the world – he was ranked sixteenth among the Top 25 Box Office Stars for 1977. However, the parts which were to be offered to him would not stretch his ability as an actor, but merely called for him to play an extension of his own personality. Asked once at an interview why he did not turn down the cardboard-hero parts at which he excelled, in order to play something with more weight to it, he replied, 'But then nothing else comes along. It just so happens that I am offered, in the main, derring-do heroes. There is an attitude among the people who put up the money for the films, and they say, "No. We know that in that type of film we will get our money back. We may be taking a risk if we use him in something else."'

Roger has also said very frequently, 'It's better to be a highly-paid personality than an out-of-work actor.'

At this time, together with his long-standing friend, producer Robert Baker, Roger was involved in the television series, *The Return of the Saint* with Ian Ogilvy, although he was not able to take an active part because of his own film commitments. However, as partner with Baker in the new venture, he earned money from the sales of the series to television.

When producer Euan Lloyd read the book *The Wild Geese* before publication he decided that, with its story of a group of mercenaries hired by an influential banker, Sir Edward Matherson, to rescue the kidnapped leader of a small African state, it was ideal film material, and he set about securing the rights to make a film based on the novel. In the screenplay that was commissioned it was decided to merge two characters from the original book into one, creating the charming, easy-going, devil-may-care Shawn Fynn, a part for which Lloyd thought Roger would be ideal. With this in mind, he contacted Roger's agent and put the proposition to him. Negotiations were slow because of what was thought might prove to be a problem of billing, and also because of the size of the role which was, in reality, no more than a supporting part. Compared with the two other lead parts among the mercenaries, Fynn had relatively little screen time, his dialogue consisting mainly of one-liners.

Meanwhile, Richard Burton's representative, having read the script, contacted Lloyd on his own initiative and told him that he felt the part of Colonel Allen Faulkner, the leader of the mercenaries, was tailor-made for his client. Terms were settled, and Richard Burton was signed for the part. By then Roger had read the script and liked it, and after confirmation that Burton had agreed to star in the film, he happily accepted the offer to play Shawn Fynn. The role of Rafer Janders, played by Richard Harris, had originally been offered to, and accepted by, Burt Lancaster, but this proved impossible. Roger Moore was second-billed after Richard Burton.

With the final cast assembled in the autumn of 1977, the film unit travelled to the tiny health spa of Tschipse, in South Africa, just below the Rhodesian border. The town, once a stopping station between Salisbury and Johannesburg, had prospered into a popular holiday resort, built around the mineral baths there. With modern facilities in the spa town, the climate, and the surrounding terrain it was the perfect location for the film. The cast and the crew took over the whole complex of about one hundred *Rondavels* (or Roundhouses), the most luxurious being allocated to the principal stars.

Within the industry there was considerable surprise when it was discovered that Euan Lloyd had cast Richard Burton and Richard Harris, both known 'hellraisers', in the film. But the situation was not as explosive as it might have seemed, as Lloyd knew that Burton and Harris were both professional men and, despite their past reputations as 'hellraisers', were dry when working and would not be drinking alcohol while they were in Africa. Both actors had been told that they were courting death if they drank and, sensibly, they abstained.

Roger, for his part, received no such threat and was able to enjoy the Martinis that he loved so much. Lloyd recalled: 'Some people get drunk on one or two drinks, but Roger can drink four or five Martinis and not even stumble over a word. He's a superb drinker – but with moderation.'

Lewis Gilbert, when directing Roger in *The Spy Who Loved Me*, had noticed that he would take particular pleasure in going out drinking with the members of the crew in the evening, particularly if Luisa were not with him on the location: 'Roger is an incredibly generous man, and it is very difficult to pick up a bill when he is around. He loves to take six or seven boys from the unit and have a real great piss-up. He likes to drink, although he is not in any way an alcoholic, and to be out with the boys, telling stories and joking, is his idea of a great night out.'

Euan Lloyd says that even if Roger had been out on a lively drinking session with the crew the night before, he would always be up and ready for work on time the next morning. Filming would start very early, as soon as there was sufficient light, because it was often too hot to shoot later in the day. At 6.30 each morning, Lloyd would make his customary circuit of the camp, ensuring that everything was in order for the day's work, and would regularly see Roger outside his hut in the camp:

Roger is tremendously fitness conscious, so he gets up in the morning and does his exercises. If he's had a few stiff ones the night before he's a little grumpy for five minutes, but it quickly disappears once he's had his eggs and bacon. Time and again I would find him outside his African hut, which was on a knoll, standing there just wearing tiny swimming trunks, holding a hose over his head with cold water pouring all over him. Then he would shake himself like a dog and say, 'Oh, dear boy! There you are. I'll be with you in two minutes.' And he'd put the hose down, go inside and off he'd go to work, and never ever show any signs of a bad night.

It was while they were on location in Africa for *The Wild Geese* that Roger celebrated his fiftieth birthday. So loved was he by everybody in the cast and crew that Euan Lloyd decided to give Roger the birthday of a lifetime, by throwing a surprise party for him in the middle of the African bush. Despite Roger's outwardly gregarious personality, he has a tendency to be bashful and modest, and would have been horrified if he had known about the planned surprise. Luisa, who accompanied her husband for half the location shooting, was sure that he would be too embarrassed to attend if he knew what was going on, and so it was arranged that, on the day, everybody would wait at the allotted spot for Luisa to deliver Roger by car. To persuade him to get into the Land Rover, Luisa told him that Richard Burton had suddenly been taken ill, and that they must go and see him. After driving for some time along dirt-track roads, deep into the African bush, Roger became suspicious and began to question her, asking, 'Where are you taking me! Richard doesn't live this way!' Luisa explained that Burton had been visiting someone when he was taken ill, and she managed to keep Roger off the scent until they arrived at the spot where the whole cast and crew were waiting.

Roger was greeted by the vision of a camp site with its boundaries marked out by a number of enormous fifteen-foot tree trunks, piled high with sticks and brush, blazing brightly, sending off sparks and flashes into the night sky. All around them on large tables were bottles of champagne and vast quantities of food – and in the unlikely setting of the African bush in the middle of the night, every member of the film unit wished him a happy birthday. Roger was thrilled and totally overwhelmed by the gesture.

Apart from this very memorable fiftieth birthday party, the location was a very happy one for all concerned. Roger had the added bonus of being able to take advantage of the abundant supply of the finest Havana cigars which, in South Africa, were cheaper than anywhere else in the world. The film was also the first occasion that he had worked with director Andrew V. McLaglen, the son of actor Victor McLaglen. Roger admired his professionalism and the two men struck up a close friendship.

Late one evening, just before filming was completed in the Transvaal and the unit was due to return to England to complete the film, Richard Burton called on Euan Lloyd at his hut in the camp, and said to him:

I'd like to talk to you quite seriously about something that's been bothering me. I've been re-reading the last scene in the picture. You know you've got one of the biggest stars in the world in the picture: Roger. We can't leave him out at the end, as the audience are going to be frustrated. Don't you think he should be with me at the end of the picture – even for a moment or two?

Lloyd readily agreed and, after Burton's suggestion, prompted only by his admiration for Roger, the character of Shawn Fynn was satisfactorily concluded in the plot, in the way a major character role should have been treated. Otherwise Shawn would have disappeared without trace after flying the survivors of the mercenary group out of Africa to safety.

Back at Twickenham Studios in England, Roger had the thrill of working with his boyhood idol, Stewart Granger, who was cast in the film in the small but important part of Matherson, the banker who betrays the mercenaries. Although Roger was not given the opportunity to share screen time with Granger, he was pleased to be working on the same film – for the first time since 1945, when Roger had worked as an extra on *Caesar and Cleopatra*. Lloyd remembers Roger and Stewart Granger being introduced when both were on call at Twickenham for some night shooting, and that they greeted each other with a great bear hug

Granger had heard the stories about Roger's adulation of him when he was a young boy, and would mention it frequently, saying, 'Why the hell anyone wants to be like me I just don't know, especially when he has risen to such enormous heights – higher than anywhere I've ever been in my life. I'm flattered, the guy must be an idiot – but he's still my buddy.'

Granger was impressed at Roger's ability to stay on top in a profession like theirs, and would say, 'He's bloody marvellous. He's up there and he's flying 55,000 ft and he's holding. Not many of us can do that. Everyone changes – but Roger doesn't.'

Roger's career continued to run at a high pitch. He was asked to head the cast in an all-star comedy thriller entitled *Escape to Athena*, playing Major Otto Hecht, the genial commandant of a prisoner-of-war camp on an island in Nazi-occupied Greece during World War II. Also in the cast were Telly Savalas, Claudia Cardinale, Elliott Gould and David Niven, whose son, David Jnr, co-produced the film with Jack Weiner. Filmed on the island of Rhodes in the spring of 1978, and ably directed by George Cosmatos, it was an enjoyable romp, in which Major Hecht, in charge of an enforced archaeological dig on the island, decides to join forces with his former prisoners when they break out of the camp. Switching allegiance to the side of the Allies, he then aids them in destroying German military installations on the island.

During production of the film in Rhodes, Roger announced his intention to become a tax exile in the near future, and just after the London premiere of *The Wild Geese* in July, in the presence of HRH the Duchess of Kent, he decided to withdraw Deborah and Geoffrey from their private school in Denham, and arranged for them to attend the exclusive Le Rosey in Switzerland at the start of the new school year in September. Shortly afterwards, Roger finally cut his ties with England when he sold their beloved Sherwood House, for a reported £160,000, and went to live in the South of France.

The sale of the house was a hard decision for Roger and Luisa who had lavished a great deal of time and effort towards making their Denham home a perfect retreat for themselves and their children. Luisa would later say: 'It was one of the saddest decisions we ever made. Roger still can't bring himself to talk about it. When we sold our lovely house I cried for a week. But you can't grieve for ever over a pile of bricks.'

The house on the French Riviera that Roger had decided to buy was in the picturesque village of St Paul de Vence, halfway between Nice and Cannes. He had first spotted it when he was staying with their friends, Leslie and Evie Bricusse, who themselves owned a house in the village. Although at the time it was only half-built, the grounds on which it was set, affording a magnificent view of the Mediterranean, were enough to convince him that he had made the right decision.

Leslie Bricusse saw the grief that Luisa suffered over the upheaval of leaving Denham, and says of her:

I think Luisa got lost when they had to leave England. She had no roots, and she went through a very difficult transitional phase, which I totally understood because an Italian mama needs to know where everything is. During this period she was very unhappy, and the lack of a base made her very fractured for a long time, and it manifested itself in all sorts of ways which I think people misconstrued as Luisa changing. But it wasn't a personality change – she was just in turmoil. She and Roger suffered a lot during that time, not knowing where they were.

It would not be until they bought their luxury chalet in Gstaad, Switzerland, an area introduced to Roger by actor Curt Jurgens, that they would finally come out of this period of limbo, and feel settled again in a real home.

In August, to celebrate the start of work on Roger's fourth James Bond film, *Moonraker*, 'Cubby' Broccoli hosted a lavish party on the fashionable Île de France boat restaurant on the right bank of the River Seine in Paris. It was a fitting opening gesture for the film, which was unusual in being a Franco–British co-production. Costs in England had become prohibitively high, and it was decided to move production over to three studios in Paris. As shooting costs were to escalate uncontrollably to a figure of thirty million dollars, making it the most expensive Bond film ever, Broccoli would have had good cause to begrudge the extravagant party on the Seine.

With the great success of *Star Wars* all over the world, and the ensuing science-fiction boom, it had been deemed more appropriate to delay production of *For Your Eyes Only*, which had been announced as the successor to *The Spy Who Loved Me*, and to turn instead to *Moonraker*. Instead of adapting the plot of Ian Fleming's original novel for the screen, which was discarded as out-of-date, the story was brought into line with modern developments in space-travel, incorporating the hijacking of an American space shuttle by the villain, Hugo Drax, who plans to breed a super-race on a space station orbiting the earth, while he destroys the earth's human population with a deadly gas.

The shooting of *Moonraker* was the usual round of globe-hopping to exotic locations all over the world. From Paris the crew moved to Italy, where they filmed in and around the canals of Venice. After a break for Christmas, production shifted to South America, but Roger had an unfortunate start to 1979 when he collapsed in Paris from the pain of a kidney stone, while en route from Switzerland, where he had spent the holiday, to Brazil. He was admitted to a Paris hospital but quickly recovered and, discharging himself, was on his way to join the unit in Rio de Janeiro by January 7th. As well as filming in Rio, they also

travelled to the spectacular Iguacu waterfalls on the Brazil–
Argentine border. With a long daily trek to the location, under
intense heat and humidity, Roger found the jungle filming exhausting and was greatly relieved when they returned to Paris to
complete principal photography. After a massive twenty-eight-
week shooting schedule, the film was completed on February
27th, with an end-of-shooting party held at Regine's exclusive
restaurant in Paris.

Though Roger could say of his previous Bond film, that it had
achieved the right balance of humour and action, this was not the
case with *Moonraker*. Although United Artists, spurred by the
huge box office success of *The Spy Who Loved Me*, had allowed
the film a considerable increase in budget, this was no recipe
for making *Moonraker* into a more entertaining film than its
predecessor.

Roger played Bond in his own inimitable style, but the humour
went to extremes with its overt emphasis on 'camp' situations,
which showed him riding on a horse, dressed as a gaucho, to the
strains of the music from *The Big Country*; rejecting the advances
of a male employee at his hotel in Rio; and driving a gondola-
turned-hovercraft around St Mark's Square to the apparent delight
of the tourists, with processed shots of pigeons doing double-takes
at the extraordinary sight. The action is handled too lightly,
most notably during the boat chase in Venice, where the action
degenerates into a series of visual jokes rather than a situation in
which Bond is fighting for his life. When Bond, wearing a gas
mask, accompanied by 'M', walks into what he believes is a
laboratory for the manufacture of a deadly nerve gas, only to
find that overnight it has mysteriously, and unconvincingly, been
transformed into Drax's office, he becomes a figure of fun. The
audience laughs at James Bond as a buffoon; he is no longer
sharing the joke with the audience – he is the joke. The film was
also marred by the return of 'Jaws' who loses all menace when,
smitten by love for a grotesque travesty of a girl with pigtails, he
becomes a sentimental oaf, turning to the side of good. The
emphasis on the gadgets and special effects swamped the story,
pushing the human characters into the background, giving director
Lewis Gilbert little hope of duplicating the success of his previous
effort. The battle in the space station at the end of the film was
too static to create any excitement, and the film generally lost all
touch with reality and stands as the weakest in the series. The
producers were justifiably swamped with letters from outraged

Bond fans who despaired at seeing their hero abused in such a way.

One asset that Roger had in the film was his leading lady, American actress Lois Chiles, who, as Holly Goodhead, gave a humorous performance which perfectly matched Roger's own, producing some of the strongest scenes between him and any Bond girl to be found in the films. Again, it appears to have been tension between them on the set which produced the necessary creative spark.

Criticism aside, when the film opened, after a spectacular Royal World Première, attended by HRH Prince Philip, on June 26th, it again did huge business all over the world, although both director Lewis Gilbert and producer 'Cubby' Broccoli were aware that they had not made as well-balanced a film as *The Spy Who Loved Me*, and sensibly determined to return to a more realistic plot-line for their next production.

Shortly after Roger had completed the shooting of *Moonraker*, he returned to the South of France to rest after the exhausting past few months. On the evening of April 7th, he and Luisa dined with Mr and Mrs Robert Dallas, the architect who designed the house they had bought in St Paul de Vence. After a very pleasant evening Roger drove home in their apple-green Range Rover. They came to the junction with the main road down to Cagnes-sur-Lieu, which was particularly dangerous as it opened on to a sharp bend where visibility of oncoming traffic was poor – and doubly worse at night. Roger pulled out into the main road, turning right, but, at the moment the Range Rover took the bend, a Citroen sped around the corner and there was a violent collision.

The owner of the Citroen was Maurice Mouillet, an airport cashier, who was driving with his 24-year-old fiancée, Isabelle Courouble. The aftermath of the crash saw Roger nursing a sprained wrist, while Luisa had been lucky enough to escape unhurt. The young couple in the Citroen were not so lucky, as their car did not have the strength to withstand the impact of the crash. The mechanic at the garage to which the wrecked car was taken said afterwards: 'The occupants were lucky to survive at all. The Citroen is a complete write-off. The entire front was caved in by the force of the impact, and there is blood all over the passenger compartment.'

Maurice Mouillet suffered a broken arm and leg, as well as cuts and bruises to his face, but most of the blood splattered around the car belonged to his fianceé, Isabelle, who had the most horrific injuries. Along with Maurice, she was rushed to the Hôpital de la Foutonne in Antibes, where she had to have a hundred stitches for three long gashes across her face. In addition, a metal splint had to be inserted into her left thigh and, according to reports, surgeons spent seven hours removing glass from the cornea of her punctured left eye, which she eventually lost.

The verdict of the accident was not decided until nearly two years later, in January 1981, when Roger, accused of 'unintentionally causing injuries' to two people in a traffic accident, was fined 2,000 francs (about £200).

At the time of the crash, Roger had been growing a beard for his forthcoming film, which had the working title of *Esther, Ruth and Jennifer*, and in fact he appeared at the premiere of *Moonraker* wearing it with pride. Earlier the previous year he had become friendly with Jack Davies, the writer and father of John Howard-Davies, the child star who had played the title role in David Lean's celebrated screen version of *Oliver Twist*, who was one of his neighbours in the South of France. Jack Davies, having just completed the script for *Esther, Ruth and Jennifer*, based on his own novel, was anxious that Roger should read it and give a professional opinion on its merits. Very generously, Roger agreed – a favour which was to pay off handsomely.

Davies unconvincingly says that he had no thought of Roger being suitable for any part in the screenplay, but when Roger popped round the next day he was very complimentary about it, telling him, 'I think it's one of the best scripts I ever read.'

Nothing further was said until three days later when Roger again wandered over to the writer's house, and asked him, 'What would you think about me playing the lead character of "ffolkes"?'

The unusually named 'ffolkes' was an underwater sabotage expert who is commissioned by Lloyd's Insurance to devise a means of overcoming a hijack attempt on an oil rig. Far from being the standard dashing man-of-action that Roger had been accustomed to playing, Rufus Excalibur ffolkes was a character he could get his teeth into. He is a gruff, no-nonsense tactician, who with his own group of personally-trained commandos, lives in a damp, windswept castle on the edge of the sea, with only his beloved cats for company. He is an old-fashioned English eccentric who dislikes women and gets his relaxation in life from needlepoint and straight whiskey. His taste in clothes, with his Edwardian-style jackets, thick sweaters and woollen bobble hats, reflects his per-

197

sonality. He is not a humorous man given to smiling or cracking jokes readily, but a total professional whose work dominates his whole life.

When Roger expressed an interest in playing the part, Jack Davies says, 'I didn't think it was an awful idea. I thought it was strange.' He asked Roger to let him think about it, and later in the day, with his proposition in mind, he rang his agent, only to discover that Roger had already contacted him about the script. He realised that Roger was serious about playing the part and said, 'It's such wrong casting that he might just be right.'

By May 1979 Roger was in Galway, on the west coast of Southern Ireland, making the film version of Davies' book, and very pleased to have something to take his mind off the terrible car crash the month before. As it turned out, he was correct in his thinking from the start and the film provided Roger with one of his best roles and a welcome departure from his accepted screen image. The story concerned two men: Kramer, the ruthless leader of a gang of terrorists wanted across four continents for his crimes, and 'ffolkes', the expert called in to combat and thwart Kramer's carefully laid plans for the destruction of an oil rig. Kramer and his men plant bombs on the supply vessel, *Esther* which they hijack, and also on the drilling rig, *Ruth* and the production platform, *Jennifer*, and then threaten to detonate the bombs if a £25 million ransom is not paid.

The film gave Roger the opportunity to work opposite one of Hollywood's finest actors, Anthony Perkins, whose portrayal of the demented Kramer undoubtedly dominated the film, although Roger held his own with a strong performance; James Mason, another of Roger's boyhood heroes, lent able support.

Lea Brodie, who played Sanna, the only woman on board the hijacked supply ship, was surprised at Roger's reaction to working with Mason:

James Mason made Roger very nervous. The first day that he turned up on the set, Roger was doing a scene with a bottle, a glass and a live cat. He doesn't like props at the best of times, and there he was juggling this really malicious moggie which was digging its claws in, trying to pour drinks and say his lines at the same time, and who should be just in that twilight beyond the lights, standing by the camera, but James Mason – just watching him. Roger told me later that he felt like a student actor with a professional watching. He was so nervous. It was

198

quite an eye-opener to see that Roger suffered from nerves just like the rest of us do.

Roger had a further reason to be nervous because the cat had been secretly drugged, and those who knew were sworn to secrecy because of James Mason's well-known love of animals – and cats in particular. Although it is common practice to sedate animals in this way, they knew that if Mason had found out he would not have listened to reason and would most certainly have walked off the picture.

Miss Brodie remembers Roger as 'very easy-going and charming – a charm which didn't break all the way through shooting, even the midnight shooting when we were all feeling sick on the high seas.'

All the location filming took place in Galway, and Roger helped Miss Brodie considerably by his thoughtfulness towards her as an inexperienced actress among such famous names as himself, Perkins and Mason. When bad weather prohibited shooting, they were all stuck in the hotel together, playing cards or table tennis to pass the time. Roger was also fortunate in having a couple of his closest friends working on the film with him: the director Andrew McLaglen and David Hedison, for whom Roger had secured the part of King. Roger introduced Lea to David saying, 'He's a great friend of mine. We go back a long way.'

Then, Miss Brodie says, 'They looked at each other and laughed. It was obviously a very jokey, long-established, relaxed friendship. They went off together a lot. It was just understood that Roger would like to see David privately and they would both walk off together, smoking cigars.' Another close friend who dropped by to see Roger while they were in Ireland was Richard Burton, who had reason to be there at the same time.

Anthony Perkins said that he found it a delight to work with both Andrew V. McLaglen, 'a sweet man', and Roger Moore whom Perkins calls 'utterly professional – a real film star'. He also adds, 'I liked Roger Moore. He has a great personality, uniquely his own. He is a very talented actor and a lovely man to work with.'

Perkins would have enjoyed playing more scenes with Roger than were allotted to him in the screenplay. Miss Brodie says, 'Roger admired Perkins. They were so totally different. Tony would psyche himself up for a scene, while Roger would tend to diffuse any tension about a scene by making a joke or a deliberate mistake when it helped.'

While on the Irish location, Lea Brodie witnessed one of the drawbacks of being a famous film star associated with tough action roles. She remembers:

Sometimes we would go into a local pub in the morning, after a night shoot, to get bacon and eggs. There would occasionally be fellows who, recognising Roger, imagined that he was James Bond. They wanted to start trouble and would look for a fight, which was a bit nasty sometimes. They would say things like, 'Oh, you think you're so terrific' or 'Are you looking at my girl?' It seems he has to meet this quite a lot, and he just used to laugh and side-step any confrontation. It is a strain for Roger, always being recognised and having people come up to him. There is that slight threat from quite a few men – there is always one who wants to prove himself. I was concerned for him because I thought that maybe I wouldn't have kept my temper so well if I'd been a man, but he just laughed and said, 'I'm a natural coward.' But I really think it is because the trouble would be continuous otherwise.

Before the film was released in the cinemas the title underwent a number of changes from its original one of *Esther, Ruth and Jennifer*. During production it was changed to *North Sea Ransom*, and before being released in Britain it became *North Sea Hijack*. In the United States the film went out under the title of *ffolkes*, which was not guaranteed to cause queues at the box office, and a fuming Roger Moore, when he heard of the change, said, '*ffolkes* means nothing!'

When the film was eventually shown on network television in the States it was retitled *Assault Force*.

North Sea Hijack did not fare as well as expected at the box office, which was a great pity since it was a tight, well-directed thriller by Andrew McLaglen which deserved better. Author Jack Davies was pleased with the final result, particularly with his friend's performance: 'I liked Roger immensely in it and I thought he made the picture. He has never done anything so good.'

The long separations, because of the amount of work that Roger was being offered, caused rumours in the press in November that his marriage to Luisa was breaking up. Both Roger and Luisa were quick to deny the truth of such rumours. What rankled Luisa was the amount of time that she was having to spend alone in the South of France, supervising work on their new home. With Deborah and Geoffrey at school in far-off Switzerland, and only young Christian with her most of the time, she felt that her whole world was falling apart. She also knew that Roger was soon to be off to India to begin work on yet another film, and she was quoted as saying, 'I miss all my friends. I miss London. I miss Rome. And I'm fed up with having the builders in here for nearly a year.'

It should have come as no surprise to Roger or Luisa that rumours of trouble within their marriage should start so easily. Their relationship had always been marked by its vitality, and the tempestuous nature of their quarrelling. Friends and newspaper reporters have witnessed their noisy arguments, and there are numerous reports of Roger having objects thrown at him, in anger, by his spouse. Roger is outwardly good-natured, easy-going and courteous, while Luisa is flamboyant, emotional and spirited – in fact, Roger is very English, and Luisa is very Italian. But their friend Leslie Bricusse asserts: 'Roger and Luisa are very compatible, while they do not appear to be, but it is a wonderful example of opposites attracting. They couldn't be more different.'

They both enjoy the excitement of their fights and arguments; Roger has always been attracted to strong personalities like Luisa. From the start their relationship was explosive, as Leslie Bricusse relates: 'Luisa has always been physically violent with Roger. When she was twenty-four or twenty-five she would say something, and she would kick or punch Roger in public – and I don't mean playful slaps – I mean really belt him.'

Too often their relationship has been misunderstood by people who tend to misjudge Luisa. Their personalities are totally different: Roger finds himself incapable of being rude or off-hand while Luisa, on the other hand, does not have the temperament to be as patient as Roger when, for example, as happens so frequently, he is asked for his autograph. Roger's natural reserve makes him avoid unpleasantness, and he is reluctant to say 'no' to anybody while Luisa, quite rightly, sees that people exploit his good nature, and tries to protect him from himself. Euan Lloyd says of Luisa: 'She's very outspoken and very direct – and that's her quality. I think he's damn lucky to have her because they are a perfect balance.'

Even when he is exhausted after a strenuous day's work, Roger will still take time to talk to his fans, and he always behaves impeccably towards them. Luisa, conversely, takes a different attitude. She has said, 'I trust nobody until they have proved themselves, but Roger, he trusts too many people and they take advantage. He has such courtesy even when he is tired but sometimes he comes home and he just screams and screams and I stay quiet.'

Although he knows that it annoys his wife, Roger will still do what he feels is his duty towards his admirers, as he once explained: 'Luisa's emotions aren't just on the surface – they're everywhere. She's completely Italian, she's Mount Vesuvius. I always get into terrible trouble with her because of people asking for autographs when we're leaving a place and she is waiting. She says I should be like an Italian star and walk out and push them all to one side.'

Often when Roger and Luisa are having a quiet dinner together in a restaurant they are interrupted in the middle of their meal by fans asking for an autograph. Even under such circumstances, when an interruption of this kind is rude and ill-mannered, Roger is unfailingly courteous. Not only does he sign an autograph, but he takes a genuine interest in those who approach him, asking their names, where they come from and what they do. It is on occasions like these that Luisa gets most exasperated.

She does her utmost to protect her husband from continual harassment, and whenever they travel together on an aeroplane she ensures that Roger sits by the window, where there is less chance of him being disturbed. When the family go skiing in Switzerland, Geoffrey also keeps watch over his father, following closely behind ready to protect him from interference, if necessary. Roger's world-wide fame has made it virtually impossible for him to walk in the street without being recognised and having people approach him.

The disadvantages of being married to a screen idol, apart from the long separations because of the vast amount of filming done on location, are considerable. In a business where marriages all too frequently break up under the pressures and temptations that are present, the role of the wife is unenviable. Luisa, like Roger, values her marriage and her family above anything else, and is fiercely determined to protect it at all cost. She is often criticised for the amount of time that she spends with him on location but, being married to a rich and handsome film star, she knows that there is no shortage of candidates only too willing to fill her shoes. Elspeth March, ex-wife of screen heart-throb Stewart Granger, through bitter experience of her own, sympathises with Luisa's position and understands why she accompanies Roger as often as possible: 'That's the way you have to be in this business because Roger is vulnerable, and I think that if a woman is determined to get a man, she can – unless she sees the shut-off sign – and Luisa has that loud and clear.'

Ever since they first met, Luisa has had to learn to become watchful of possible rivals for her husband. A number of people have commented on the marked change in Luisa's character from the sweet young girl whom Roger brought back from Italy in the early 1960s to the harder woman of today. But the experience of living under the pressures that she does has taught her the need to adopt a strong attitude towards potential threats. On one occasion, soon after they had first met, when they were filming *The Rape of the Sabine Women* in Yugoslavia, Luisa went back to their hotel room to fetch a coat, and discovered a pretty female fan lying naked in the bed, in the hope that Roger might come into the room. Seeing an equally startled Luisa, she grabbed her clothes and ran out. When Roger was making *The Saint*, actress Sylvia Syms remembers Luisa getting particularly annoyed when they had an au-pair girl living with them at home, because every time Roger walked into the room the girl, who was meant to be looking after their children, would just stare at Roger as if she were in a trance until he left the room.

Luisa has adopted a very sensible attitude and admits that she always makes a point of making friends with the beautiful girls who work on the Bond films because, she says, 'As friends they lose all thoughts of seducing my husband.'

Leslie Bricusse says of her: 'She protects her husband and her children as only an Italian mother can. She is a wonderful woman, she has got a huge heart, she is generous, she is kind, and she is very strong.'

Bricusse remembers one incident when he and his wife Evie were dining at the White Elephant restaurant in London, with Roger and Luisa, in the late 1960s when the mini-skirt had just come into fashion. As both couples were enjoying their meal the door opened and in walked a very pretty girl, wearing a mini-skirt. Roger and Leslie stopped eating and stared at her as she walked over to a table, accompanied by her escort. Bricusse recalls that 'Luisa turned round, looked at Roger, and belted him across the face.'

A startled Roger said, 'What was that for?'

'That's-a just in case!' came Luisa's quick reply.

It must be difficult for her to deal with the adulation that Roger receives. He is always the main focus of attention, so far as the public is concerned, and this is not easy to cope with for a woman as glamorous as Luisa, who occasionally has minor regrets about abandoning her own career. Naturally she found it unbearable when she had to spend her time in the South of France, supervising the completion of their house in St Paul de Vence, pushed into the background while her husband fulfilled work commitments all over the world.

Ten

In DECEMBER 1979, after spending only a week at his home in St Paul de Vence, Roger flew to India to start work on *The Sea Wolves*, adapted from James Leasor's book, *The Boarding Party*, published the previous year. The story centres on a group of ageing civilians, members of a volunteer cavalry regiment – the Calcutta Light Horse – which had last seen action in 1900 during the Boer War. In 1943, bored with a life of useless inactivity during wartime, they undertook a hazardous mission to silence a German spy ship, the *Ehrenfels* which was transmitting the whereabouts of Allied shipping to Nazi U-boats from the safety of the neutral port of Marmagoa in the Portuguese colony of Goa, on the Indian Ocean.

Once again the film was directed by Andrew McLaglen. It also reunited Roger with Euan Lloyd, the producer of *The Wild Geese*. While making the film in Goa, Roger said: 'I have been very fortunate that every film I have made over the last few years has been with a director who is a good friend, with whom I have a rapport and who has basically the same sense of humour.'

As well as McLaglen, with whom he was working for the third time, he cited Lewis Gilbert, who had directed *The Spy Who Loved Me* and *Moonraker*, his most recent Bond films. It is possible that Roger's preference for working with friends may have affected the limitations he has put on his acting. Throughout the history of film-making some of the most successful results have been achieved by the combination of a big star and a first-class director, human yet unyielding to his cast and crew in the pursuit of the best possible results. The fact that Roger has worked endlessly with friends at the helm of his films could be the reason for his not having attained the dramatic eminence of contemporaries such as Peter O'Toole, Richard Burton, Paul Newman and Robert Redford.

Although *The Wild Geese* had been popularly accepted in Britain and some other territories, it had been less successful in the United States. Euan Lloyd saw in *The Sea Wolves* another yarn for his three *Wild Geese* stars but, by 1979, he found it difficult to secure the finance for such a venture based on the

205

same three actors. The Americans stated quite definitely that a Hollywood star must play the role of Lieutenant-Colonel Lewis Pugh, of the Special Operations Executive in India, in charge of the mission.

While Roger Moore was most acceptable for the part of Captain Gavin Stewart, also of the SOE, Pugh had to be played by a top Hollywood star, capable of assuming a near-perfect English accent, or what the Hollywood people would call a Bostonian-type accent. The only suitable actor, who was still a name to be reckoned with at the box office, was Charlton Heston. Though only three years older than Roger Moore, he was offered the role and the producers awaited his acceptance with high hopes. Heston had kept his career on an even keel and was still a great favourite with the mass audience of filmgoers, but unfortunately he did not like the script and promptly turned it down out of hand.

The problem became acute, and the only actor who came to mind and who, in terms of age, was a better choice was Gregory Peck – who was some eight years older than Heston, although he had long since lost his position as a top box office star. Producer Euan Lloyd was inspired to cast Gregory Peck in the film after seeing him in Roger's company at the Dorothy Chandler Pavilion in Los Angeles after the Academy Award ceremonies. Lloyd says: 'After the show I stood on the steps of the theatre looking down into the foyer and there they were, standing together. Peck by this time had grown a moustache and the image was exactly what I wanted. They looked so good together that the following day I made my moves.'

As Peck was in dire need of a film, an affirmative answer was received soon after he had read the screenplay. Lloyd had originally intended to cast Richard Harris in the other principal role of Colonel Bill Grice, but he was really too young for the part, and again the Americans wanted a third, more 'bankable' name above the title. Gregory Peck suggested his friend and neighbour in the South of France, David Niven, who would obviously be acceptable to Roger – the other member of the Riviera triumvirate. Euan Lloyd readily agreed that his old friend Niven would be both an ideal choice for the part and a 'name' above the title, and the planned line-up of Peck, Moore and Niven was deemed more acceptable to the money men in 1979 than the previous Burton, Moore and Harris team.

Unbeknown to producer Lloyd, however, the agents for all three men had sent a copy of the screenplay to Mr Niven, at Mr

Peck's request, and he had turned it down. Gregory Peck was determined that his friend David Niven, an actor most suitable for the part of Bill Grice, should be in the film – but the problem was how to persuade Niven to reverse his decision.

Lloyd met with the agents, who told him, 'We can't make the deal for the picture unless Mr Niven plays that part.'

It became apparent to Lloyd that for a higher salary Niven might waive his objections and accept the role. The agents told him, 'Maybe for a lot of money he would consider doing the picture.'

Lloyd recalls: 'The talks went on for hours, and in the final analysis they wanted to double Niven's money.' It was obvious by now that David Niven had to appear in the picture. Lloyd says: 'The only way I could agree to it was that he would get my salary, and mine would be deferred out of profits – and that's exactly what happened.'

Roger did not find out until the party for the end of shooting in Goa. He went up to Lloyd and said, 'Euan, I've heard the story and I know it's true. It's not one of the happiest stories to come out of Hollywood, is it?'

So David Niven received the princely sum of half a million dollars for his contribution, while Lloyd says he was not paid for the three years' work he put into setting up the film. When it was shown, it was obvious that David Niven's mortal illness had commenced, altering him radically into a rangy, thin man with a drawn look on his face. His voice had lost much of its earlier appeal, and that he was obviously ill may in part have been the reason that Niven first turned the picture down. His agent, Dennis Selinger, felt that it could not have been pure greed that spurred the actor to accept; he says, 'David Niven never wanted for money. He liked to earn good money and had made a fortune.'

The location shooting in the paradise spot of Goa, where Lloyd had once again quartered his actors in luxurious comfort right on the edge of the sea, was particularly enjoyable for Roger, who was co-starring with two of his closest friends, as well as working with Lloyd and McLaglen again. David Niven said of Roger at the time, 'I don't know another actor in the business who is so grateful for what has happened to him, and so enjoys it.'

They were working in gruelling temperatures, sometimes reaching 140 degrees, and there was great relief at the end of each day's shooting. Lloyd recalls: 'When he got back after finishing his day's work, Roger was the first to rush into the ocean – clutching his

Martini in his hand. He was followed in rapid succession every night by Gregory Peck, David Niven, Trevor Howard and everyone else in the cast.'

Luisa accompanied Roger on the location, pleased to be with her husband rather than alone at their house in the South of France, although occasionally she would fly out to Bombay or New Delhi on shopping trips. Young Christian was with his parents throughout the filming, and sixteen-year-old Deborah visited them briefly before having to return to school in Switzerland.

Roger regarded the film as one of the happiest he had ever worked on. This cannot be said for close friends, Peck and Niven, who had a very unfortunate week during production. Lloyd remembers: 'Something happened one day when Niven passed a remark that upset Mrs Peck, and they didn't speak to each other for about a week. It was very unpleasant, but I can't remember what it was about.'

He adds, 'The problem with Niven was that you were never sure whether he was serious or not, because he was so witty with his remarks.'

Roger would run away from trouble of this sort, sensibly avoiding involvement in arguments between friends. Niven, perhaps aggravated by the heat and his increasing frailty, would also occasionally let remarks slip out that were unkind towards Roger, and not nearly so charitable as his remarks to the press.

If Euan Lloyd and director Andrew McLaglen had problems with the cast, or the excessive heat was causing tension on the set, they always had a helpful ally in Roger. The producer is full of praise for his ability to diffuse trying situations:

Having Roger around is like having a shower in the middle of the jungle where the humidity is unbearable. Sometimes the temperature on a film becomes very difficult to live with but Roger, just by walking on the set, by his presence and a quick remark – never unpleasant, but some intelligent remark – can cool a situation. Time and again I have seen him take the heat out of a potentially dangerous situation.

The finished film leaves one in some doubt as to whether Euan Lloyd's decision that fateful night in Los Angeles at the Dorothy Chandler Pavilion was a correct one. Moore's name on the marquee most certainly brought in the public, but it is questionable whether Gregory Peck, with the exception of his performance in *The Omen* in 1976, was any longer in the forefront of current motion picture stars after his 1966 film *Arabesque*. In the film Mr Peck gave such a low-key performance as the real-life hero, Colonel Pugh, that all credibility and tribute to him were lost. David Niven's participation in the film was, for whatever reason, sadly dismal. The rest of the *Sea Wolves* were made up of distinguished character actors from Great Britain who shared little action and less dialogue.

Roger Moore, direct from another triumph as James Bond, was a fine piece of casting as Captain Gavin Stewart, and he gave a very good account of himself in the film. Unfortunately for Roger, he did not have a thoughtful, clever and persuasive ally in a strong position close to producer Euan Lloyd – there was no Richard Burton to draw Mr Lloyd's attention to the fact that his star, Roger Moore, was barely represented at the conclusion of the story, when most of the action takes place.

The story, based on fact, was a good one and was well worth telling. The production values of the film were fine, but Andrew McLaglen was hampered by what can only be admitted as the miscasting of Roger's co-stars. As a successor to *The Wild Geese*, it was not in the same class, and the lead players did not have the same on-screen rapport as those in the former film. The film was dedicated to Earl Mountbatten, who had been helping with research for it before his tragic assassination in August 1979, and who was himself an honorary Commander of the Calcutta Light Horse.

In early 1980, just before Roger finished shooting *The Sea Wolves* he flew to Los Angeles to receive the Hollywood Foreign Press Award as World Film Favourite. At the time there was talk of Roger's next film being *High Road to China*, in which he would co-star with Bo Derek but, for whatever reason and luckily for Roger, the film never came to fruition and was later made with Tom Selleck and Bess Armstrong in the lead roles.

After completing *The Sea Wolves*, Roger went skiing with David Niven in Gstaad, but interrupted the holiday to continue his hectic working schedule. He flew to France, where he was to be directed, for the first time, by his old friend Bryan Forbes in *Sunday Lovers*, an anthology of four comic stories based on the common theme of adulterous weekends in different countries. Each segment was made by a separate director: Gene Wilder wrote and directed the American episode, Edouard Molinaro directed the French, Dino

Risi the Italian, and Bryan Forbes the English. The screenplay for the episode in which Roger appeared was written by his friend, Leslie Bricusse, and was filmed on location at Roquetailiade Castle near Bordeaux. The French location was chosen because the castle looked suitably English; it had belonged to Oxford University in the fifteenth century and was also convenient for Roger, now living as a tax exile in France. Shooting in Bordeaux meant that he would not have to sacrifice any of the precious few days he was permitted to work in Great Britain.

In the Forbes segment Roger was cast as a lecherous cockney chauffeur, alongside Lynn Redgrave as the nymphomaniac Lady Devina. Reminiscent of a traditional English sex farce, the action involves the goings-on when the lord of the castle goes away for the weekend, and the chauffeur takes his place. The butler, who is gay and a transvestite, and was played by Denholm Elliott, has also invited a dizzy air hostess, performed by Priscilla Barnes, over from a Heathrow hotel, and both she and Lady Devina end up in bed with the chauffeur at the same time. Both actresses enjoyed working with Roger, and Miss Barnes said, 'He is an actress's dream. He's helpful, generous and isn't on an ego trip. They don't make men that way any more.'

Roger hoped that the film would at last give him an opportunity to display his touch for light comedy, but unfortunately it had a very limited release, and came and went so fast that director Bryan Forbes says that he never had a chance to see the completed film.

Immediately after making *Sunday Lovers*, Roger was scheduled to make a guest appearance on *The Muppet Show*, recording his contribution in May, although it was not due to be broadcast until October, when it would launch the last series of this popular television show. Working with the Muppets gave Roger the chance to spoof his own image as James Bond. Looking immaculate in his dinner jacket and black tie, he performed a comedy sketch with Miss Piggy, in which she tries to seduce him. She serenades him with 'I'd like to get you on a slow boat to China', while Roger stares at the camera in disbelief, confiding to the audience, 'I can't believe it. She's singing to me!' Roger tries to fend off her advances, telling her that he is expecting his date to arrive at any moment. She arrives and turns out to be another pig – called Annie Sue!

Walking off-stage Roger treads in a custard pie which has been left carelessly on the floor, and he points out to Kermit what he

210

has done. After Roger has retired to his dressing room, Kermit says, 'He's so suave I never would have noticed unless he'd mentioned it.'

In the second half of the show Roger sang 'Talk to the Animals' from Leslie Bricusse's musical *Doctor Dolittle*. The choice of song was a good one since it was tailored for the wholly individual style of Rex Harrison, who had starred in the film. Roger was able to give a fair imitation of the inimitable Harrison in a very pleasant performance, surrounded by furry animals, who greeted him with a familiar 'Hi, Rodge', as he passed by singing the song. Midway through the performance he found himself involved in a battle on-stage in which he despatches spies, who have disguised themselves as cute little animals, with kicks and karate chops. He clearly enjoyed immensely the opportunity to send up his screen image, which he did with all the urbane charm one would expect of him.

Roger's performance gives an interesting indication of his possibilities as a musical performer, especially in view of his declared ambition to be in a musical. His friend Leslie Bricusse had written the musical version of James Hilton's *Goodbye Mr Chips*, which was made into a film with Peter O'Toole. The film became one of Roger's own favourites, and he had often told Bricusse that he would like to perform it on the stage one day. When Sir John Mills starred in the Chichester Festival Theatre production in August 1982, he was very disappointed. Bricusse says: 'I never realised that Roger was serious about *Goodbye Mr Chips*. Every year he used to say to me, "I'm saving that for my old age. I'm going to do that later on." He knew all the songs inside out and backwards.'

The next time that Roger saw Bricusse after Mills had done the show he said, 'You bastard! You let someone else do *Chips*.'

Bricusse replied, 'Well, you couldn't have done it anyway.'

Roger had to agree, but said, 'I was saving that for later. It was going to be my swan-song.'

Bricusse feels sure that Roger has the ability to perform *Chips*, and he qualifies this by saying, 'Roger has got a pleasant voice and he can sing in tune. If he worked on his voice to prepare for a production, to the extent that Chips needs to sing, he could do it.'

Roger has also said that he would like to work on a film musical, and once admitted that he desperately wanted to direct the film version of Sandy Wilson's *The Boy Friend*. He was not at all

211

happy with Ken Russell's extrovert production. So far, Roger's heavy work schedule has left him with insufficient time for him to be able to embark on such ventures.

After *The Muppet Show* Roger was cast as one of a number of guest stars, including Farrah Fawcett, Dom De Luise, Dean Martin and Sammy Davis Jnr in Burt Reynolds' latest starring vehicle, *The Cannonball Run*, directed by Hal Needham. About an illegal coast-to-coast road race, it was a typical Burt Reynolds action film, with endless stunts and car chases, bolstered by the comic appearances of its array of guest stars. It was a sure indication that Roger had reached the top rank of international popular stardom, when he was offered the cameo role of Seymour Goldfarb Jnr, a rich Jewish boy who thinks he is Roger Moore. Roger's light-hearted contribution proved to be the most memorable in the film, poking fun at his own image. The principal cast met on only three occasions, as for the most part they spent the entire film in separate cars. Roger said, 'I was ordered to shoot my piece in a week, and I had two months off in the middle of it.'

In July, when he was in London for the Royal Premiere of *The Sea Wolves*, Roger appeared to have finished with James Bond forever. In the previous February, he was reported to have said, 'I don't want to take another six months out of my life playing James Bond again.'

By July, negotiations between Roger and 'Cubby' Broccoli over his fee for the next film, *For Your Eyes Only*, had broken down. Roger felt himself to be in a particularly strong position after the success of his last two Bond films. The amazing box office records established by *The Spy Who Loved Me* had been smashed with the release of *Moonraker*, and Roger knew that, with a winning formula on their hands, he could afford to push his price up. Shooting on *For Your Eyes Only* was due to start on September 15th, but at this late stage no deal had been concluded that satisfied both parties. Of the accepted trial of strength over Roger's salary before each new Bond film, Broccoli says: 'Peculiarly enough, we have put Roger in the fortuitous position that he is in. I think it is fortuitous being Bond, but having done that we normally get pummelled by the agents to get more money.'

Broccoli, in order to prepare himself for the possibility that Roger might not agree to play Bond for the fifth time, had been testing newcomers for the part. Roger discovered what was happening, and at the *Sea Wolves* press conference in London he stated firmly that he would not be playing Bond again. Although Roger's cat-and-mouse game with his producers was all too familiar, on this occasion he appeared to be in earnest about forsaking the role that had made him an international film star.

Since there was a chance that another actor would be playing Bond in *For Your Eyes Only*, the first scene in the script was tailored to give the newcomer to the part a link with the past, by showing him in a country churchyard putting flowers on the grave of Tracy Bond, his wife of one day who had been killed by Blofeld in *On Her Majesty's Secret Service*. Inevitably, by September a contract with Roger had been signed, but it was decided to keep the scene in the screenplay for Roger to perform. Roger's sharp business-sense in refusing to commit himself to another three-picture deal after finishing *The Spy Who Loved Me* was beginning to pay dividends with a reputedly seven-figure fee.

The film's story involves Bond's search for the top-secret ATAC (Automatic Targeting Attack Communicator) system, which has been sunk in the Mediterranean in a trawler used by the Royal Navy. Bond meets a beautiful young girl, called Melina Havelock, after she has killed assassin Hector Gonzales at his hillside retreat with a bolt from her crossbow, in revenge for the murder of her parents, who had been trying to trace the secret device for the British government. Melina joins forces with Bond on his search, which takes them to Cortina in Italy, as well as to the beautiful Greek islands and mainland Greece itself. With the help of a Greek smuggler, Columbo, Bond sets out to thwart the plans of millionaire businessman Aristotle Kristatos, who intends to sell the ATAC system to the Russians.

Shooting began, as planned, on September 15th at the luxurious Villa Sylva at Kanoni on the island of Corfu. The hillside villa was used as the setting for Hector Gonzales' hide-out and, as has become standard in the Bond films, was decked out with glamorous girls lounging around the swimming pool. One of the girls was a six-foot-tall, twenty-seven-year-old model from England, who worked under the name of Tula.

Tula had not always been the busty, green-eyed beauty with long, golden-brown hair who appeared in the film. In 1974, at the age of twenty, she had undergone the last £1,000 operation, at London's Charing Cross Hospital, which transformed her from Barry Cossey to Caroline Cossey. The story did not break until after the film was on general release, when the *News of the World*'s headlines read: 'James Bond Girl Was A Boy' and 'Tula – The

Sex-Change Model'. She had supposedly been recognised by residents of the small town of Brooke, in Hampshire, where Barry Cossey spent his youth. Her big break came when she was selected from among many hopeful models to appear in the latest James Bond film and was flown to Corfu for the filming. She enjoyed working with Roger, and especially admired his sense of humour, although she admitted that it was very difficult to keep a straight face when they were filming, because of the remarks Roger made. She remembers getting on particularly well with Roger, when she and a couple of the other girls were invited out to dinner with him and director John Glen, because they both spoke Italian.

Roger was not in the best of health while he was making the film. He had been told by doctors that he had a high cholesterol level in his blood, and so was forced to adhere to a strict diet of grilled fish during location filming in Greece – not very pleasant for a man who has highly cultivated gourmet tastes. He was also taking antacid pills to relieve heartburn, and admitted to having trouble with his back, which was aggravated if he sat in a draught or slept awkwardly. This problem was not helped when he was badly knocked about during filming of a fight sequence in an ice-hockey rink in Cortina, early in the New Year.

Five weeks were spent filming in Corfu, after which the unit moved to Kalambaka in mainland Greece, where the climax of the film was shot at the 600-year-old Meteora monastery, perched precariously on top of a thin rock outcrop. Filming continued at Pinewood Studios and on location around the London area, moving to Cortina D'Ampezzo, high in the Dolomite mountains of Northern Italy, after Christmas.

While in Cortina they received the tragic news of the death of Bernard Lee, who had played 'M' in all the Bond films up to *Moonraker*. Shortly before his death he had been preparing to make another appearance as 'M', but when he went on the set at Pinewood he was unable to remember his lines. A month later, in February, tragedy again struck the unit in Cortina itself, when the twenty-three-year-old Italian, Paolo Rigon, was killed when the bobsled he was in flew off a bend in the bob-run, crashing into a clump of pine trees. They had been filming a sequence when Bond, following the sled on skis, was being pursued by a man on a spiked-wheel motor cycle, adapted to grip snow and ice. Other problems occurred in Cortina because of the unseasonable lack of snow in the town itself, which necessitated transporting lorry-loads from higher ground to the town centre for filming. By the end of April, Roger completed the film and flew to Hollywood.

For Your Eyes Only marked a deliberate return to the older values of the James Bond films. While filming in Corfu 'Cubby' Broccoli said: 'We are concentrating on the character. We don't need to compete with *Star Wars*. This is a story where the character shines through.'

There was a more realistic approach to the violence in the film than had been apparent in the recent productions in the series, and Roger as Bond comes in for considerably more physical punishment than before, giving the character more vulnerability than had been the case in *The Spy Who Loved Me* and *Moonraker*. Under director John Glen, Bond is presented as a more ruthless agent, most notably when he disposes of Locque, another assassin, by kicking his car off the edge of a cliff, where it is precariously balanced. John Glen recalled afterwards that Roger had been reluctant to play the scene as it was written. Glen was convinced that the scene would be effective and argued the point with him, but Roger kept insisting, 'It's not me. I don't do that sort of thing.'

Glen eventually persuaded Roger that Bond's action was a quite natural reaction under the circumstances, and the scene was shot as originally planned. Roger's leading lady, twenty-three-year-old French actress Carole Bouquet, said of him, 'He's very nice. He reminds me of my father.'

This impression also carried over to the film, Bond's relationship with Melina Havelock being one of paternal protection towards her. The final fade-out clinch between them is in keeping with the traditional ending of a Bond film, but in the context of this film it was certainly not such an inevitable conclusion to their working partnership. Screenwriter Richard Maibaum had originally intended Bond's continual attempts to make love to Melina to be interrupted at the crucial moment by emergencies that arise in the plot that he has to deal with. He intended Bond's lack of success to be a running-gag throughout, until at the end of the film he finally succeeds without interruptions. However, director John Glen decided to put less emphasis on this aspect of the screenplay, and to concentrate instead on the action sequences. Maibaum was not happy about this change. He has also commented that Roger has a habit of changing some of the lines in the script.

Just after completing *For Your Eyes Only*, Roger accepted the title role in a proposed film version of James Clavell's wearily-long novel *Tai Pan*. The deal was subject to a budget and a rewrite of the screenplay, but problems arose with the Swiss banks who were to finance the project, and it collapsed. Fortunately the project had gone no further than consideration for the principal casting.

Roger rested at his home in the South of France before returning to England in June for the premiere of *For Your Eyes Only*, which was held once again at the Odeon, Leicester Square in the presence of HRH Prince Charles and Lady Diana Spencer, shortly before their marriage. It was marvellous publicity to have the couple attend the première at a time when their every movement was monitored by the press from all over the world.

After the London première, Roger began his worldwide tour to promote the film, beginning with a day-long press conference in New York. In July, with the exhausting publicity tour completed, he returned to the Riviera for a cruise on the Mediterranean in the family yacht. There was a moment of drama on the trip when seven-year-old Christian fell down a stairway during a storm. The boy was bleeding badly, and Roger had to sail the yacht ten miles through a gale to reach Portofino on the Italian coast, where he was taken to hospital. The wound needed ten stitches.

At about this time Roger decided to buy a chalet in Gstaad. Up to then, since first discovering the place in 1977, they had rented chalets for the winter months, but with his life becoming once more settled into a regular routine, he decided to make an offer for the nine-bedroomed house they had rented for the past couple of years. When given the choice, the children had asked to go to school in Switzerland, and becoming a settled property-owner in Gstaad enabled Roger to spend more time with them. When asked by a journalist why he had settled there, he said: 'The reason I'm living in Switzerland is so that when I finally kick off, maybe in the not-too-distant future, I can leave enough money to my children. I think the death tax in England is the most insidious, appalling thing. You spend your life working, manage to save a bit, and then when you're dead they take it from your family.'

Now that they had two proper homes of their own on the Continent, Roger began to limit the amount of work that he accepted as, having made a considerable fortune, he wanted to spend more time with his family before they grew up and left home. His life now became a regular routine in which he would spend the winter in Switzerland, summer in the South of France, also visiting the United States frequently. The Moores employ a permanent staff for their homes in Europe, who commute from one to the other, with the couple, as required. Roger likes to spend the winter skiing, and then in April or May, usually just before the Cannes Film Festival, drifts south to St Paul de Vence, where the summers are spent playing tennis and enjoying the sunshine.

After finishing *For Your Eyes Only* Roger's next film appearance was a brief comic appearance, bumbling around with his head covered with bandages, in *Curse of the Pink Panther*. The film also featured David Niven who, by this time, was very seriously ill, and whose voice had to be dubbed by another actor because it had deteriorated so much. It was a sad experience for Roger, seeing his old friend in such a fragile condition, but since he was spending much more time in the South of France and in Switzerland, where Niven also had houses, he was able to keep a close check on the actor's health.

While relaxing at one of his homes, Roger keeps in touch with the latest films and television programmes by watching video cassettes which he arranges to be sent to him. David Hedison says: 'A way of relaxing for Roger is to watch television. The only way that he can take a nap is for the television to be on in the background with the sound full on. One time I was with him in the evening, and Roger was sleeping. I wanted to leave, but I made the mistake of turning the television off – and he woke up immediately.'

Roger is also an avid reader; he takes all the important daily newspapers, which he tries to get through, as well as tackling the *Daily Telegraph* crossword puzzle, which he has done regularly for years. Much of his time in Gstaad and St Paul-de-Vence is given over to ploughing through the enormous number of books that he orders during the year. He always makes sure that all the latest bestsellers are sent to him, as well as the most recent show-biz biographies, which he particularly enjoys reading. His favourite authors are Rudyard Kipling and John Steinbeck. Roger also pursues his love of art and frequently sits down to sketch and draw caricatures.

An enjoyable evening out for him is to go to one of the many local restaurants for a good meal. As he has grown in stature as a worldwide celebrity, so his tastes have become cultured and sophisticated, and he appreciates well-prepared food and good wines. Whenever they are in Los Angeles, Roger and Luisa are frequently to be seen dining at the Colombe D'or and Ma Maison restaurants, surrounded by their numerous friends. They both enjoy socialising and love having people to stay. Fred de Cordova, the producer of the *Tonight Show* with Johnny Carson, often visits the Moores in Los Angeles with his wife, Janet:

Whether at his house or at other people's homes, Luisa will sing and Roger will play a guitar and tell stories. The children are remarkably well brought-up and precocious – in the nice sense of the word. It's a lovely house to go to, and it is one of those occasions that you know will not be a stuffy evening. When we are there, it is rarely dinner for two – it is usually dinner for ten or twelve, and mostly people who fall into the category of those you are delighted to see. The dinner is perfectly served, and there is often a discussion of what Roger has prepared and what Luisa has prepared. Certainly the wines and cigars are first-rate Havana cigars and first-class wines.

David Wardlow says of Roger: 'Like Niven, Roger does not particularly like to work. He loves to ski, he loves to play tennis, he loves to go out for great meals. He could actually think of a year-round of events not to work.'

Although Roger has certainly not stopped working, he has decided to spend more time relaxing than he has done in the past.

In many ways, he leads two different lives, having two almost distinctive and separate groups of friends. Since becoming a rich film star he has naturally moved in higher social circles, and both he and Luisa particularly enjoy mixing with those people who are high in the social scale in Hollywood, like the Gregory Pecks, the Kirk Douglases and the Louis Jourdans. Among others, they also mix regularly with David and Bridget Hedison, Linda Evans, Jackie and Joan Collins, and Sean Connery and his wife.

Many of Roger's old friends from the days before he took over James Bond feel awkward about contacting him today, especially since his wealth and fame have become so great; they do not want to appear to be hanging on to his coat tails. But his friends do him an injustice, as Bryan Forbes states: 'Roger's great saving grace is that he has never altered. Success has not altered him, except to make him more generous. It's a fight to get Roger to let you take him out to dinner. He's the most generous host.'

Just before work began in preparation for *Octopussy* Albert R. Broccoli received filmdom's highest award when, on March 29th, 1982, at the Academy Award ceremonies he was presented with the Irving G. Thalberg Award, 'given by the Academy of Motion Picture Arts and Sciences in Hollywood for continued production excellence'.

In terms of both the profession and filmgoers throughout the world, there could have been no more deserving a recipient. Like the great David O. Selznick, Broccoli has always taken a dynamic part in all aspects of the film productions in which he is involved. He says: 'I like to be on the set. To me the fun of making a picture is to be where the action is. Little things come up and changes are made under the camera, and I like to be there.'

By being given the Thalberg Award, Broccoli was in distinguished company, previous recipients including such great names as David O. Selznick, Hal B. Wallis, Darryl F. Zanuck, Alfred Hitchcock, Jack Warner, Samuel Goldwyn, Walt Disney and Cecil B. De Mille.

For his sixth Bond film, *Octopussy*, American actor James Brolin was being dangled in front of Roger as his possible replacement, but Brolin was to be yet another victim in a long line of pretenders keen to oust him from the role when, in July, after several months of negotiations, Roger once again put his signature on a contract to play James Bond.

Faye Dunaway had originally been rumoured as a strong possibility for the title role of 'Octopussy', the glamorous lady jewel thief, but it was eventually given to Maud Adams, the Swedish model who had achieved fame as Scaramanga's mistress in *The Man With The Golden Gun* ten years earlier. The story, about the smuggling of priceless jewels from the Kremlin in Moscow, interwoven with a plot by a mad Russian general to start a nuclear war by destroying a US Air Base in West Germany, entailed a great deal of location work. Most of the scenes set in Eastern Europe were shot in England, but it was necessary for Roger to spend three weeks filming in India, which was an uncomfortable experience for him.

Shooting began on August 10th in Berlin, where a scene was shot at Checkpoint Charlie in which Bond is briefed by 'M', played by Roger's close friend, Robert Brown, replacing the late Bernard Lee. Brown remembers that wherever Roger went he would be mobbed by fans anxious to get his autograph and catch a glimpse of their hero. Even when they secretly booked a table under another name at one of the best restaurants in the city, the news somehow leaked out that Roger would be dining there, and when they arrived they were confronted by a mass of fans waiting for them. Roger, despite Luisa's unwarranted protestations, lingered to talk to them and to sign autographs, in his usual exemplary manner.

After finishing work in Berlin they returned to England for a week's shooting at the privately-owned Nene Valley Railway near Peterborough in Cambridgeshire, which had been converted into an East German border post for the film. Production continued at an RAF base at Northolt, Middlesex and at a United States Air Force Base in the Midlands.

The principal unit then flew to India, and on September 12th began an intensive three-week shooting schedule at Udaipur, in Rajestan. The Lake Palace Hotel, on Lake Pichola, once the home of the rich Maharaja of the district, was used to represent Octopussy's island retreat. Roger was very open about the problems of filming in India:

A lot of location work means a lot of travelling, and the hazards of the places where you are shooting, like India where it can affect the stomach and you've still got to work. And when you're on location it's a six-day week. And, as Bond, I'm an idiot running around in a black tie and dinner jacket while everybody else is in a sari. Tearing around in that heat is arduous; we have laughs but it's a slog. I enjoy it because I don't mind work.

Producer Broccoli says in reply to Roger's often-quoted claims about how exhausting the six months spent on making each Bond film are: 'It's always hard, but we make Roger's life quite easy. We're not that tough on him. We give him time at Christmas to go home, and all of these things he now wants. We are cooperative to one another. The main point is to get the film made, and get it made happily.'

The 120-degree heat in India made it necessary for Roger to change continually into clean shirts for each shot, in order to ensure that James Bond looked fresh and unruffled for the cameras. Interviewed on the location, he explained another of the hazards which faced them: 'Somebody introduced me to a local drink that's had me running to the toilet ever since.'

Throughout the filming in India the cast and crew were all

220

plagued with trouble of this kind, as stunt arranger Bob Simmons recalls: 'We all had stomach bugs. Roger had a bad tummy, and all the way home I don't think he sat in his seat on the plane – he sat in the toilet.'

A couple of days into the shooting at Udaipur, Roger heard the tragic news of the death of Princess Grace of Monaco, a day after her car had swerved off the road and crashed down a hillside. Roger was unable to attend the hastily arranged state funeral, as was another of her close friends, David Niven, who was too ill in his villa at Cap Ferrat to make an appearance. Roger and his family had always been welcome at the Palace in Monte Carlo when they were there in the summer, and Deborah and Geoffrey had become very friendly with Prince Albert and Princess Stephanie. Roger had always made a point of sending Grace an enormous bouquet of flowers on her birthday.

Roger's friend Louis Jourdan, who played the villainous Kamal in *Octopussy*, was equally saddened by the death of Princess Grace. He had acted opposite her in *The Swan* in 1956, in a part that Dore Schary had wanted Roger to play. However, he had been unable to persuade director Charles Vidor that Roger would be suitable, and the part had gone to Jourdan.

Hanging over the production of *Octopussy* was the knowledge that Sean Connery was at last making his return as James Bond in *Never Say Never Again*. Since 1975 'Cubby' Broccoli had been determined that he should be the only producer of James Bond films. Many times it had seemed that Broccoli had won his battle, and that Connery's attempt to return to the role would come to nothing, but by the autumn of 1982, two Bond films were in production, both with a projected release date of summer 1983. A great deal was made of the competition between Roger Moore and Sean Connery, although both men denied that any personal rivalry was involved. The men were close friends, and when they were filming their respective Bond productions in England, they frequently used to meet for dinner in the evenings.

Broccoli says: 'We didn't go out to compete, saying "We're going to be the best Bond" – the public's going to decide that anyway. So it always annoyed me to see in the press: this Bond was fighting that Bond, which was really not so, at least as far as we were concerned.'

Fred de Cordova, talking about the relationship between Connery and Moore, says: 'They seem to be very good friends – they always speak nicely about each other. There doesn't seem to be the slightest personal antagonism even though they are playing "the same character" for different people.'

After returning from India, shooting on *Octopussy* continued under great secrecy at Pinewood right up until Christmas Eve, when Roger left England to fly to Switzerland to spend Christmas at home in Gstaad. He was back at work at Pinewood on January 3rd of the New Year, completing principal photography on January 21st, after which he and Luisa spent a weekend in Paris.

In September of the previous year, Deborah had started her acting training at LAMDA (the London Academy of Music and Dramatic Art), having been rejected by RADA. She was sharing a flat with Bryan Forbes' daughter, Emma. Roger said to Robert Brown, who is Deborah's godfather, 'Of course, everything is for art's sake now!' He also said that Deborah criticised him for the films that he made, telling him that he should do something more worthwhile, and was herself keen to appear in a play with her father.

Roger still continued his work for the Stars Organisation for Spastics, helping them to raise much-needed funds at a time when they were particularly desperate. For the first nine months of 1982 Roger allowed his picture to be used on the cartons of Ski yogurt, the royalties from which he donated to the SOS. In October, to mark the end of the campaign, a Gala Ski Dinner was held at the Europa Hotel in London where Roger, along with HRH Princess Michael of Kent, accepted a cheque for £146,000 from Ski on behalf of the SOS.

After skiing in Switzerland in the early part of 1983, on completion of the Bond film, Roger flew to America. In May, he was among a host of world-famous celebrities, including Frank Sinatra and Dinah Shore, who paid tribute to Elizabeth Taylor at the Waldorf-Astoria in Manhattan, when the Friars Club, a show business fraternity, honoured her as 'Woman of the Year'. Roger had paid a similar tribute to the much-admired Elizabeth Taylor a couple of years earlier, when he appeared alongside Bette Davis, Gregory Peck and other Hollywood luminaries in Hollywood's own Filmex Gala Tribute to the great star. The occasion had been expertly produced by the prolific film director Curtis Harrington, who says: 'Roger was by far the best in the whole show. He was amusing, entertaining, lucid and exceedingly easy to work with – a joy.'

Octopussy was premiered at the Odeon, Leicester Square, as planned, on June 6th, attended by the now-married Prince and Princess of Wales. Roger then spent the next month promoting the film, which included a visit to Japan. The plan to release *Never Say Never Again* simultaneously with *Octopussy* had sensibly been shelved, and the Connery film was not released until the autumn.

On July 29th, early in the morning, David Niven died at his home in Switzerland, after a long illness which had wasted his muscles away, turning him into a gaunt and pale figure – a shadow of his former self. The two men, who had first met when Roger was only sixteen, had become close friends, particularly after Roger had settled near to Niven both in the South of France and in Switzerland, where they spent a great deal of time together. During Niven's protracted illness Roger used to visit his friend as often as possible, and otherwise would keep a regular check on his condition by telephone, from wherever he might be.

Although Roger knew that Niven was dying, it came as a terrible blow to him when he heard the news. As soon as he was told, he immediately made the seven-hour journey from St Paul de Vence to Niven's home in Switzerland, accompanied by Deborah, who was able to comfort the actor's two daughters, Fiona and Christina, with whom she was friendly. As Roger was the first to arrive at the house, he made most of the funeral arrangements and put everything in order, while awaiting the arrival of David Niven Jnr, who was flying over from Los Angeles. Mrs Niven heard the news in the South of France.

Roger made a statement to the press, who early on had begun to congregate outside Niven's house. In an obviously shaken state, he said of his friend: 'He'd started gaining weight again, and was increasing his exercise, and that's why it came as such a shock. We thought everything was going to be okay.'

Niven's death, coupled with the tragic death of Princess Grace less than a year before, completely changed life in the South of France.

Never Say Never Again was released initially in America, and a month later reached the cinemas in Britain. Roger's only recorded comment was: 'It's the only film I've been criticised for which I wasn't even in.'

There was much talk of Sean Connery showing audiences how Bond should be played, and that Roger Moore with his light-hearted approach would be finished. The producers of *Octopussy* were sufficiently confident that Roger had kept his public to announce, only a couple of days before *Never Say Never Again* opened in Britain, that Roger would be playing Bond in their next production, to be called *From A View To A Kill*, although the title was to be shortened later on. Roger Moore and United Artists had come to an agreement remarkably quickly over his salary for the film, avoiding the cat-and-mouse game between Roger and 'Cubby' that had come to be expected.

Connery's return did not wipe Roger Moore off the screen as Bond, as some had predicted. If anything, Connery had been forced to change his own interpretation of the character and, with age, had become a more humorous man to the point of appearing almost benign. As 'Cubby' Broccoli rightly says: 'To judge the success of any film, the box office receipts are the truest indicator of what the public wants to see. In all territories of the world, with one exception, *Octopussy* had 20–30% higher attendance figures.'

Ironically, the one exception was in Italy, where Connery's film had a slight edge over Moore's. When Roger heard this he said, 'I'll have to speak to Luisa about that.'

For fifteen years Roger had nursed the ambition to make a film version of Sidney Sheldon's thriller, *The Naked Face*. When he was approached by film producers Menahem Golan and Yoram Globus to star in a production for them, his first choice of a property was the Sidney Sheldon novel that he had liked so much. Roger also suggested that they employ his long-time friend, Bryan Forbes, to write the screenplay and to direct the film, which they were happy to do. Roger also had a say over the principal cast, and he asked that David Hedison be given the part of Dr Hadley, his brother-in-law in the film. Also in the cast were two Academy Award winning actors: Rod Steiger as an embittered Chicago cop, Lieutenant McGreavy, and Art Carney as Morgens, a private detective down on his luck; Elliott Gould played McGreavy's outwardly more sympathetic colleague, Detective Angeli.

Roger felt that the film would give him a much-needed change of pace from the world of 007. He remarked: 'I have more lines in one scene in *The Naked Face* than in all seven Bond pictures.' Wearing glasses for the part, he was cast as Dr Judd Stevens, a successful Chicago psychiatrist who innocently becomes embroiled with the Mafia and a jigsaw of red herrings that were totally incomprehensible to film audiences, and must have been equally so to the actors.

Bryan Forbes directed the film with a sure touch, and Roger, up against a strong performance by Rod Steiger, gave a credible picture of a man in fear of his life, with none of the flippancy of his portrayal of James Bond. He shows the desperation of the doctor – a man unused to violence – as he attempts to find out why his life is being threatened.

Much of the film was made on location in Chicago, and while shooting there Roger received a message that his mother had suffered a massive stroke at her bungalow in Frinton-on-Sea, Essex, where his parents had retired. He heard the news at just after midnight and immediately contacted Bryan Forbes, telling him, 'I think my mother is dying. She has had a massive heart attack.'

Roger was anxious to rush to his mother's side in hospital, but was concerned about holding up production of the film. Forbes told him not to worry, assuring him that he would be able to shoot around him until he returned. Roger and Luisa quickly packed for the journey to England, while Forbes booked seats for them on Concorde. From Chicago they flew to New York, and then by Concorde across the Atlantic. On arrival at London's Heathrow Airport, they hired a helicopter to take them to Colchester, and from there drove to Essex County Hospital.

Roger and Luisa checked into the nearby Colchester Mill Hotel, whose Greek proprietors, Maria and Emilio were surprised and happy to have such a famous celebrity as their guest. Maria remembers that on the first day she glimpsed Roger going in and out of the hotel, looking horribly worried and silent. On the second day, Saturday, October 1st, Roger received encouraging news about Lily, and saw for himself that she had turned the corner and was on the long road to recovery – she was off the danger list. He returned to the hotel later that day and happily joined the proprietors and other guests in the cosy bar for a drink. Maria says he was a changed man, and on the Sunday, he lunched with Luisa, Deborah and his father, and even took time to pose for a birthday photograph with the owner's young son.

With Lily now out of danger, he thanked Maria and Emilio effusively for the way they had looked after him and his family during this great crisis in his life. In the centre of the hotel lobby there hangs a colour photograph of Roger, inscribed with his gratitude and love.

On the Monday a cautiously thankful Roger was able to return to Chicago to resume filming, while Luisa stayed on with her father-in-law for a further couple of weeks, until Lily was able to return to their small bungalow, St Olaves, situated on the main

Walton Road between Frinton and Clacton. Whenever Luisa and Roger visited George and Lily, they used to stay at a local hotel in Frinton. Unhappily for Luisa, at about the same time that Lily fell ill, she lost her own mother in Italy.

Shooting *The Naked Face* took about ten weeks, after which Roger could look forward to Christmas at his chalet in Switzerland, with himself in charge of preparing and cooking their traditionally English Christmas dinner. They invited their friends, Leslie and Evie Bricusse, to stay with them, along with David Hedison and his wife, Linda Evans, and Robert Wagner, and threw a lavish party for their guests.

However, the festive season was not the trouble-free rest that Roger had hoped it would be, as Luisa began the skiing season with two unfortunate accidents within the space of one month. The first occurred when, skiing down a hill, she swerved to go around a small chalet, and crashed straight into a stone wall. Her face smashed against the wall, but luckily her forehead bore the brunt of the impact, and she avoided breaking her nose. The Bricusses left Gstaad after the New Year's Day celebrations, by which time Luisa had recovered from this accident. Soon after their departure an undaunted Luisa took to her skis again but this time fell and broke her leg, and was taken to hospital where it was put in plaster. After the upsets of the recent deaths of Luisa's mother and David Niven, as well as his own mother's serious illness, from which she was making a slow recovery, Roger was not particularly pleased to have an invalid on his hands. Charlie Isaacs, a friend in Hollywood, says: 'Roger doesn't like to hear about sickness and death. He shies away from it. He likes to hear about happiness. He wants life to be beautiful and happy.'

Roger enjoys the close relationship that he has with his family. Whenever he is in England, his first priority is to go and see his parents in Frinton-on-Sea, and he loves to have them to stay at Gstaad or St Paul de Vence whenever possible. Having been fortunate enough to have had a very happy and contented childhood himself, he wants the same for his own children. Agent Dennis Selinger says: 'There's no argument that you won't find a better father anywhere in the world. He's marvellous with the kids – he dotes on them and is with them at any opportunity.'

Roger's film contracts always provide air fares for Luisa and the children, so that they can come out to see him if he is working on location. He finds it difficult to refuse them anything, and Luisa has said of her husband: 'He loves the children very much, but he is too soft. I say you can be hard and still you can love.'

Roger, for his part, has said: 'I think I'm fairly just with my children. I've never raised a hand in anger or love. I feel that in life you shouldn't tread on other people's toes, unless you want yours trodden upon.'

Roger dislikes being unpleasant with anyone, and cherishes the image of being a 'great guy'. Dennis Selinger says: 'Roger's greatest ambition is that he wants to be a nice guy. He doesn't want to hurt anybody, as he sees no reason to be unkind, or spiteful, or malicious.'

Director Terence Young, paying tribute to his character, says: 'I can't imagine Roger hating anybody or trying to destroy anybody. I don't think he's got any malice in him at all.'

Although Roger is always happy to listen to other people's problems and do what he can to help, when it comes to any private worries of his own, he keeps them to himself. Even David Hedison, who is probably his closest friend, says: 'Roger is a very secretive person and he never talks about anything that is bothering him.'

Above all, Roger believes in keeping everybody laughing – he will make light of things which mean a lot to him, rather than show himself to be vulnerable. Lewis Gilbert, who directed him in two James Bond films, and is a good friend, says:

> None of Roger's troubles were ever told to you as serious troubles. They were always made to sound very, very funny. However sad it was underneath, it would sound funny. I think that is Roger's protection from the world – that's the way he gets through life. He doesn't show himself very easily. Roger will never reveal his true self. However down he is, however sad he is, whatever problem he has – he always covers it up with a veneer of humour.

Luisa said that when she first met George and Lily, they never kissed when they greeted but that, under her influence, they do now. She thought their natural reserve to be very English. Roger has inherited his parents' characteristics, which is in complete contrast to his wife, who is always open in her opinions – if she dislikes something she will say it. She once said: 'I have problem, I say what I feel. If I order something in restaurant and the wrong thing comes Roger says, "Eat it." I ask: "We live in 1983, we go to the moon and I cannot say, 'You make mistake'?"'

Roger has admitted, on rare occasions, that he does have insecurities and does sometimes suffer depressions, but he will not discuss them. This side of his character he keeps to himself, refusing to unburden himself in public or to wear his heart on his sleeve as so many actors do. When asked during the filming of *The Sea Wolves* why he always cracked jokes and made fun of himself, Roger said: 'Self-defence – make people laugh before they laugh at you. It is better that they laugh with you.'

He laughs along with everybody else about the interminable criticism of his acting ability, but in private he is not as unconcerned as he likes to make himself out to be. Bad reviews do upset him, although he will not admit it directly, and with friends dismisses them lightly, saying 'What a bore' or 'Not another one!' Bryan Forbes recently asked him if he ever thought about how he might die, and with characteristic humour, Roger replied: 'Oh yes, I know exactly how I'll die. I shall wake up one morning, get my first good notice and die of a bloody heart attack!'

He prefers to be known as a witty and amusing chap, rather than as someone who is insecure and has 'hidden depths'. He always admired David Niven's ability as a raconteur, and basks in his own reputation for telling stories very well. Fred de Cordova, the producer of the *Tonight Show*, says: 'It is always welcome news to hear that Roger is back in the States and available for the show. Roger remembers jokes and tells them very well. I think he is pleased with his performance as a story-teller.'

After the show's host, Johnny Carson, had first met Roger one summer in the South of France, he told de Cordova, 'Gee, that Roger Moore is amusing and bright and funny. Any time we can grab him for the show, please do.'

Roger loves entertaining people with his enormous fund of stories and jokes. Making people laugh and enjoy themselves is one of the great pleasures of his life. Leslie Bricusse says that whenever he meets Roger, he always knows all the new jokes and will proceed to trot them out one after another. Bricusse says, 'One in five is good.'

Leslie Charteris regards him socially as '. . . a terrific entertainer. He just has got that gift. I don't think Roger is ever boring. He can be one of those "life of the party" people because he has this tremendous repertoire of stories that he can tell very well.'

And John Howard-Davies says of him: 'If he weren't so famous it would be possible to meet a Roger Moore as a more colourful character in a pub.'

In 1984, Roger had no film commitments until August, when he was due to start work on the new Bond film, now entitled *A View To A Kill*. In the interim he spent his time travelling between his homes in France and Switzerland, and in April he appeared at the Academy Awards ceremonies in Los Angeles, to introduce veteran director Frank Capra, who was presented with a special award for the brilliant work throughout his career.

Euan Lloyd, when setting up the proposed sequel to his popular film, *The Wild Geese*, to be directed by Peter Hunt, had hoped again to cast Roger opposite Richard Burton, but the shooting schedule clashed with that of *A View To A Kill*, and he was unable to accept. However, Burton did not live to make the film as he died suddenly on August 5th, at the age of fifty-eight, at his home in Switzerland, only days before production was due to begin in West Germany.

On August 1st, Roger started work on *A View To A Kill* at Pinewood Studios. Shortly before beginning work on the film – the fourteenth in the series and Roger's seventh – 'Cubby' Broccoli said, 'I think it's a phenomenon myself, and I'm amazed to find ourselves in it to this great extent. We're happy it has been successful because it has kept a lot of us working in England and America.'

All the Bond films have been major productions and major successes throughout the world. It is hard to imagine any other series of films in the major league running to four productions, let alone the number the Bond series has reached – an achievement unlikely to be equalled, and certainly not in the twentieth century.

The enormous lead that the Bond films have over all other subjects is due to one man – a showman with a great vision: Albert R. Broccoli. By virtue of his enormous achievement as a film-maker of such prominent success and box office might, he certainly has earned his place beside those like Mayer, Warner, Goldwyn and Selznick. And Roger Moore's contribution to Mr Broccoli's success has been quite considerable. Through his presence in the films, Roger enabled the series to continue well after its originator had left. He succeeded Sean Connery as James Bond which, in itself, was a daring feat and, to his eternal credit as an actor and a personality, he has made the character of James Bond his own. Only when another actor comes to tackle the role will Roger's unique skill in playing the part with such charm and professional ease be fully appreciated.

After all the criticism, both good and bad, is considered, the

229

major fact that emerges is that the James Bond films, collectively and individually, are among the most popular of all time throughout the world.

When *A View To A Kill* is premiered in June 1985, Roger will be nearing his fifty-ninth year, still handsome and possessed of a fine figure, but he will not play the role again. To see him out of Bond, producer 'Cubby' Broccoli has bestowed upon Roger a singular honour – casting Oscar-winning actor Christopher Walken as the villain, the first time that an actor of such standing has been cast in a James Bond film. Roger, with his usual common sense, has picked the right Bond film in which to make his final exit. The actor who is chosen to take over the part from him will find his success very hard to follow.

It has been suggested to Roger by friends and fans alike that he should follow so many film stars and reappear before a live audience. When this was put to him while he was in London for the premiere of *Octopussy*, he said: 'The longer I am away from the theatre, the more nervous I am about going back. I should get out and exercise my legs, but I'm so exhausted by the time I finish a picture. I don't want to go and rehearse a play – I'd much rather enjoy myself. I'd be a sitting duck – the critics would love to think, "Here's a bloody movie actor on the stage."'

But possibly the truth is not quite as Roger tells it, and he is sensible enough to realise that he has neither the training nor the experience to assure a successful theatrical appearance. He never had any success in the theatre and, with hindsight, it is doubtful that he ever would have done if his career had not taken the lucky path that it did, both in television and in films. Despite his enormous success in this field, he has admitted to a minor feeling of regret that he has never known triumph in the theatre: 'I suppose from the ego point of view it would be nice to get wonderful reviews in a marvellous play somewhere, but that is not the path I took when I had the choice between Hollywood and Stratford. I took Hollywood – I was greedy.'

Shooting finished on *A View To A Kill* at the beginning of 1985, and Roger went back to the bosom of his family at his chalet in Switzerland. But the Moore family will not be together for long after the New Year. Deborah, his eldest child, has completed a very successful course at London's prestigious Academy of Music and Dramatic Art, and will be seeking her own way as an actress on the world's stage. Geoffrey, fully grown, having shown an increasing interest in film production when accompanying his father on location, will be off searching for his own niche in the industry, while Christian, at the age of twelve, will be reaching out and preparing for adulthood. Luisa, comfortably into middle age, will be by Roger's side as he decides what to do next, whether in front or behind the camera, as actor, or producer or director. But as he sits back, alone in his study at his Gstaad home, he will be able to reflect on his own life – a career full of success in spite of itself, riches beyond anyone's dreams, and blessed still with loving parents, wife and children. In the final analysis, with all human frailties and human circumstances taken into consideration, it is a well-deserved success, for Roger George Moore, first and foremost, is a really good man.

The Films of Roger Moore

Roger Moore's film career started with walk-on parts in the following British productions:

1) CAESAR AND CLEOPATRA (GB 1945) Rank. Producer: Gabriel Pascal, Directors: Gabriel Pascal/Brian Desmond Hurst. With Vivien Leigh, Claude Rains, Flora Robson, Stewart Granger
2) PERFECT STRANGERS (GB 1945) MGM. Producer: London Films, Director: Alexander Korda. With Robert Donat, Deborah Kerr, Ann Todd
3) GAIETY GEORGE (GB 1946) Embassy Production. Director: George King. With Richard Greene, Ann Todd, Hazel Court. (US Title: Showtime)
4) PICCADILLY INCIDENT (GB 1946) ABP. Director: Herbert Wilcox. With Anna Neagle, Michael Wilding
5) TROTTIE TRUE (GB 1949) GFD–Two Cities. Producer: Hugh Stewart, Director: Brian Desmond Hurst. With Jean Kent, James Donald, Hugh Sinclair
6) PAPER ORCHID (GB 1949) Ganesh–Columbia. Director: Roy Baker. With Hugh Williams, Hy Hazell, Sidney James

Speaking roles:

7) THE LAST TIME I SAW PARIS (US 1954) MGM. Producer: Jack Cummings, Director: Richard Brooks. With Elizabeth Taylor, Van Johnson, Walter Pidgeon, Donna Reed
8) INTERRUPTED MELODY (US 1955) MGM. Producer: Jack Cummings, Director: Curtis Bernhardt. With Eleanor Parker, Glenn Ford, Cecil Kellaway
9) THE KING'S THIEF (US 1955) MGM. Producer: Edwin Knopf, Director: Robert Z. Leonard. With Ann Blyth, Edmund Purdom, David Niven, George Sanders
10) DIANE (US 1955) MGM. Producer: Edwin Knopf, Director: David Miller. With Lana Turner, Pedro Armendariz, Sir Cedric Hardwicke
11) THE MIRACLE (US 1959) WB. Producer: Henry Blanke, Director: Irving Rapper. With Carroll Baker, Walter Slezak, Katina Paxinou, Elspeth March
12) GOLD OF THE SEVEN SAINTS (US 1961) WB. Producer: Leonard Freeman, Director: Gordon Douglas. With Clint Walker, Robert Middleton, Chill Wills
13) THE SINS OF RACHEL CADE (US 1961) WB. Producer: Henry

Blanke, Director: Gordon Douglas. With Angie Dickinson, Peter Finch, Juano Hernandez

14) THE RAPE OF THE SABINE WOMEN (Il Ratto Delle Sabine) (Italy–France 1961) Producers: FICIT/CFPI, Director: Richard Pottier. With Mylene Demongeot, Luisa Mattioli

15) NO MAN'S LAND (Un Branco di Vigliacchi) (Italy–France 1962) Producers: FICIT/Coliseum Film/Contact Organisation, Director: Fabrizio Taglioni. With Pascale Petit, Frank Villard, Luisa Mattioli

16) CROSSPLOT (GB 1969) Tribune Productions. Producer: Robert Baker, Director: Alvin Rakoff. With Martha Hyer, Francis Matthews, Bernard Lee

17) THE MAN WHO HAUNTED HIMSELF (GB 1970) ABP. Producer: Michael Relph, Director: Basil Dearden. With Hildegard Neil, Anton Rodgers, Freddie Jones

18) LIVE AND LET DIE (GB 1973) Eon/UA. Producers: Albert R. Broccoli and Harry Saltzman, Director: Guy Hamilton. With Jane Seymour, Yaphet Kotto, David Hedison

19) GOLD (GB 1974) Avton Film Productions. Producer: Michael Klinger, Director: Peter Hunt. With Susannah York, Ray Milland, Bradford Dillman, Sir John Gielgud

20) THE MAN WITH THE GOLDEN GUN (GB 1974) Eon/UA. Producers: Albert R. Broccoli and Harry Saltzman, Director: Guy Hamilton. With Christopher Lee, Britt Ekland, Maud Adams

21) THAT LUCKY TOUCH (GB 1975) Fox–Rank. Producer: Dimitri de Grunwald, Director: Christopher Miles. With Susannah York, Shelley Winters, Lee J. Cobb

22) SHOUT AT THE DEVIL (GB 1976) Hemdale International. Producer: Michael Klinger, Director: Peter Hunt. With Lee Marvin, Barbara Parkins

23) THE SICILIAN CROSS (Gli Esecutori) (Italy 1976) Aetos Produzioni Cinematografiche. Producers: Manolo Bolognini and Luigi Borghese, Director: Maurizio Lucidi. With Stacy Keach, Ettore Manni

24) SHERLOCK HOLMES IN NEW YORK (US 1976) TCF/NBC TV-movie. Producers: Nancy Malone and John Cutts, Director: Boris Sagal. With John Huston, Charlotte Rampling, Patrick MacNee

25) THE SPY WHO LOVED ME (GB 1977) Eon/UA. Producer: Albert R. Broccoli, Director: Lewis Gilbert. With Curt Jurgens, Barbara Bach, Richard Kiel

26) THE WILD GEESE (GB 1978) Richmond Film Productions/Rank. Producer: Euan Lloyd, Director: Andrew V. McLaglen. With Richard Burton, Richard Harris, Hardy Kruger, Stewart Granger

27) ESCAPE TO ATHENA (GB 1979) Pimlico Films/ITC. Producers:

David Niven Jnr and Jack Weiner, Director: George Cosmatos. With David Niven, Claudia Cardinale, Telly Savalas, Stefanie Powers

28) MOONRAKER (GB 1979) UA/Eon. Producer: Albert R. Broccoli, Director: Lewis Gilbert. With Lois Chiles, Michael Lonsdale

29) NORTH SEA HIJACK (GB 1979) Cinema Seven Productions/CIC. Producer: Elliott Kastner, Director: Andrew V. McLaglen. With Anthony Perkins, James Mason, David Hedison, Lea Brodie

30) THE SEA WOLVES (GB–US–Switzerland 1980) Richmond Light Horse Productions/Lorimar/Varius. Producer: Euan Lloyd, Director: Andrew V. McLaglen. With Gregory Peck, David Niven, Trevor Howard, Barbara Kellerman

31) SUNDAY LOVERS (GB–US–Italy–France 1980) MGM. Director: Bryan Forbes (RM episode). With Lynn Redgrave, Denholm Elliott, Priscilla Barnes

32) THE CANNONBALL RUN (US 1980) Golden Harvest/20th Century-Fox. Producer: Albert Ruddy, Director: Hal Needham. With Burt Reynolds, Farrah Fawcett

33) FOR YOUR EYES ONLY (GB 1981) Eon/UA. Producer: Albert R. Broccoli, Director: John Glen. With Carole Bouquet, Julian Glover, Topol

34) OCTOPUSSY (GB 1983) Eon/MGM-UA. Producer: Albert R. Broccoli, Director: John Glen. With Louis Jourdan, Maud Adams

35) CURSE OF THE PINK PANTHER (GB 1984) MGM-UA. Director: Blake Edwards. With David Niven, Ted Wass, Robert Wagner, Joanna Lumley

36) THE NAKED FACE (US 1984) Cannon Films. Producers: Menahem Golan and Yoram Globus, Director: Bryan Forbes. With Rod Steiger, Elliott Gould, Art Carney

37) A VIEW TO A KILL (GB 1985) MGM-UA. Producer: Albert R. Broccoli, Director: John Glen. With Christopher Walken, Tanya Roberts, Grace Jones

Index

Note. The abbreviation RM is used throughout for Roger Moore; M for the surname Moore.

MOORE, ROGER GEORGE
birth, 10; childhood, 13–22; family, 14; education, 16–22, 23; wartime evacuation, 18–20; first job, 23–4; as film extra, 26–7, 32–3; enters RADA, 27–8; National Service, 31–40; courtship and first marriage, 31, 35; second marriage, 55; divorces, 51, 54, 129, 136; third marriage, 130–1; children, *see* Moore, Christian; Deborah; Geoffrey

career: in repertory at Cambridge, 31; early stage and film parts, 42–3, 45–7, 51–2; modelling jobs, 43–4; television debut, 54–5; on Broadway, 55–6; in Hallmark Theatre series, 56–7; screen test for MGM, 57; disenchantment with theatre, 58; arrives in Hollywood, 59; undergoes speech therapy, 76–7; film work, 232–4 *and under individual titles*; major television